THREE POWER PLAYS

T0348047

David Pinner

THREE POWER PLAYS

THE DRUMS OF SNOW
RICHELIEU
PRINCE OF TRAITORS

OBERON BOOKS
LONDON

First published in 2006 by Oberon Books Ltd.

521 Caledonian Road, London N7 9RH

Tel: 020 7607 3637 / Fax: 020 7607 3629

e-mail: info@oberonbooks.com

www.oberonbooks.com

A catalogue record for this book is available from the British Library.

ISBN: 1 84002 597 2

Cover illustration: Andrzej Klimowski

Contents

Preface

I WROTE MY Anglo-French *Three Power Plays* over a period of ten years, beginning with *The Drums of Snow* in 1966, followed by *Richelieu* in 1972, and completing the trilogy with *Prince of Traitors* in 1976. *The Drums of Snow* deals with the power struggle between Charles I and Oliver Cromwell. Contemporaneously, *Richelieu* focuses on Cardinal Richelieu, who acquired power to pacify and stabilise Louis XIII's war-torn and anarchic France. *Prince of Traitors* explores Bishop Talleyrand's extraordinary political acumen as he survives the French Revolution to become Napoleon's Foreign Minister. After which Talleyrand helps to bring about the fall of the despotic Napoleon, which in turn earned Talleyrand the dubious appellation of 'Prince of Traitors'.

The Drums of Snow is a macrocosmic play that examines the economic, political and religious reasons for the English Civil War. The main protagonists are Charles I, the closet Catholic, and Oliver Cromwell, the messianic Puritan. John Lilburne, the radical Leveller, comments ironically to the audience on the King and the Ironsides' General as they open the Gates of Hell to bring forth the Four Horsemen of the Apocalypse. The play is a historical fiction that is grounded firmly in fact. It should be played on a bare stage in order to achieve the necessary epic fluidity to illustrate the frenzied anarchy of civil war and its bloody consequences. In Lilburne's words:

> Out of the dark we come,
> Into the murk we go.
> Men have only the drum
> And the hopes of the starving crow.
> One king is king today,
> Then come the drums of snow.
> A screech of the axe;
> His head rolls away.
> In his eyes dead lilies grow.

The Civil War is being waged by the upwardly-mobile Puritan 'business class' against 'the Divine Right' pretensions of the autocratic King Charles, who is abetted by his Catholic French consort, Henrietta Maria. Unlike the French Revolution, the English Civil War is a middle-class/aristocratic affair, which unfortunately ensures that the majority of the working-class never benefit from Charles' subsequent execution. Despite Cromwell's injunction to his soldiers to 'Begin the labour to love – which is harder than death', once he becomes the Lord Protector, within a very short while, Cromwell replaces Charles' despotic Star Chamber with his own narrow-minded religious regime, which leads to even more repression.

It is Lilburne (who has been imprisoned at different times by both the King and Cromwell) who gives voice to the terrible paradox of aspiration and fulfilment in the final ballad:

Oh listen to the drums of snow,
Into, into dark we go.
All that's left for us to do
Is to watch the darkness grow.
The future's all left up to you.

At the same time as Cromwell and the Puritans are destroying the power of the King and creating a divided nation, in *Richelieu,* the young Richelieu, as Bishop of Luçon, is beginning his life's work. He sets out to persuade the weak, stuttering Louis XIII to embrace the Divine Right of Kings, in order to pacify and unify France. So although both *Richelieu* and *The Drums of Snow* are epics, the power goals of the protagonists are completely different.

As Bishop Richelieu steps onto the world's stage, France is still composed of warring dukedoms and principalities. It requires the political genius of this reluctant cleric to transform France's anarchy into a genuinely integrated nation with secure borders. Richelieu is 'a reluctant cleric' because he wants to be a soldier, but as he is the youngest son, Richelieu's father insists that he becomes a priest.

Richelieu reveals a very different Richelieu to the 'self-serving, cruel and sinister villain' as depicted by Alexandre Dumas in *The Three Musketeers*. Indeed Richelieu, who always has poor health, continually sacrifices his own personal life for the greater glory of the King and France. As a result, he makes innumerable enemies, and he survives exile and two assassination attempts. When Richelieu fails to respond to the sexual advances of the Queen Mother, she screams: 'Take my hate then, you treacherous cleric. By God's Eternal Grace, I'll have your sex hacked off and forced down your dying throat.' Although Richelieu 'exalts' the King, and is rewarded for his services by being elevated into a Cardinal, the emotionally-tortured Louis still loathes Richelieu: 'I feel I am nothing more but an extension of your will, Eminence. I would give anything to forget my wife, my mother, you – and even France – for one moment of friendship.'

So what are Richelieu's final achievements? As the Cardinal says towards the end of the play on his deathbed: 'I have brought peace to the kingdom. In so doing, I have sculpted France out of the veined marble, and given it the piercing features of my death mask for the next hundred years. But the Sun King is coming.' Richelieu is responsible for the 'god-like golden' reign of Louis XIV, but the pleasure-loving Sun King proves to be a tyrant to the majority of his underprivileged nation. Then the Divine Right of Kings' despotism becomes even more draconian under Louis XVI, which, in turn, leads to the bloody excesses of the French Revolution – but it also ushers onto the world stage another cleric, Bishop Talleyrand, the Great Survivor.

The central figure in *Prince of Traitors* is the old, dying Talleyrand, who is surrounded by tailors' dummies. They accuse him of betraying not only Louis XVI, and then the French Revolution, but also Napoleon, who appears, screaming: 'Talleyrand, you Prince of Traitors, you're nothing but shit in a silk stocking!'

Talleyrand responds: 'I only betrayed you, Bonaparte, after you had betrayed yourself in your hunger for power, because Racine was right when he wrote: "Treachery is noble when its target is tyranny".' Talleyrand proceeds to enact his 'Defence to Posterity' to the audience. Like Richelieu, he too was forced to become a cleric by his parents. In Talleyrand's case, he acquired a club-foot because of a childhood accident that prevented him from going into the army.

As an influential bishop, Talleyrand soon finds himself in the presence of Count Artois, the King's brother: 'Highness, the People of France are starving, so if the coming harvest is as calamitous as the last, Robespierre, Marat and the other revolutionaries will incite the mob to hack off your royal heads. Your only hope is to persuade the King to become a constitutional monarch like the King of England, and to set up a parliamentary democracy after the English model, before the Deluge engulfs us all.' For his pains, Talleyrand is thrown out of the palace – but he remains a passionate Anglophile for the rest of his life.

Talleyrand is appointed as the Chaplain of the Revolution, and although he is an aristocrat, Talleyrand still manages to outwit the blood-thirsty Robespierre, by persuading Danton to send him to England as France's ambassador. Two years later, Talleyrand sails to America where he acquires a black mistress while making his fortune on the Stock Market. When he learns of Robespierre's execution, Talleyrand returns to France where he becomes Napoleon's Foreign Minister. Then he tries to prevent the self-appointed Emperor from plunging Europe into a world war. Napoleon ignores him, so Talleyrand 'betrays' the Emperor to the Allies with the words: 'You promised me, sire, that we would not become traffickers in nations. I can no longer stomach the waste of human life, the stench of carnage and the rape of Liberty.'

His crowning victory is the Congress of Vienna, during which he persuades the Allied Nations to allow the recently defeated France to regain some of her former glory. History remembers the reluctant bishop for his indefatigable belief in peace, democracy and political moderation, but it is his 'seditious survival' skills that make all his considerable achievements possible.

Another of Talleyrand's famous dictums was: 'War is the first recourse of the power-hungry scoundrel, so war should only ever be embarked upon when every other avenue has been explored and exhausted.' As there are no shortage of 'power-hungry scoundrels' in the world today, these *Three Power Plays* are a reminder that peace and liberty are always under threat.

DP, 2006

THE DRUMS OF SNOW

Author's Note

The Drums of Snow is a modern play about modern dilemmas using historical syntax. I manipulate history in order to lay bare the present.

Costumes and settings should be grounded in the past, but savouring of the present. The Puritans can be in dark, utility leather. Everything about them is business-like, anticipating war. The Royalists are clothes-conscious, with their lace collars and their long hair.

The action of the play takes place mainly on a bare stage, though two or three stage levels would be useful. Only essential props are used, and change of location is suggested with a chair or a banner. The action is continuous, with often three things happening on the stage simultaneously. The songs can be sung or chanted.

The play should move with great pace like a political dance, with the audience as an integral part of the play. They are 'The People' who are hectored and pushed about, but who are rarely understood by the combatants.

Characters

The Royal Family

KING CHARLES I of England

HENRIETTA MARIA, his Queen

PRINCE CHARLES, their son, later CHARLES II

The House of Commons

MR JOHN PYM, First Minister of England

MR EDWARD HYDE, the Speaker in the Commons

MR DENZIL HOLLES, Member of the Commons

SIR JOHN ELIOTT, Member of the Commons

MR OLIVER CROMWELL, Member of the Commons

SIR THOMAS WENTWORTH, later Earl of Strafford and
Deputy of Ireland

The House of Lords

THE EARL OF MANCHESTER

THE MARQUIS OF NEWCASTLE

THE EARL OF ESSEX

GEORGE VILLIERS, the Duke of BUCKINGHAM

LORD DIGBY

The Church of England

WILLIAM LAUD, Bishop of London, later Archbishop of
Canterbury

The King's Army

PRINCE RUPERT

The Parliament Army

SIR THOMAS FAIRFAX

The Scottish Army

THE DUKE OF ARGYLL

THE DUKE OF MONTROSE

Others

JOHN LILBURNE, the Leveller

JOHN BRADSHAW, a lawyer

Lords, Ladies, Soldiers, the Mob, Whores, Boys etc.

The Drums of Snow was first performed at the Stanford Repertory Theatre, California on 8 April 1968 with the following cast:

LILBURNE, Terry J Hinz

CHARLES I, Andros Thompson

HENRIETTA MARIA, Sheila Mahoney

PRINCE CHARLES / ROYALIST COCK,
    Michael R Murphy

PYM, Roger Hardy

HYDE / MONTROSE / PURITAN COCK,
    Dick Leonard

HOLLES / BRADSHAW, Wes Finlay

ELIOTT, Paul Willis

CROMWELL, Gene L Engene

WENTWORTH, Eugene Kustere

MANCHESTER, Richard Kite

NEWCASTLE, Marcel M Hernandez

ESSEX / ARGYLL, Bruce Janger

BUCKINGHAM / DIGBY, Christopher Bennion

LAUD, Charles Feinstein

RUPERT, Paul Willis

FAIRFAX, Richard Carp

FIRST WHORE, Suzanne Bales

SECOND WHORE, Patricia Hanley

HEADSMAN, Roger Hardy

SOLDIERS, Charles Feinsten, Art Hager, James Hinz, Eugene
    Kusterer, Dick Leonard, Michael R Murphy, Tom Sather,
    Jim Spickard

Original Music Theorore Antoniou

Director John Chioles

Designer Robert Franklin

Choreographer Shirlee Dodge

Costumes Sally Shatford

Lighting K Clarke Crandell

Sound Shawn Murphy

PART ONE

The play opens on a glowing cyclorama.

JOHN LILBURNE, the Leveller, runs onto the forestage. He comments on the proceedings.

LILBURNE: September third Sixteen Fifty-Eight. Cromwell is dead is Cromwell dead is dead.
   (*Enter a Drummer and a Trumpeter playing a joyful fanfare that becomes 'God Save the KING'. Edward HYDE, the Speaker of the House of Commons, enters with all the ROYALISTS. They kneel in a semi-circle facing the audience.*)

HYDE: The Beast is dead. Cromwell is dead. God save King Charles the Second.

LILBURNE: May twenty-ninth Sixteen Sixty.
   (*Enter KING CHARLES II.*)

CHARLES II: That is most enchanting of you, ladies and gentlemen. The bended knee adds a sweet sweep to the thigh that appeals. (*He touches a Lady's cheek.*) Yes, laugh, my pretty one, and your breasts will laugh with you. Come to us tonight. And come. (*He crosses himself.*) My poor father – where is his poor head? Do lilies grow there? Or rosemary?

LILBURNE: (*Singing.*)
   Out of the dark we come.
   Into the murk we go.
   Men have only the drum,
   And the hopes of the starving crow.
   One king is king today,
   Then come the drums of snow.
   A screech of the axe;
   His head rolls away.
   In his eyes dead lilies grow.

CHARLES II: How dared they execute my father? Dig Cromwell out of his grave.

HYDE: Isn't it a little early in the morning for necrophilia, sire?
   (*The KING glares.*)

We have anticipated your wishes, Majesty, and we have already dug him up.

(*HYDE claps his hands and the bodies of CROMWELL and JOHN BRADSHAW are dragged onto the stage.*)

Allow me to introduce Mr Oliver Cromwell, Your Majesty, and Mr John Bradshaw. As I am sure you remember, Bradshaw convicted your father of high treason.

CHARLES II: (*Covering his nose.*) They stink!

LILBURNE: I venture to suggest, Your Majesty, when you have been in the grave as long as they have, you, too, will not smell of eau de cologne.

CHARLES II: I did not give you permission to speak.

LILBURNE: No one ever did. That was the trouble. But they couldn't stop me. Your father often flayed my back, but as you see, I survived.

CHARLES II: Arrest him!

HYDE: But he is Mr John Lilburne, the popular Leveller.

CHARLES II: And I am Charles the Second of England, Scotland, Wales and Ireland!

HYDE: And we sincerely hope you remain so, sire, but now you never know in England.

CHARLES II: (*Laughing.*) So this is the awesome Oliver Cromwell. (*He turns CROMWELL's body over with his foot.*) Very disappointing. He's decomposing so slowly. And he doesn't look sufficiently monstrous. Was he a human being? He laughed once, I remember. Hang him anyway. And hang this Bradshaw thing.

(*Two ROYALIST SOLDIERS stand on chairs with dangling nooses. Other ROYALISTS assist in the hanging of CROMWELL and BRADSHAW.*)

ROYALISTS: (*Singing.*)

We've waited for this.
We've hated for this.
To see them stark on the killing rope;
Confectionery for earth.
You Puritan swine,
Now is the time
For your second death on the killing rope,
And in hell, your second birth!

LILBURNE: (*Singing.*)
> Poor old Cromwell's had his day.
> Lust and Charlie's here to stay.
> (*The dead bodies jerk into grotesque positions, then freeze.*
> *BRADSHAW's tongue protrudes from his mouth.*)

CHARLES II: And cut Bradshaw's tongue off. It offends me.
> (*HYDE obeys.*)

LILBURNE: Of course, in reality, Cromwell's body is a
> Heavenly Host – of worms.
> (*CROMELL's dead slumped head responds.*)

CROMWELL: But the Lord God anointed my head with steel,
> So I will haunt England until God fails,
> Or until He takes it for His Own with Fire!
> But let us peruse the beginnings.
> (*CROMWELL removes the noose from his neck.*)
> I came with Christ's Cruciform sword.
> My ironsides rode like human tanks.
> Our feet were dragons. Our eyes were lizards.
> Like wet green corn under the iron hail,
> Charles the First fell beneath God's flail.
> It was God! Always remember it was God!
> It was never me.

LILBURNE: He believes, you see. There are many excuses
> for handing out death – and God is the best one thought
> of yet. Cromwell only sounds like words now when he
> justifies himself, but you should have seen him on a horse.
> He was a horse and a man together. And I loved him.
> Once.

BRADSHAW: (*Sneering at CHARLES II from within the confines*
> *of his noose.*) If I were alive now – which unfortunately I'm
> not because I'm one of the lesser ghosts – a sneaky-creak
> ghost.
> But were I alive now,
> I would try *you*, Charles the Two,
> And when I had finished saying all that was to be said
> About the corruption of kings, they'd chop off your head;
> But I can't, alas, 'cause I'm dead.
> (*BRADSHAW exits with his noose.*)

HYDE: Your Majesty, although I'm enjoying all this hanging as much as the next man, nevertheless, in my role as the Speaker of the Commons, I do feel that we must begin to re-order most of the laws, not to mention reforming the Church. Well, we must do something! Anything!

CHARLES II: (*Swaggering off.*) Come, everyone, it's time to banquet in my wife's boudoir.

HYDE: (*Following and pleading.*) But the laws, sire…

CHARLES II: (*Overriding him.*) Poor father, why did you take everything so seriously? I did warn you.

(*CHARLES II and the ROYALISTS dance off, with the spluttering HYDE in the rear.*)

LILBURNE: (*Singing.*)
I was born into a country of pain.
The Few ruled the Mob in God's name.
Death was the only way of life.
The People were castrated by the King's knife
In Sixteen Twenty-Five.
(*Speaking.*) It was dying then to be alive!
(*Singing.*) I was born nothing but a whipping song,
And England belonged to the King.
Cromwell was a country thing
When it all began to fester wrong
In Sixteen Twenty-Five.
This fop's father, Charles the First,
Was twenty-five when *his* father died.
Charles took the throne as King James' hearse
Rolled the wisest fool in Christendom
Into the fires of Kingdom-come.
It seems England cannot do without a king,
So let the royal death-bells ring.
James the First of England's dead!
Charles the First will fool instead,
'Til Charlie loses his foolish head!
(*The Court enters with a satirical fanfare. The Court includes the Puritan JOHN PYM, who is First Minister; THOMAS WENTWORTH, Pym's Second in Command; Sir THOMAS FAIRFAX; the EARL OF ESSEX; the MARQUIS OF*

MANCHESTER and DENZIL HOLLES, a Member of Parliament.

CROMWELL stands aloof.

They form an aisle as CHARLES I appears in full coronation regalia. The arrogant DUKE OF BUCKINGHAM walks beside him. ROYALISTS bring up the rear.

Everyone but the KING, BUCKINGHAM and CROMWELL kneel.)

COURT: (*Singing.*)
Charles is King
By Right Divine.
Let angels sing:
The world is thine.
Now let the King ascend his throne.
He is King of heart and bone.

PYM: (*Aside to WENTWORTH.*) While all his bloody subjects groan! (*Confronting the King.*) Now, sire, it is imperative that you recall Parliament. Despotic law in England will bring tyranny.

BUCKINGHAM: His August Majesty is not disposed to talk of trifles today, Mr Pym.

PYM: I'm sorry, sire, but as First Minister, I must insist...

BUCKINGHAM: (*Overriding him.*) Jumped-up tradesmen are not in a position to insist on anything, sirrah.

PYM: (*To CHARLES.*) I demand that you recall Parliament!

BUCKINGHAM: Why? His Majesty is governing very prettily without them.

PYM: (*Under his breath to WENTWORTH.*) Charles is certainly repeating all his father's mistakes.

BUCKINGHAM: God's wounds!

PYM: And without the assistance of Parliament, soon the King won't have enough money to entertain such perfumed frills as *you*, my Lord Buckingham.

BUCKINGHAM: Puritan, I advise you to return to managing your nefarious companies, or whatever miserly thing it is you do. Leave the ruling of England to those whose birth it befits.

WENTWORTH: (*Now nose-to-nose with BUCKINGHAM.*) Well, that certainly doesn't include you, stable boy!

BUCKINGHAM: (*With his hand on his sword.*) God's teeth, Sir Thomas Wentworth, how dare you...?

WENTWORTH: (*Relentless.*) Because everyone knows that your swollen head is a direct result of your swollen codpiece, in King James' bed!

BUCKINGHAM: Christ's bowels, Wentworth, I'll have you racked for this!

WENTWORTH: You, sir, will do nothing, sir, because you, sir, are a fool, sir. Well, you were defeated ignominiously by Cardinal Richelieu at the siege of La Rochelle. What's more, every man in England remembers this, and knows you now for what you are: the King's catamite clinking the King's purse.

PYM: Who bares his bum-boy's arse in the continuous service of Rome!

BUCKINGHAM: Charles, how can you remain silent in the presence of these jackals?

WENTWORTH: (*Indicating BUCKINGHAM.*) Your Majesty, for England's dear sake, cast this expensive primrose into the Thames.

PYM: Then there will be a chance that we can financially redeem you.

BUCKINGHAM: Christ's loins, I will not be...

WENTWORTH: (*Overriding him.*) It's either Buckingham, Majesty, or your kingdom!

(*BUCKINGHAM flashes his glove across WENTWORTH's face. With an imperious gesture CHARLES stops the quarrel from escalating further. The KING has a pronounced stutter when he is moved or angry.*)

CHARLES I: My c-crown is in the direct line of King D-David.
So when the p-puffed-up n-nightingale
Attempts to enchant the b-bloated owl,
Then the Hawk of G-God will rip out their eyes and lives.
And I am the Hawk of God.
So my will supersedes everything and ev-everyone.
The rest is immaterial.

PYM: Parliament still represents the People, Majesty. I do not wish to presume but there *are* people in England. Some two odd million who *should* have rights. But don't let that worry you.

CHARLES I: I won't.

PYM: They need help from their King.

CHARLES I: (*To BUCKINGHAM.*) Dear George.

BUCKINGHAM: Yes, Your Majesty.

CHARLES I: You will ensure that my subjects receive the j-justice that they deserve, by assisting their King with a few minor t-taxes; tonnage and poundage – at the rates of two shilling per t-tun on wine, and sixpence per p-pound sterling on all other merchandise. And, what's more, for the rest of our l-life.

PYM: Parliament will refuse to endorse such iniquitous taxes.

BUCKINGHAM: Traitor!

CHARLES I: Parliament d-dare not d-deny me!

PYM: At best, the members will grant you tonnage and poundage for the first year of your reign only. I know them.

BUCKINGHAM: Then we will hang them!

WENTWORTH: Your Majesty, there is another way.

CHARLES I: Yes, Sir Thomas?

WENTWORTH: But first you must remove Buckingham from under your cloak.

BUCKINGHAM: Christ's navel, hang 'em all, and instantly!

PYM: One day very soon, George Villiers, you will find that you are eating death for your breakfast.

CHARLES I: G-Gentlemen! If you persist in thwarting my desires, I shall be forced to consign y-you and P-Parliament into oblivion. By the by, I intend to m-marry tomorrow.

PYM: (*Nonplussed.*) But, Majesty…?

WENTWORTH: Is that wise, sire?

BUCKINGHAM: Yes, Charles…

CHARLES I: (*Smiling.*) Perhaps.

(*The sound of jubilant marriage bells. A Boy enters swinging an incense censer, followed by the French Princess, HENRIETTA MARIA, and Bishop LAUD. HENRIETTA has a beautiful face but she has a slightly humped back.*)

LAUD: (*Chanting.*) Sweetness of marriage
Comes from the sweetness of Christ.

PYM: (*To WENTWORTH.*) Despite his Church of England trappings, Bishop Laud is a Papist!
(*Singing.*) Out of the Roman darkness comes
The Ave Maria of idolatrous hell.
Against this French armada sound the drums,
And ring the bloody Doomsday bell.
(*During the singing, HENRIETTA and CHARLES kneel before LAUD.*)

LILBURNE: (*Singing.*)
The incense, of course, was not really there
But the stench hung metaphorically in the air.
Henrietta Maria, our Queen-to-be,
Is a Roman Catholic, you see,
So there is a hell of a lot to fear.
(*The marriage ceremony is completed tout de suite. CHARLES and HENRIETTA face one another.*)

HENRIETTA: (*Pulling her train around her protectively.*)
A people of ice!

CHARLES I: Don't be frightened, Henrietta, my love. I am the sun.

LAUD: (*Singing his blessing.*)
May summer always cradle you
In its sunlit fingers.
Blossoms are blown by Christ across your eyes
To take the darkness from them,
So do not shut Christ's Light out.

PYM: (*To WENTWORTH.*) Archbishop Laud positively stinks of Rome. He must be watched, Sir Thomas.

WENTWORTH: You are too hasty, Mr Pym, as is your wont. You never think anything through to its logical conclusion, do you?

PYM: Like what?

WENTWORTH: Bishop Laud will bring some much needed order into the Church. He will keep the People's lips firmly pressed to the flagstones. Never forget that the stronger the Church is, the stronger we are.

PYM: Blasphemy! God is not a sponge to squeeze the People with.

WENTWORTH: Then why do *you* squeeze money out of the People in *His* Name? Why do you build your Puritan businesses under the sanctity of His Cross?

PYM: God's tripes!

WENTWORTH: You sound just like Buckingham.

PYM: And you, Wentworth, sound like the condescending nobility, and as such, the People will very soon treat you as you deserve. Every last man jack of you.

WENTWORTH: Oh I am sure you will try. That is why all you money-grubbers make such good businessmen. You equally hate those above you – as much as you hate those below you. But you are still hypocritically willing to sell your souls to either, for the right price.

PYM: Just as I thought; you really despise us, don't you? So why do you consort with us, then?

WENTWORTH: Because, temporarily, we need one another.

PYM: (*Brushing WENTWORTH's shoulder with his fingertips.*) You have incense on your shoulder, Sir Thomas. Take care or the dogs will urinate against you.

WENTWORTH: You will not touch me until Buckingham's disposed of. And even then – we shall see.
(*During this conversation, dance music is playing quietly. CHARLES and HENRIETTA enter, with BUCKINGHAM and his Lady. On the opposite side of the stage, the Members of Parliament gather around PYM. CROMWELL continues to watch from the side.*)

CHARLES I: (*Dancing with HENRIETTA.*) Your fingers are ice, my dear.

HENRIETTA: It's the climate, my love. (*Shivering.*) And the People. They hate me for being a Catholic.

CHARLES I: As long as there is love between us, no one can touch you.

HENRIETTA: Never doubt me, Charles. Will you?

CHARLES I: No, but ensure that your n-nuns are well hidden in your private Chapel. Keep everything to do with R-Rome out of the public eye – for both our sakes.
(*HENRIETTA's diamond necklace slithers to the ground. With an elaborate bow, BUCKINGHAM returns it to her.*)

BUCKINGHAM: Your Highness, allow me.

HENRIETTA: Thank you, my lord.

CHARLES I: This is my Lord of Buck-Buckingham. The hooded eyes behind my smile. Or is it vice versa? Love him, dearest, as I do. He has an interest in your religion – which I sense could prove to be dangerous.

BUCKINGHAM: Charles, are you aware of what's happening?

CHARLES I: Of course.

BUCKINGHAM: Pym is trying to pass the Bill of Rights through Parliament.

CHARLES I: So?

BUCKINGHAM: They intend to draw our teeth. Soon we will only be able to tax our servants.

CHARLES I: They have always wanted to curtail my power but I have always prevented them.

BUCKINGHAM: But this time they want more. Much more. The Puritans want to rule. And they control the trading, remember. They have the money.

CHARLES I: I forbid you to use that w-w-word in my presence!

BUCKINGHAM: And with all their money, they plan to rule in a very different way. With no single Puritan taking full responsibility for anything because each is in the other's pocket.

LILBURNE: (*To the audience.*) Which explains a lot.

BUCKINGHAM: Arrest Pym! Dissolve Parliament! Or they will stifle us, Charles. Already they are invoking the Magna Carta, and they are petitioning against your right to tax and imprison whomever you want. They're cutting holes in your privileges. Pym even has the Queen watched!

CHARLES I: You are pre-presumptuous, sirrah, to…

BUCKINGHAM: (*Relentless.*) And Pym has her servants watched. Also he has informed the Commons that *you* yourself intend to become a Catholic!

HENRIETTA: (*To CHARLES.*) Well, don't you, dearest?

CHARLES I: E-E-Enough!

BUCKINGHAM: Charles…

CHARLES I: I said enough! Because you were favourite to my father – (*Dangerously.*) and I know how – sometimes you sicken me with your sly smiles. My f-father would dr-dribble in your beard.

BUCKINGHAM: You wrong me!

CHARLES I: Do I? Do I? I know how you fla-flatter, my f-friend. Or *are* you 'my friend'? Is anyone? (*Pause.*) Sometimes I...

(*CHARLES trails off.*)

BUCKINGHAM: Yes, sire?

CHARLES I: Sometimes I wonder why men want to r-rule. Oh I know *you* want to, George. As Pym does. And Wentworth. Even that upstart, Cromwell, as he hovers between the tradesman and the mob, pretending to be both; he, too, wants to rule.

BUCKINGHAM: So break them all on the rack!

CHARLES I: (*Staring at the motionless CROMWELL.*) Yes, they would all break – save Cromwell. He says little but he disturbs me. Look at him brooding on his obscene Jehovah.

HENRIETTA: It amazes me, dearest, that you should take that pock-marked churl so seriously.

CHARLES I: I amaze myself. But then I only sit on the Right Hand of God the Son. I am not ambitious. I wear C-Christ's earthly crown. But we are not im-immortal. Yet.

HENRIETTA: (*Provocatively.*) But you could be, dearest.

CHARLES I: It is a pity that each of us needs a p-private Christ. Although it does have a consoling aspect. It ensures that Our Lord is extremely adaptable.

BUCKINGHAM: Then stop playing games, Charles. Arrest all your enemies. Dissolve Parliament forever. Rule by Right Divine. Here is the power. (*He kisses CHARLES' ring.*) Without this ring and your signature, England does not exist. Have you ever thought of that? So use them like God, and the People will love you for it. They don't mind you stepping on their necks – as long as you are wearing *royal* slippers.

CHARLES I: I wish... I wish that I was k-king enough to...

HENRIETTA: (*Eagerly.*) To do what, my sweet?

CHARLES I: ...To do without you all!

BUCKINGHAM: I pity you.

CHARLES I: How d-dare you?

BUCKINGHAM: You are the King of England, and yet you want to be loved. Bizarre. All you have in your crown is death, and your duty on earth is to hand out death as imaginatively, and often as possible. The mob will love you for it. They need entertaining – like everyone else.

HENRIETTA: The Pope wishes to be remembered to you. He says the sunlight in the Vatican will burn the ice of England into Roman water.

CHARLES I: Silence, w-woman!

HENRIETTA: (*Touching her womb.*) I have life here, beloved. Your life.

CHARLES I: I know. I have you watched. I am not King for nothing. And, Henrietta – be careful. Do not use my son as a weapon.

(*CHARLES I and his Court dance into the shadows.*
PYM harangues the Commons.)

PYM: We will blast the King with this petition, and throw Magna Carta in his face, because we are too old, gentlemen, too tired, and far too abused to tolerate a second John Lackland in England. And that is exactly what Charles is trying to become. He is trying to circumvent our privileges as Englishmen by forcibly billeting troops in our homes against the will of the Commons. He is taxing us indiscriminately, making trading unprofitable, and then imprisoning innocent dissenters. Yes, gentlemen, he is ripping up the lilies of the field while his rank hemlock, Buckingham, and that deadly nightshade, Laud, the brothel bishop, between them they are poisoning the garden of England. Even the Star Chamber, under Queen Elizabeth, was only ever used for protecting the direct interests of the monarchy and the clergy, but it has now become a Torture Chamber, a Second Inquisition, that Charles and his cronies are employing continuously and callously against the Common People. The King is flouting the

Common Law! Flouting our rights as individuals. Indeed no man may speak his mind for fear the torturers break his spine. So, gentlemen, we must now strike at the centre of evil. The Star Chamber. It must be instantly revoked, dismembered, and then hurled into God's Furnace like stubble in the whirlwind. Because God is with us! We are doing God's Work.

(*During this speech, a large black star is lowered and hangs suspended centre-stage.*

LAUD appears beneath the star. He calls to LILBURNE.)

LAUD: You.

LILBURNE: Me?

LAUD: Yes, you!

LILBURNE: 'Sir' usually follows my name. Were you addressing me or someone else?

(*Two Guards knock LILBURNE to the ground while CHARLES and HENRIETTA continue to dance in the shadows.*)

Oh, you did mean me.

LAUD: (*Waving a piece of parchment at LILBURNE.*) Did you publish this seditious drivel, John Lilburne, concerning His Imperial Majesty?

LILBURNE: (*Snatching the parchment from him and reading the contents outloud.*)

'Charles the First, by Right Divine,
Loves the Pope and Roman wine.
He blows his wind up England's nose.
It pongs worse than cheesy toes.
And he thinks as long as he's the King,
His dung sweetens anything.
But I'm a free-born Englishman
And I intend to belch his pong
Back to Scotland – whew, it's strong! –
Where it can sweeten a Scottish man.
I'm not saying that Charlie's sinned,
I just don't like his wind!'

Do you mean did I compose this delicious little ditty?

LAUD: Yes!

LILBURNE: No. But I wish I had.

LAUD: You appear to be obsessed with the rear end.

LILBURNE: From what I hear from your choristers, I'm not alone.

LAUD: Enough of your bawdy badinage! You are here to be judged.

LILBURNE: By whom, and for what?

LAUD: By *me*; and for taking the King's name in vain.

LILBURNE: Even if I did write this – which I didn't – you can hardly call it seditious. And, anyway, why are *you* involved? When it has nothing to do with the Church.

LAUD: *Everything* has to do with the Church. Are you suggesting that you possess any rights, other than those bestowed upon you by your Bishop and your King?

LILBURNE: Certainly. I'm a free-born Englishman. The King's jurisdiction ends with my body, as the Church's ends with my soul. My heart and my mind are only answerable to me, sir.

LAUD: They are immaterial when the King can wrack your body, and the Church can damn your soul.

LILBURNE: Listen, I'm telling you the truth. I didn't write this. And I refuse to cower before you. The Star Chamber cannot judge me, and you know it. If I had committed a crime – which I haven't – I should be judged under civil law, not by the corrupt clergy.

LAUD: (*To the Guards.*) Silence him!

LILBURNE: (*As the Guards kick him.*) You'll never do that, mates, until you cut off my head. What's more, there are millions more like me, waiting in and out of the womb, to flame you into Purgatory. So do not try our patience. We are very hungry.

LAUD: John Lilburne, I find you guilty of insubordination; the essence, if not the practice of treason; of libel; and the beginnings of blasphemy.

LILBURNE: Really? Well, I find you, my no one's lord, guilty of coldness; of the essence of hate and its practice; of defecating on England; and the beginnings of hell. (*Despite being kicked, he manages to kiss LAUD's ring.*) Congratulations. Oh and…give my regards to His Majesty. You're a wonderful watchdog.

(PYM, leading the House of Commons, begins to sing. The song starts quietly, and can barely be heard above the royal dance music, but it soon builds to a discordant climax.)

PYM / COMMONS: Free John Lilburne
Free born free him
Give him freedom
Or we'll claim him
We'll unchain him
Dung disease
May you freeze
Bishop
Star chamber
Satan's rainbow
Bishop
We've had enough ceremony
We've had enough of Death to see
You've made the Church into a whore
Shaking her breasts against Hell's door
You've no right to try him so
Listen to the drums of snow
Plague and desperation's here
We have passed the Church of Fear
Listen for your death is near
Free John Lilburne
Free-born free him
Give him freedom
Or we'll maim you
Yes we'll brain you
Freedom!
Freedom!

(CHARLES, HENRIETTA, BUCKINGHAM et al are still dancing.)

CHARLES I: *(To BUCKINGHAM.)* George, dissolve Parliament. They're getting rather excitable.

PYM: *(To the COMMONS.)* We won't give the King a single farthing!

LAUD: John Lilburne, you will be flogged from the Abbey to Fleet.

LILBURNE: Well, that's freedom, anyway – from *you*, for a start. But then one must never be over-ambitious in England. We are a quiet, cruel, conservative race. Long may we continue.

(*A Soldier strips the shirt off LILBURNE's back, and then proceeds to whip him around the perimeter of the stage.*)

(*Singing.*) Here we go – the pain.

Whip – whip – whip again.

Cut my back, but not my brain.

Freedom! Freedom!

Strap me on the rack.

Split my rib-cage – crack.

Leave my brain. Cut my back.

Freedom! Freedom!

(*LILBURNE and the Soldier exit. The dance music becomes more sensuous.*)

HENRIETTA: (*To CHARLES.*) A beautiful man, my Lord of Buckingham. His fingers uncurl like water lilies. I would like him to be – my champion in the hunt tomorrow, dearest.

CHARLES I: The hunt of what, Henrietta?

HENRIETTA: The little one inside my womb. Shall we call him 'Charles' after his father?

CHARLES I: Does your b-back hurt you, my love?

HENRIETTA: Why must you always remind me of my deformity?

CHARLES I: Does it cause you distress, carrying Charles, is what I meant, my dear?

HENRIETTA: Buckingham doesn't notice my back. George Villiers doesn't notice. George doesn't notice.

CHARLES I: My sweet, the extra wave on your shoulders
G-God made so that the swan of your throat
Can ride in its beauty more freely.

(*CHARLES and HENRIETTA dance off. BUCKINGHAM dismisses the Lady he was dancing with. Then he draws his sword and proceeds to dance and fence in front of a mirror that is lowered in front of him.*)

During this, the Commons also retreat into the shadows – while
PYM, WENTWORTH and CROMWELL watch the fop,
BUCKINGHAM.
LILBURNE re-enters, swabbing his blood-stained back.)

LILBURNE: (*To the audience.*) We are now vaguely in the year
Sixteen Twenty-Eight.

PYM: (*To WENTWORTH.*) Buckingham is madly in love
– with himself.

WENTWORTH: (*Approaching BUCKINGHAM.*) George
Villiers, I wish to warn you of the dangers of corrupting
the realm, of intriguing with Cardinal Richelieu, of Roman
Catholic tendencies – and also of possessing a dirty mind.
(*BUCKINGHAM stops his mock-fencing in the mirror, and
levels his sword at WENTWORTH's throat.*)

BUCKINGHAM: I see life bores you, sir. So let's finish
with your life. Unsling your sword; if you are not entirely
leprosy inside.

WENTWORTH: Oh you could easily kill me, Villiers. But,
sadly, I cannot allow you the pleasure. Unlike your own,
my life is invaluable to England.

BUCKINGHAM: You merchant banker!
(*PYM clicks his fingers. CROMWELL steps out of the shadows
– like a gunfighter in a Western.*)

PYM: Mr Villiers, may I introduce you to the new Member of
Parliament for Huntingdon, Mr Oliver Cromwell. He is a
real swordsman. Not a dilettante, like you.
(*BUCKINGHAM advances on CROMWELL with his
sword drawn but CROMWELL's flickering blade instantly
disarms him. The tip of CROMWELL's sword touches
BUCKINGHAM's throat.*)
See what I mean. They say the Royal Hump would like
you to give chase, Villiers.

BUCKINGHAM: What villainy is this?

WENTWORTH: (*As CROMWELL sheathes his sword.*) Yes, Mr
Pym, there is no cause to attack Her Majesty.

PYM: (*Clutching his stomach.*) My apologies. I have a recurring
abdominal pain, sir, that plays havoc with my sentence
construction. What I meant was…they say that Her Majesty
would like Mr Villiers to give chase in the Royal Hunt.

BUCKINGHAM: (*Picking up his sword.*) Yes...then I will leave
it to the King to order your heads to be spiked on Traitors'
Gate in the morning. The Hawk of God will tear out your
lives while the Nightingale sings over the marshes of your
blood. And *I* am the Nightingale.
(*BUCKINGHAM returns to his fencing in the mirror.*)

CROMWELL: Sir, because you copy the King's mode of
speech, do not think you are the King. You are not.

BUCKINGHAM: (*Continuing to fence with himself.*) So the
religious assassin can talk, can he? Your father was some
kind of udder-jerking farmer, wasn't he?

CROMWELL: I do have earth in my fingernails, yes.

BUCKINGHAM: And God in your codpiece, I hear. Must be
tricky for you both – with the ladies.

CROMWELL: (*Drawing his sword again.*) You may sneer at
me, Villiers, but I will rip out your soul if you desecrate
God's Ineffable Name.

BUCKINGHAM: (*Nervously.*) You actually mean what you
say, God help us. I mean... It's just so unsophisticated.
'Fact it's almost obscene. But don't worry; I'll have you in
your grave by dinner.

CROMWELL: First there, first served. And you...look
premature to me.

PYM: (*Under his breath.*) He's a dead man, so it's hardly
surprising.
(*WENTWORTH, CROMWELL and PYM exit.*)
Ring the bells. Summer is coming.
(*LILBURNE watches BUCKINGHAM loving himself in the
mirror.*)

LILBURNE: The Duke was dappled in firelight.
The moon was sweet at midnight,
And the Gentleman Caller is coming tonight
to give you one hell of a goodnight fright.
(*Re-enter WENTWORTH, putting on a black mask. Then he
follows BUCKINGHAM, unseen.*)

BUCKINGHAM: (*Singing.*)
I would love to stroke Henrietta's crooked spine,
And kiss her foreign lips with England on mine.

I will hunt the Royal Hump in the morning,
While Parliament loses its head as a warning
To all the Freedom Seekers in the morning.
(*WENTWORTH stabs BUCKINGHAM in the back with a
knife, then he drags off the corpse.*)
LILBURNE: (*Singing.*)
Never to taste her royal wine,
Never to see the morning.
Stuck with a crooked knife in a straight spine.
The Freedom Seekers give their first warning.
(*Speaks.*) The Duke of Buckingham comes back in our
proceedings – as Lord Digby. Well, there's always a king's
favourite, waiting for the odd earldom to be dropped as a
scrap to a dandified dog under the table. And the king's
favourite is usually a dandified dog.
(*Re-enter WENTWORTH, without his mask. He approaches
LILBURNE.*)
WENTWORTH: You write well, Lilburne. Be my scrivener.
I'll need one where I'm going.
LILBURNE: Oh, where's that? A political brothel.
WENTWORTH: (*Smiling indulgently.*) No, on the contrary,
I intend to bring a great deal more money, trade and
prosperity into the kingdom. In fact I will fulfil the dreams
of all men, by beneficently ruling over all men.
LILBURNE: Find another Puritan, Sir Thomas. I do not
follow other men – in anything but dying.
WENTWORTH: Naïve! You are being led by the groin as
the rest are. England – like the world – is in the balance,
seething between unrest and total madness. It has the
choice to either naturally decay – or to make use of the
Establishment's almost limitless power. So don't be a
martyr to the People, Lilburne. They do not give a fig if
you rot. They only live for their own flabby, insular lives.
That's why we must contain them before they devour us.
We must make the Law absolute – so that at least *some* will
prosper. If not, there is only Anarchy.
LILBURNE: My God, Sir Thomas, I did not realise that you
were – *are* – so appallingly ambitious.

WENTWORTH: Only for England! There has to be the fist in the night. The bodkin rammed into the brain. Otherwise the peasants will take us by the throat, and choke us in our own blood.

LILBURNE: By Christ, I hope they do! I hope *we* do! It's *our* turn now, and we will build a new and infinitely better world.

WENTWORTH: You're deceiving yourself, man. You will only succeed in being more inefficient, more selfish, more brutal – and finally more loathed. But I can use you. Because underneath you are just like me. You're dangerous because you really believe that you are always right. And you're willing to die for it. Just think of it, Lilburne. With my cunning and my imagination, and your energy and your popular sentimentality – for that's what it is – together we could do anything. So come with me to the King.

LILBURNE: Treacherous autocrat!

WENTWORTH: The King is our only hope. And by 'King', I do not mean that vain, weak man, Charles Stuart. No, I mean – the Throne, the Power and the Glory. That is why we must prevent the King from stuttering into the abyss, because if he does, then everything we know and love will be null and void. And in his stead, a more desperate, bitter creature will claw its way into power, and tyrannise the land. I can see him in my mind's eye; a religious zealot, with hate in his veins. Then the spirit of England will wither. There will only be God and money – and grey faces – and even more money. Although in the right hands, of course… (*Producing a purse full of money like a magician.*) …money becomes something else.

LILBURNE: In *your* hands, for instance?

WENTWORTH: In *our* hands. (*He dangles the purse under LILBURNE's nose.*) Take it.

LILBURNE: No, thanks. Lucre stains the mind, you know.

WENTWORTH: Not if it's used to make a king into a King.

LILBURNE: You're insane.

WENTWORTH: Am I?

LILBURNE: Pym will hate you for turning coat.

WENTWORTH: Pym cannot smell beyond the garlic on his breath. Now Buckingham is dead, someone must help Charles to rule. Someone must help him to understand – this. (*He rattles the purse.*) Which, unfortunately, he seems to have a royal aversion to. But you and I know that *without* this, he is King in name only. He's merely a decorative bauble. So Charles must be trained to like money, to collect money, to save money, even to hoard money – for the greater glory of the realm. So I intend to teach him.

LILBURNE: And if you lose your head in the process?

WENTWORTH: I will be yet another failure in history's comedy. So be yourself, Lilburne. Use this money for the King. It's either Charles, or the faceless usurers. The spectres. Choose. Come with me to the King. We can use one another.

LILBURNE: No one uses me, sir. Not even God. And no matter what you think, you can't do it without the People.

WENTWORTH: Wrong. As usual. Even in a hundred, a thousand years' time, the People – as you call them – will still be willing to remain enslaved by the System – the System that they stupidly thought was created for them.

LILBURNE: If you're right, there'll never be any progress.

WENTWORTH: Quite. No one learns anything from another man's pain, so there's no such thing as progress. Except in surface sophistication.

LILBURNE: (*Touching WENTWORTH's shoulder.*) You have incense on your shoulder, Wentworth. Watch it.
(*LILBURNE moves away from WENTWORTH as CHARLES, HENRIETTA and LORD DIGBY enter.*)
And here's Lord Digby. What did I tell you about a dog dandified.

DIGBY: Sire, I intend that Buckingham's funeral will be even more elaborate than your wildest dreams.

CHARLES I: Thank you, Digby. It is good to have f-friends. Poor George… (*To HENRIETTA.*) …He died defending your honour, my dear.

HENRIETTA: His fingers uncurled like water lilies in the sun.

CHARLES I: Digby, when will Van Dyke finish our portrait?
I foster artists but they're all so incredibly l-lazy.

DIGBY: Indeed you speak the truth, sire. (*Indicating WENTWORTH.*) I've heard from certain unimpeachable sources that Sir Thomas Wentworth has changed his coat again. But don't trust him, Majesty. We don't need him.

WENTWORTH: (*Kneeling before the King.*) Your Majesty, I...

CHARLES I: (*Interrupting.*) I know. You want to serve me.

WENTWORTH: But I told no one.

CHARLES I: Eyes watch you. Your rheumatics. The dryness of your lips. The order of your prayers – when you remember them. And you're a-ambition – for England, of course.

WENTWORTH: (*Kissing the King's hand.*) Your Majesty.

CHARLES I: I require ob-obedience above everything.
(*PYM and CROMWELL enter.*)

PYM: (*To CROMWELL.*) Sir Thomas Wentworth is a true King's man – and a traitor to the Realm. Which is original, to say the least.
(*CHARLES, HENRIETTA and DIGBY exit.*)

CROMWELL: Poverty in England. Unbelievable.
My feet are frozen.
Look, the horses are steaming.
How can we help the People, Pym?
I pray for guidance but it does not come.
Christ seems to be...

PYM: ...Dead?

CROMWELL: (*Distraught.*) No! No. Christ must be amongst us. He must. He is.

PYM: Sometimes I...
(*PYM trails off.*)

CROMWELL: He is!

PYM: Sometimes I wonder why we go on trying.

CROMWELL: We are compelled.
(*PARLIAMENT gathers, including HYDE, who is carried in on the Speaker's Chair, and HOLLES and BISHOP LAUD. WENTWORTH joins them.*)

LILBURNE: (*To the audience.*) So we bumbled our way to Sixteen Twenty-Nine.

LAUD: The Prayer Book is to be changed. Vestments are again to be worn by priests. Once more the altar will be placed in the apex of the church, and Sunday will be reverently observed because the Church has lost its style.

PYM: No, no, no, no! Nothing related to the Church will be changed. And also no more tonnage and poundage will be collected in the realm. The King has more than had his year of privileges. Henceforth, taxes will only be imposed by Parliament. And the King must rule through Parliament. (*The Puritans cheer.*)

HYDE: (*Banging his gavel.*) Order, gentleman, gentlemen! And Mr Pym is *out* of order! (*To PYM.*) You exceed your Puritanical rights, sir.

WENTWORTH: I agree, Mr Speaker. So: to return to the King's requirements. His Majesty is a great supporter of the Arts, as you know. But he must have money. And more money because it is imperative that the Monarchy have style.

LAUD: And the Church needs more money because it, too, must have style.

CROMWELL: The Monarchy and the Church have style, but no bloody content! If you'll forgive my bluntness.

PYM: Yes, Bishop, you dress the Church up in the wantonness of popery.

WENTWORTH: You are bigoted, sir. How can the Mob be expected to understand Christ but through the romance of symbols? And symbols are expensive. (*The seventy year-old Sir JOHN ELIOTT enters, tired and late.*)

ELIOTT: You do not understand the Mob, as you call them, Sir Thomas. Apologies for lateness, gentlemen. The Mob is composed of individuals, many of whom are starving. And they are not hungry for candlelit altars. But they *are* hungry. Very hungry. And stained glass is not food.

PYM: (*Applauding.*) Yes, you tell them, my dear Eliott, you tell them. Would that you spoke more often.

ELIOTT: If I did, Prime Minister, *you* would not be Prime Minister. But I'm not interested in your thirst for power, Pym. Nor in the horses charging behind Cromwell's eyes. Or the fancy dress delusions of the Bishop. Or in Wentworth's misguided stratagems. No, I am only interested in hunger. I can smell hunger. I have been possessed by it. It jerks the bowels out of control. You vomit up the contents of your stomach which happens to be bad air. You gnaw rotten fingernails when you're hungry. The sun smells of plague, and the moon hangs in your eyes like leprosy when you're hungry. And all the symbols of Christ only increase the need for miracles – to relieve your hunger. Miracles that *never happen,* but they go on teasing you that they will. So you grow to hate yourself and all mankind. You become evil with hunger. And we, gentlemen, are the apex of the hopes of the hungry. But what do we do? We tax the People's hunger. We build churches, awash with gold and silver, on the backs of their hunger. Gentlemen – all of us here – myself included – make me wish that Man had never corrupted the Light by existing at all!

(*Enter CHARLES in his full pomp.*)

CHARLES I: Parliament is dissolved, gentlemen – for ever. If words are said contrary by any gentlemen, any gentlemen will breakfast in the Tower.

(*CHARLES exits, and is followed out by LAUD and WENTWORTH who are smiling. There is a roar of disapproval from the Commons.*)

LILBURNE: (*To the audience.*)

The Triumvirate of England begins.

And, Hallelujah, listen to the bloody din!

HYDE: (*Banging his gavel.*) Gentlemen, Parliament will adjourn indefinitely!

PYM: (*Snatching the gavel from HYDE.*) No, Hyde, we will pass a couple of laws before we go.

HYDE: The King will declare them illegal!

ELIOTT: Let the King hang himself in his Portrait Gallery!

HOLLES: We pass that tonnage and poundage are illegal from this day forward.

HYDE: I protest, Mr Holles…

CROMWELL: Protest all you like, but from this day, any alterations in the Puritan laws of the Church will be greeted with severe punishment.

HYDE: Once I leave my chair as Speaker, this Parliament is illegal.

PYM: Sit on Mr Hyde, Mr Cromwell.

CROMWELL: Certainly. (*Forcibly CROMWELL sits on HYDE.*) He's a bit bony.

PYM: Anyone who aids the King's soldiers in the extraction of arbitrary taxes, other than those imposed by Parliament, is a betrayer of the Liberty of England, and, forthwith, should be fed to the Dogs of Hell. (*To a Secretary.*) Have you got all that?

HYDE: I protest! This violence towards me only indicates the unlawfulness of your proceedings!

ELIOTT: I agree. (*Drawing his sword.*) This must be done without violence!

(*ELIOTT tugs PYM's beard.*)

HYDE: (*Throwing CROMWELL off his knee, and drawing his sword.*) For the King! For England and Peace!

(*Everyone draws their swords. Pandemonium breaks loose. CHARLES enters, followed by WENTWORTH and LAUD. The fighting stops.*)

CHARLES I: Thank you for standing, gentlemen. I arrest, in my name, as a traitor to the realm... Whom shall I arrest as a traitor to the realm?

WENTWORTH: Pym, Your Majesty. He is the most dangerous.

CHARLES I: Tomorrow perhaps. But today – ah, let me see... Mr Eliott, I think.

ELIOTT: You have no right to be in this Parliament, Charles Stuart.

CHARLES I: Impertinent gadfly!

ELIOTT: ...Unless you are invited! These constant displays of despotic power...

CHARLES I: To the Tower with him!

(*ELIOTT is seized by Soldiers.*)

PYM: Your Majesty...

CHARLES I: Do you wish to join him, Mr Pym?

PYM: No, Your Majesty. I hope you enjoy the recess.

CHARLES I: I will.

WENTWORTH: Take the initiative, sire. Hang Pym and Cromwell!

CHARLES I: I would I could. But as you have taught me, Thomas, without them, there is no money. And without money I cannot r-rule. (*To the Members.*) A hundred years ago I would have had you drawn and quartered – all of you!

LILBURNE: (*To the audience.*) So, you see, there are compensations for living today.

ELIOTT: I speak out rarely but when I do, I'm certainly heard.

(*CHARLES, WENTWORTH and LAUD exit.*)

(*Singing.*) Let's sing out for Liberty

Because Charles the First is certainly

Preparing the hate in me,

To burst open hungrily.

Loose all the Poor of England on him!

Goodbye, the Royalty. *The People Are Coming!*

(*ELIOTT is dragged off. CROMWELL is about to start something but PYM shakes his head. The PURITANS exit in silent protest.*

DIGBY enters, carrying CHARLES' hunting gear, and boar spears for CHARLES, WENTWORTH and LAUD. A hunting horn is heard.)

CHARLES I: Ah, this is so pleasant.

LAUD / WENTWORTH: (*Singing and dancing together.*)

A-hunting we will go

To trap the wild boar in the fen.

We'll tax England for the King,

And we'll melt the Puritan snows.

LILBURNE: (*Singing.*)

Eleven years they taxed the land.

And reformed it as well, you must understand.

(*The Royalists search the ground for boar tracks.*)

WENTWORTH: The boar passed this way, Highness.

(*Off, the Boar is heard snorting.*)

The Treasury is filling nicely. (*Pointing to LILBURNE.*) That fellow there owned this land recently.

CHARLES I: Have you seen the boar, sirrah?

LILBURNE: (*To the audience.*) I told you, 'sir', usually followed my name. (*To CHARLES.*) It was snuffling for your Majesty. (*A Puritan, wearing a Boar's head, snarls into view. Warily the KING, WENTWORTH and LAUD circle the Boar.*)

The baited boar snarls at the sky.

His crimson eyes of pig and hate

Charge at the gold of Royalty.

Goodnight. Bad dreams, Your Majesty.

CHARLES I: At him, my lords. I see Parliament in his eyes! (*The Boar charges at the KING. The KING stumbles. The Boar is about to rip out the KING's throat with his tusks. WENTWORTH charges with his spear, wounding the Boar in his left flank. Blindly the Boar leaves CHARLES, then he attacks WENTWORTH. LAUD wounds the Boar in its right flank. The Boar is now mad with pain. CHARLES lands the killing blow. Roaring and screaming, the Boar flails into death. The KING removes the Boar's head with his spear. Triumphantly he holds up the Boar's head. Then the KING looks with horror at the dead body: OLIVER CROMWELL.*)

Oliver Cromwell! I have hunted you in my dreams.

WENTWORTH: (*Perplexed.*) Who, my liege?

CHARLES I: (*Pointing at the body.*) The beast, Cromwell.

LAUD: But it's only a dead boar, sire.

CHARLES I: No, under the mask of the animal is the human hatred. The Puritans are hungry for me. The aristocracy is dying. The tradesmen are here. Everywhere there's the taste of money – because that is what the Puritans carry in grubby bundles under their sackcloth and ashes. I am stifled by bankers and lawyers. So I have no choice but to sit upon their heads.

WENTWORTH: And, in turn, the bankers and lawyers sit upon the heads of the People. A pleasant arrangement. We're frightened of the Puritans, and *they're* frightened of the People.

CHARLES I: We're *all* frightened of the People. My lords, in order that we few survive, we must suppress the animals around us, so I will now bestow upon you the power to keep them in cages. In the year of our Lord, Sixteen Thirty-Three, I appoint you, Sir Thomas Wentworth – Earl of Strafford and Lord Deputy of Ireland. And you, William Laud, I appoint as Archbishop of Canterbury. As for you, Digby: you shall wear the boar's head. It suits you.
(*CROMWELL's body is removed.*)

WENTWORTH: It would be prudent, Majesty, to arrest all the ringleaders in Parliament.

CHARLES I: (*Laughing.*) What p-parliament?

WENTWORTH: The members plot in secret against you.

CHARLES I: On what charges can we arrest them? Bad breath? Nightmares involving the King?

HENRIETTA: Charles, for once, try to rule like the Sun. It could prove to be a pleasant occupation. And also his Holiness, the Pope, approves.

WENTWORTH: No, Madam, we must be more subtle. Let the Archbishop subdue the Scots. In the name of God, of course. And I will subdue the Irish. Then – when both the Scots and the Irish are grovelling – together, with our armies, we can converge on rebellious England, and, if necessary, storm and occupy London. But we need time. Time! And we must be secret.

CHARLES I: Are you suggesting that you want me to declare w-war on my own c-country?

WENTWORTH: Why not? They have all but declared war on you. And you have every right to legally occupy what is yours already.

CHARLES I: And I wanted to be a cr-creative King. (*Pause.*) Oh, do as you think best, Thomas.
(*CHARLES and HENRIETTA dance off together. DIBGY follows. WENTWORTH and LAUD remain on opposite sides of the stage. A giant green shamrock is lowered behind WENTWORTH.*)

WENTWORTH: (*With his arms wide-stretched.*) I insist upon equal judgement here in Ireland, now that I am Lord

Deputy. I rule in the King's name because Parliament no longer exists. We will have order for the first time ever in Ireland.

(*Enter an IRISH LORD.*)

IRISH LORD: That won't last long.

WENTWORTH: I will train a magnificent army. Trade will expand. Navigation become safe. Personally I will supervise the expansion of the linen and flax industry.

IRISH LORD: But who, in the name of the Mother of Jesus, is going to do the fecking work?

WENTWORTH: (*To the audience.*) You are! – and you are! – and you are! – and you are! I appoint the Archbishop of Canterbury as the new Chancellor of Dublin University. Art will prosper. Word jewels will light the peat bogs.

IRISH LORD: We had art here, boyo, when you and your countrymen were still painting your arses blue.

(*The IRISH LORD exits. WENTWORTH watches LAUD to see how the Archbishop is faring.*)

LILBURNE: (*To the audience.*) Meanwhile back in the Scottish bush, Sixteen Thirty-Seven, clickity-click.

LAUD: (*Calling off.*) Boy, bring me the wedding dress of Christ.

(*Two Choirboys enter, carrying the Archbishop's mitre, the Bible and the Common Prayerbook.*)

(*As they dress him.*) So tired. Not so roughly, boy. Leave it! It is well enough. These Scottish peasants are incapable of learning. They're much too proud.

(*ARGYLL and MONTROSE, two of Scotland's most important lords, dressed in kilts, enter. They begin to poke the ARCHBISHOP with their claymores.*)

MONTROSE: Were ye gabbin' about the Lord Argyll and mesel', ye religious turd ye? 'Cause you pong o' Papery, Bishop mon.

ARGYLL: Ay, ye reek o' niffy Papery.

LAUD: How dare you enter God's House armed?

ARGYLL: Ye'll find that Lord Montrose and mesel' will do absolutely anything to uphold our beloved Scottish Covenant. 'Cause we dinna like your Papish symbols, turning our Kirk into a poxy brothel. See, we ha' a great abhorrence o' stained glass, poncey altars an' sic!

LAUD: Blasphemous lords, these symbols are necessary to educate the Scottish people.

MONTROSE: Not only are they obscenely Papish, but they also cost money – mickle money! – which we here in Scotland dinna have too much of! 'Cause ye've already sucked us as dry as an old whore's dugs, Archbishop Bumhole. (*Cutting the Prayerbook in half with his claymore.*) And we'll not be havin' ye shitty Prayerbook, neither.

LAUD: You have no choice! You will use the Prayerbook as instituted by me, and you will respect the Kirk – I mean, of course, the Church – as much as I respect it.

MONTROSE: Oh we've a naughty, wee, wanton manikin here, Argyll.

LAUD: Out of my way, you vermin! I have a Service to officiate. And serving God is hard. His Exact Instructions are often misinterpreted from the Bible – so, in future, *my* interpretation is the only one that counts!

ARGYLL: Yes, he's a truly degenerate bum-bruiser, Montrose.

LAUD: Christ was disciplined. Man is not. So I intend to make man like Christ!

MONTROSE: There's no way that'll happen, Blubberchops.

LAUD: But you must see – it is the only way. Scotland is riddled with vice and anarchy. You are not even faithful to your King.

MONTROSE: Why the devil should we be? Charles Stuart only tramples us into the peat bogs.

LAUD: Obedience is everything!

ARGYLL: Ay, but that's only if *you're* the one that's bein' obeyed.

MONTROSE: That's why *we're* takin' things into our own hands now, 'cause we're very short o' cash, y'see.

LAUD: I fail to see what…

ARGYLL: So we're acomin' to London, to collect that cash.

MONTROSE: Canny trews he wears, Argyll. What say you we borrow them?

(*ARGYLL and MONTROSE walk round LAUD, jabbing at his vestments with their claymores.*)

ARGYLL: I like his neat, wee helmet.
(*ARGYLL removes LAUD's mitre, and then places it on MONTROSE's head.*)
LAUD: This is insufferable!
ARGYLL: Oh ye'll make a bonny wee priest, Montrose.
LAUD: I protest! (*They start to strip the Archbishop.*) You cannot unfrock the Archbishop of Canterbury!
MONTROSE: Just watch us! (*Removing LAUD's cope and tying it around ARGYLL's waist.*) Oh ye got a great paunch on ye, Tub Guts.
LAUD: Respect! I demand respect!
ARGYLL: Ye mean, you've no understanding us? He doesna ken our meaning, Montrose.
MONTROSE: Ah well, it's war that we're wantin', Bishop Turd. An' it's war, we're gonna have.
(*He twists the top of LAUD's crook off, to reveal a spearhead.*)
LAUD: The King will not like this!
MONTROSE: (*Grinning.*) Nay, but, nevertheless, he's gonna get it. (*Snatching the Bible from LAUD.*) Oh ye musna read such mucky books. (*He throws the Bible off-stage.*) See, we're sick o' bein' the underdogs.
ARGYLL: Ay, we're goin' to be free! An' war's the way to freedom! War!
MONTROSE: War!
(*By now they've stripped LAUD down to his underwear. The Choirboys laugh. MONTROSE pricks LAUD's arse. Yelping, LAUD exits, followed by the laughing Choirboys.*)
LILBURNE: (*To the audience.*) This, of course, only happened in the Scots' over-fertile imaginations – but they did declare war in November, Sixteen Thirty-Nine.
(*MONTROSE and ARGYLL march round the stage. Soldiers, with large red beards and in kilts, join in the march. They all sing together.*)
SCOTS ARMY: We're acomin' for ye, Charlie,
To strip ye bare, Charlie!
See, we've got enough Charlies
Of our own, Charlie,
Without the bloodyness of ye, Charlie!
Beat, beat, beat the drum!

Here comes Scotland, here we come!
We suffer much, but we're not dumb!
Beat, beat, beat the drum!
We'll sit ye, Charlie, on yer bum!
(They conclude with a brief Highland Fling.
CHARLES enters with DIGBY and LAUD. They are armed for
war. WENTWORTH, who has been watching the proceedings,
speaks to CHARLES.)

WENTWORTH: Charles, you and the Archbishop should
barricade the Border Land, but do not declare…

CHARLES I: War! …is declared.
(CHARLES signals to his Soldiers off-stage. Four very ragged
Soldiers pant into view, beating their stomachs with their
palms.)

ENGLISH ARMY: *(Singing.)*
We wish, we wish, we had a drum.
We wish, we wish, we hadn't come.
We're starving, and it isn't fun!
Beat, beat, beat the tum!

MONTROSE / ARGYLL: Charge! For Scotland and the
Covenant!
(The Scots begin to charge, but a cry from CHARLES brings
them to a halt.)

CHARLES I: Just a min-minute! You've got many m-more
than we have, and that isn't fair. It's just not English. I
think we'll have a t-treaty. Treaties are very E-English.

MONTROSE: Fine, but it'll cost ye more than ye ken Charlie.
'Fact it'll cost ye a Scottish Parliament, and a Scottish
General Assembly under the Covenant!

CHARLES I: *(Very tired.)* Have it as you will. But I will hawk
you when the t-time is right.

MONTROSE: We'll be waitin'. *(To his MEN.)* Come awa' now.
We'll be back.
(The Scots go out at a galloping speed.
CROMWELL and PYM enter.)

CHARLES I: *(To WENTWORTH who is on the opposite side of*
the stage.) Come back from Ireland, Thomas. I need you.
(At the back of the stage PYM and CROMWELL talk.)

PYM: We have him, Oliver. Charles needs money. That means he needs us. And in return, we will remove both of his evil advisers.

CROMWELL: Yes, we will be moderate. As always.

WENTWORTH: (*To CHARLES.*) Promise me, Charles, that my wife and children will continue to live in safety when the axe comes for me.

CHARLES I: Would I betray my P-Peter? The Rock on which my throne is built.

WENTWORTH: You are Christ's Deputy, so your responsibility is not to me, but to the heritage of our beloved England. Look! (*He points at the sky.*) That hawk – flashing into the sun.

CHARLES I: So?

WENTWORTH: Learn from him. Scream out of the sky, Charles, and tear those religious vermin out of your path. Execute Pym, Fairfax and Cromwell before they suck our blood.

CHARLES I: You are old, my friend. Old. So I have decided to employ c-cunning instead.

WENTWORTH: No, you're simply vacillating as usual, Charles. You will have to recall Parliament. Without them, you will have no money to pay the Scots.

LILBURNE: (*To the audience.*) We have now conger-eeled our way to April thirteenth, Sixteen Forty.

CHARLES I: (*To PYM.*) Mr Pym, I wish…

PYM: (*Interrupting.*) Nothing. (*Signalling for the rest of Parliament to come onto stage as he continues to address CHARLES.*) There is nothing in this Kingdom for you but hatred, and hunger, and pain.

CHARLES I: I am not interested in your op-opinions, Mr Pym.

LILBURNE: (*Singing.*)
One king is king today,
Then come the drums of snow…
(*Off-stage we hear a drum beating quietly – like a heart beat. This should continue on and off at the director's discretion until the end of Part One.*)

(*To the audience.*) Drums are lonely. Drums are animal guts tightened to a screech for men to thump war out of.

CHARLES I: (*To PYM.*) I want an army! I want money! I want armour! I want guns! I want p-pikes! I want...!

PYM: ...God? Well, He is displeased with you. So Parliament will not give you one penny, Majesty, not one belch until summer flows from you. I have one million grievances, in England's name, that must be redressed first!

CHARLES I: Parliament is ab-abolished!

(*Parliament, save PYM and CROMWELL, exit.*)

LILBURNE: (*To the audience.*) That was only three weeks after it was re-opened. Remarkable.

WENTWORTH: Charles, you will have to use my Irish troops. They're cheap, obedient and well-trained, so, with God behind us, we'll push Parliament and the Scots, into the abyss.

CHARLES I: No, there must be another way. Perhaps Cardinal Richelieu will help me to...

(*CHARLES is drowned by the Scots Army song, off.*)

SCOTS ARMY: We're acomin' for ye, Charlie,
To strip ye bare, Charlie.
See, we've got enough Charlies
Of our own, Charlie,
Without the bloodyness of ye, Charlie!
Beat, beat, beat the drum.
Here comes Scotland, here we come.
We suffer much, but we're not dumb.
Beat, beat, beat the drum.
We'll sit ye, Charlie, on ye bony bum!

WENTWORTH: Use my army, Charles, while there is still time!

(*HENRIETTA enters, frightened.*)

HENRIETTA: The Pope must help us.

CHARLES I: (*Above the singing and the drumming.*) It's coming.

CROMWELL: Coming.

PYM: Coming.

WENTWORTH: Coming.

CHARLES I: Is my crown safe no-nowhere in England?
Must I continue to build palaces in bl-blood and mire?
God, for C-Christ's sake, show me something other than a
landscape of faces that hate me!
(*The Scots march into view. Then four ragged English Soldiers
charge at the Scots.*)
ENGLISH ARMY: For death and hunger!
To live no longer!
(*The Scots slash the English to death with their claymores.*)
MONTROSE: (*Sitting on a dead body.*) We'll feed 'em to the
Campbells. What say ye, Argyll?
ARGYLL: Ay, Montrose, there's nae thing like a dead
Sassenach to the Campbells – save, of course, twa dead
Sassenachs!
(*Laughing, MONTROSE and ARGYLL point their claymores
at the KING's throat.*)
Ye word...
MONTROSE: ...Or ye kingdom!
WENTWORTH: Please, Charles, use my army while you still
can! Do not...
CHARLES I: ...Recall Parliament!
LILBURNE: (*To the audience.*) November third, Sixteen Forty.
(*PYM signals. Parliament reappears.*)
PYM: (*To CROMWELL.*) We have him. (*Approaching
CHARLES.*) You wanted us, Majesty?
WENTWORTH: I played dice for England. I lost the dice,
and England.
CHARLES I: I must have money to pay off the revolting Scots.
LAUD: You must not plead with them, Charles. Well, I have
been silent long enough. Arrest Pym and Cromwell, and
then try them for treason in the Star Chamber.
(*The Black Star of the Star Chamber is lowered.*)
CROMWELL: Down with the Star Chamber!
(*Parliament tears the Star to pieces.*)
LAUD: I will go to Westminster Abbey to pray for
deliverance. God may yet help us because Man is lost. One
thing is certain, if Sir Thomas loses his head; shortly after, I
will be minus mine.
(*LAUD goes out.*)

CHARLES I: Which way now, Thomas?

WENTWORTH: Oh, for God's sake, Charles, impeach Pym for High Treason! Our heads are wavering in the twilight. And, as yet, I have achieved so little. Law in Ireland. But only Law. I seem never to have shared anything with anyone – other than the rules.

CHARLES I: You're such a morbid soul. How say you, Henrietta?

HENRIETTA: Usually Wentworth is too outspoken, but for once I agree with him.

(*CROMWELL approaches the KING.*)

Start with Cromwell, Charles. Arrest him first.

CHARLES I: Oliver Cromwell, in England's name…

CROMWELL: (*Overriding CHARLES and turning on WENTWORTH.*) …I arrest you, Thomas Wentworth, erstwhile Earl of Strafford and Deputy of Ireland, as a consummate traitor to England and to her dominions. The Archbishop of Canterbury will be arrested discreetly in the Abbey.

(*Two Soldiers exit. John BRADSHAW enters.*)

BRADSHAW: (*To the audience.*) This is where I come in. For the trial – because I'm what's known as a 'trying' man. (*Laughing at his own joke.*) You'd nearly forgotten me, hadn't you? I'm your favourite venomous slug with slimy intentions. Creaky ghost, Third Class. (*To WENTWORTH.*) To the various charges of High Treason, how do you plead, Thomas Wentworth?

WENTWORTH: Nothing.

CHARLES I: You cannot t-try him.

CROMWELL: We can. We will. We are. Watch us.

WENTWORTH: What I did was England's good.

BRADSHAW: You took bribes in Ireland.

WENTWORTH: Where are the witnesses against me?

BRADSHAW: John Lilburne.

LILBURNE: Wentworth is a man. That is sufficient guilt in the eyes of the earth.

BRADSHAW: And, worse, Wentworth, you corrupted the mind of our beloved King.

CHARLES I: N-n-no!!

WENTWORTH: I fulfilled the King! So it is impertinent to threaten me.

BRADSHAW: Insidious whispers in corridors, Thomas, candlelit stratagems.

WENTWORTH: Anything you ask or demand of me, Bradshaw, my answer will always be Charles. (*Clutching his heart.*) I have not time now for this…insufferable pain.

BRADSHAW: Did you or did you not corrupt the King, take bribes in Ireland, rule arbitrarily in Ireland, encourage the King to use tyrannical power in England, and also persuade the King to rule without Parliament?

WENTWORTH: Bradshaw, do they pay you well? Are your claws stroked with promised power? But you don't cry out for the majority of England. None of you do! You cry out for the Middle Class. All politicians in England have, do, and always will, cry out for the Middle Class.

PYM: How dare you besmirch the machinery of England? Without us, the Poor would starve for ever!

WENTWORTH: And with you, they will, Mr Pym! Only your gut will bloat from over-eating.

CHARLES I: Be gentle with them, Thomas. I will save you, I pro-promise!

WENTWORTH: There's no point in pretending, Charles. The sea is coming. So prepare for the sea-wolves.

BRADSHAW: Answer these charges against you, sirrah. Your seditious rhetoric will not preserve you from the rigours of the Law.

WENTWORTH: I say again – if you try me – you try all of England.

PYM: Arrogance of the dead.

WENTWORTH: I am Charles…

HENRIETTA: His arrogance is beyond thought, Charles.

CHARLES I: His neck is bearing the royal axe, my dear, so one cannot b-blame him for a little arrogance.

WENTWORTH: (*To Parliament.*) I am finished with you, gentlemen. Return me to my quarters.

(*WENTWORTH moves to go.*)

PYM: Stay! You are no longer impeached for High Treason.

WENTWORTH: Free? Am I free, then?

PYM: I did not say that.

WENTWORTH: Charles, remember: Peter may fail Christ, but Christ dare not fail Peter.

CHARLES I: My word is eternal.

PYM: (*Producing a document.*) He is no longer impeached, Majesty. But under this Bill of Attainder, Wentworth is guilty of being an Enemy of the People, by implication only, which is sufficient condemnation in the eyes of the Law at the time of a national crisis. (*To CHARLES.*) So sign.

CHARLES I: In-insolence!

PYM: As I said: sign this.

LILBURNE: (*Singing.*)
The wolf is coming to the gun.
The bat is blinded by the sun.
Do not laugh at Justice done.
Death is the essential fun
That man from man has won.

CROMWELL: Thomas Wentworth only loves himself. He judged other men, and found them wanting. To the axe with him.

CHARLES I: But where is his c-crime?

CROMWELL: He is. Everything he is. *That* is his crime. One man cannot rule an empire. Not even a king. Not even if the king is good. Or a saint. The People must rule the People. Even if Anarchy comes. Sign.

CHARLES I: No. Oh, I do not love him. But he is my right hand.

WENTWORTH: (*Clutching his pain-wracked chest.*) Sign, Charles! It's the only way they will give you the money.

CHARLES I: Money has nothing to do with…

WENTWORTH: (*Overriding him.*) Money has everything to do with everything! When will you learn, Charles? Money is the centre. And without it, you don't exist.

CHARLES I: But I abhor everything to do with money.

WENTWORTH: But that is how you live, Charles – how we all live.

CHARLES I: N-n-no!

WENTWORTH: How you rule!

CHARLES I: No, I rule because...

WENTWORTH: Yes?

CHARLES I: Be-be-because...

WENTWORTH: ...Of taxes, your armies and your land
– and create money! But if you at least learn this, then my
death will have been worthwhile. Therefore I beg you to
give England back her glittering glory before these drab
business men suffocate your kingdom. So sign my death
warrant, and collect the money. Sign!

CHARLES I: But I gave you my word that I'd...

WENTWORTH: I know you, Charles. Under all your regalia,
you are gasping to sign. Be true to yourself. England is
stretched to her uttermost. So you must be free to act like
a King.

CHARLES I: I pr-promised...!

WENTWORTH: I love. Not England. Not you, Charles. But
the essence of both. Sign.

HENRIETTA: Yes, he is a necessary sacrifice, Charles.
England needs his blood in order that the roses may riot
again in the quietest gardens of England. Sign.

PYM: Sign. Your power in England will grow, Majesty. Death
is the only reward for singularity. Sign.

CROMWELL: Sign. God is. Man is not – without God.
Wentworth is without. Sign.

WENTWORTH: You cannot beat them, Charles, so join
them. I am convulsed with heart-stopping pain, and I am
very tired. The earth aches for me. I love. It is enough that
I love, and that I'm willing to die – for the Treasury. So
sign.

CHARLES I: But I pr-promised you...

WENTWORTH: (*Relentless.*) You are King. A king promises
for one moment of time only. And that moment is history
now. Sign for the future. Let me go now. Sign.

HENRIETTA: Sign!

PYM: Sign!

CROMWELL: Sign!

WENTWORTH: For mercy's sake, sign!

CHARLES I: (*Stuttering badly.*) I s-s-s-sign!

CROMWELL: (*Triumphant.*) England to England!

WENTWORTH: Gentlemen, see that the King is well paid.

LILBURNE: (*Pleading.*) Anyone! God! Anyone! HELP US!
   (*Blackout.*)

PART TWO

LILBURNE, on his hands and knees, enters out of the enveloping darkness.

LILBURNE: (*Singing.*)
> We're preparing for the night.
> Wentworth's head's upon a spike.
> Charles and Cromwell are alike.
> They're preparing for the night.
> Hush, my friends, nothing's right.
> You will not sleep deep tonight.
> (*To the banging of percussion, the Cast dance onto the stage.*
> *CROMWELL holds up a giant striped Maypole with*
> *WENTWORTH's head spiked on top of it. The Cast dance*
> *around the Maypole, clutching the streaming ribbons. During the*
> *following song, the dance and singing rise to a fever pitch.*
> *CHARLES and HENRIETTA watch the proceedings.*)

ALL: (*Singing.*)
> His head's, his head's a nice old head.
> He was nice alive but he's better dead.
> He didn't die on the job in bed.
> We're doing the job for him instead.
> So come, my darling, let's get wed.
> Or, better still, go straight to bed.
> We'll save our wedding 'til we're dead.

CHARLES I: (*Singing.*)
> I love you, Thomas, I tell you true,
> But not half as much as God loves you.
> Oh I know
> I let you go
> To the drums of snow
> Where only the sneaky maggots grow.
> Forgive me for the things I do.
> But I had to let you go
> To know
> That all the things you said were true.
> And now I'm the pea

In the Parliament stew,
And they'll gobble me
Like they've gobbled you.
(*CROMWELL tugs WENTWORTH's head off the spike on the Maypole. Then he swings it over the audience's heads like a gigantic ball on a string.*)
ALL: (*Singing.*)
Wentworth's rotting now, my lad.
Cromwell will drive Charlie mad.
Still, Pym and Cromwell aren't so bad,
But when they're dead won't we be glad
To see their heads on spikes of grass.
Then we'll blow our wind and wipe our arse,
And sing of how they lost *their* heads
While we ploughed their wives in bed;
'Cause we'll make love 'til we are dead;
'Cause that's what life is, when all's said!
His head's, his head's a nice old head.
He was nice alive but he's better dead.
Now we're loving hungry in his bed,
'Cause we're the people who aren't fed.
We listen to whatever's said,
But talk won't do instead of bread.
We're randy hungry 'til we're dead!
(*Still singing, they all surge off, leaving CHARLES and HENRIETTA. DIGBY lights a candelabrum in the gathering shadows.*)
CHARLES I: (*Sitting in desolation.*) Both Ireland and Scotland are in revolt. And soon m-my England will…
HENRIETTA: (*Overriding him.*) Everyone whispers against us. For pity's sake, my love, let us go to my brother, Louis, in France. He will tell Cardinal Richelieu to protect us.
CHARLES I: (*Placing a finger over her lips.*) Hush, my sweet. Pym has you watched. (*Pointing at the candelabrum.*) Look, how the shadows flee from the candles. I wish to God that I were not the flame.
HENRIETTA: You should take your cue from the implacable Richelieu. Then everything would be different.

CHARLES I: No! By making the Monarchy absolute in France, Richelieu only postpones the wrath of the People. He is simply stoking up hatred against the crown. (*He puts his arm around her.*) I know, I know; in England, the hatred has already arrived. And so has C-Cromwell.

HENRIETTA: He's nothing but a country clod!

CHARLES I: Nevertheless the People are behind Cromwell. (*Eating an apple.*) Even though they fear him.

HENRIETTA: But what is his mystique?

CHARLES I: If I knew, I'd have Cromwell prostrated at my feet. (*Discarding the apple.*) Even the apples are tart this year. But there must be some weakness in the man. Some humanity. If we can find it, why, then, there is hope because then we can destroy Cromwell.

HENRIETTA: Oh you're so absurdly innocent, my love.

CHARLES I: You un-underestimate him!

HENRIETTA: No, he's just a man like any other. Striving for power because of personal inadequacy. He's only dangerous because he's unpredictable. You see, he believes that God has given him *carte blanche,* to carve his initials on England's forehead.

(*CHARLES grips the calf of his leg in pain.*)

CHARLES I: A stitch! One ripple of pain, and we are no longer im-immortal. Where is our Charles-the-Second-to-be?

(*PRINCE CHARLES appears in the shadows.*)

PRINCE CHARLES: In the shadows, father, waiting to come into the light.

CHARLES I: Only when I'm dead, boy. So what will you do when you are King, Charles?

PRINCE CHARLES: Laugh, my lord.

CHARLES I: P-Parliament's not very f-funny.

PRINCE CHARLES: (*Laughing.*) Oh nothing's really serious, father.

CHARLES I: (*Clutching his calf.*) Not even growing old? Rehearsing owl-notes for the g-grave?

PRINCE CHARLES: That's the funniest part. You can do nothing about death but laugh. So laugh. Come to that, why don't you just give Parliament what they want?

CHARLES I: You are not my son! My son would wither them for the p-pain they cause his father.

HENRIETTA: Don't snarl at the boy, dearest. He still rules the universe in his head. He hasn't tried the terrors of trying to rule Little England yet.

CHARLES I: You must grow up, Charles.

PRINCE CHARLES: Oh father, father. I am already more mature than you. Give Parliament what they think they want. They don't want it really, they just *think* they do. Or at least tell them a joke or two. Jesus had the right idea about giving, but He didn't have a sense of humour; so unfortunately the joke is now on *us*.

CHARLES I: B-Blasphemous boy! Your flippancy will cost you the k-kingdom.

PRINCE CHARLES: On the contrary, father; it might make England fit to live in.

CHARLES I: Don't you see that by jibing at Our Saviour, you will encourage the m-mob to do the same?

PRINCE CHARLES: I see that you, my father, are using Christ like a bull, to gore the majority of England.

CHARLES I: Christ is all we have to…

PRINCE CHARLES: (*Finishing his father's thought.*) …To protect *you* from the People.

CHARLES I: And *you,* Charles. He also protects you.

PRINCE CHARLES: Our way of life revolts me. And, sometimes, Christ revolts me.

HENRIETTA: (*Crossing herself.*) God forgive you, my son, because I do not know if *I* can.

PRINCE CHARLES: We would be better without Christ. All He has bequeathed us is the obscenity of guilt, fear of damnation, and the overwhelming lust to murder all our enemies in His name. So, Christ Jesus, are You pleased with this…this endless death toll that Your Followers trail behind them? You are the greatest murderer that ever lived.

HENRIETTA: For God's sake, stop his mouth, husband!

CHARLES I: When will you learn, my son? When? You are only wrenching your own heart. Whatever you may *want* to be, you will always be a predatory eagle – like me. Oh, one day there may be a time for humanity – centuries ahead – but not yet! Today, there are only the Leaders and the L-L-Led. Our laughter and our crying we must imprison in our skulls, or we will be replaced. Remember that.

(*DIGBY who has been standing in the shadows, moves forward.*)

DIGBY: Your Majesty, Cromwell has been impertinent enough to demand an interview. Shall I...?

(*CROMWELL enters, brushing DIGBY aside. He gives a letter to the KING.*)

CROMWELL: Highness, read.

CHARLES I: At my l-leisure.

CROMWELL: Now, Highness. I recommend now.

HENRIETTA: Insubordinate, sir!

CROMWELL: I have no way with speech, madam. Read, Highness.

(*Moving away CHARLES begins to read.*)

PRINCE CHARLES: (*To CROMWELL.*) Your collar's dirty. Just there. (*Recoiling.*) It's blood. How can you give my father orders when you can't even shave without cutting yourself?

CROMWELL: Prince, I am a man. That should be enough.

PRINCE CHARLES: Do you like my father?

CROMWELL: I love the King. But I am not sure if I love Charles Stuart.

PRINCE CHARLES: Love? I said nothing of love.

CROMWELL: That is all there is. Consuming love. Christ said: 'Love thine enemies.'

PRINCE CHARLES: How convenient. He said nothing about *liking* them.

CROMWELL: Prince, you presume...!

PRINCE CHARLES: (*Overriding him.*) What would you do if I told you that God was dead? That we are on our own, and that we always have been.

CROMWELL: (*Losing his temper.*) By the Living God, I will
scour such disbelief from England! I will…!

HENRIETTA: (*Smiling ironically as she interrupts him.*) '*You*'
will? It seems that everything is 'you', Mr Cromwell.
And don't lecture me on 'love', sir. Love is outside your
comprehension. The only thing that consumes you, is your
obsession with yourself. Your blank passion.

CROMWELL: On the contrary, madam, since my feet first
moved one in front of the other, I have only loved and
believed in Freedom. God is freedom. God will kill for
freedom. And I will kill for God. So beware me. Words
hurt me as I talk. My meaning is often contorted. But, by
the living Christ, I mean what I say. So do not laugh at my
difficulty because I have a long memory. And one thing
is very certain: I will save the country from your whims,
madam. I will make her grow. Europe belongs with us.

PRINCE CHARLES: (*Laughing.*) Really? When did God tell
you all that?

CROMWELL: Presumptuous whelp! This fist…is where God
lives. In the name of the People, I am the Lord's Hammer!
(*CHARLES thrusts the letter under CROMWELL's nose.*)

CHARLES I: How dare Pym? How dare he?

HENRIETTA: What does he want?

CHARLES I: Ev-everything!

CROMWELL: (*Taking the scroll from him and reading rapidly.*)
We, the House of Commons and the House of Lords,
have suffered for far too long the arbitrary government of
a despot. This must cease forthwith. The Army must be
controlled by Parliament, and it must crush the rebellion
in Ireland. The King's Ministers must be selected by
Parliament, for Parliament. Forthwith, there must be
a new reformation of the Church by Parliament, and
henceforward…

HENRIETTA: No, no!

CROMWELL: (*Relentless.*) …Bishops will no longer be
permitted to influence political decisions. For the first
time in our history, the Church will be subservient to the
Common Law. The King must bow to the People. (*Turning
on CHARLES.*) Or we will crush you… *I* will…

CHARLES I: (*Interrupting.*) YOU? There is no such thing
as YOU, Mr Cromwell. There *is* no you. Oh I see your
eyes – who could miss 'em? Stunned with their own des-
desolation. I can smell your acrid sweat and your erupting
skin. I can hear that drum you use as a voice. But where
are YOU, Oliver Cr-Cromwell? WHAT ARE YOU?

CROMWELL: (*Almost inarticulate.*) Do not...intrude...upon
ME!

CHARLES I: How can a Th-Thing have privacy? The day
you gave up your mother's milk, you gave up everything.
Henrietta, look at the sterility in his face. See how he wants
to bl-blubber back into childhood.

CROMWELL: Wrong! Wrong!! It is *you*, Charles Stuart, who
is still playing hobbyhorse with England. But this is the
New Age! The age of Control. Discipline!

CHARLES I: Out of my sight, h-half man! Tell P-Pym there
is but one King. As my realm is, so it will remain. *You* must
be King elsewhere. T-T-Tell him!

CROMWELL: Yes, Highness. (*Pause.*) Highness?

CHARLES I: Yes, Mr C-Cromwell?

CROMWELL: I hope tomorrow is kind to you. *God* be with
you, because soon no one else will be.

PRINCE CHARLES: I see you crucified against your own
soul.

CROMWELL: And I see you, Prince, whimpering, with
blood in your hair.

PRINCE CHARLES: Whose blood, Mr Cromwell?

CROMWELL: England's, boy.
(*CROMWELL strides off. PRINCE CHARLES smiles.*)

CHARLES I: I will have P-Pym's head! A head for a head.
(*Staring sightlessly in front of him.*) Poor T-Thomas.

HENRIETTA: Cromwell is infinitely more dangerous than
Pym.

CHARLES I: Yes, but Cromwell is dead – as you saw.

PRINCE CHARLES: For a moment I thought...

CHARLES I: What, my son?

PRINCE CHARLES: I thought I touched the man...inside.

CHARLES I: You touch a w-wraith…that haunts my crown. (*Shivering.*) I fear the darkness is hungry for me. I will arrest Pym m-myself!

HENRIETTA: But, Charles…

CHARLES I: And then I will watch him hang!

(*CHARLES, HENRIETTA, PRINCE CHARLES and DIGBY exit.*

PYM leads the Puritan section of the Commons in a hymn-cum-song. They enter on their knees, singing.)

PURITANS: O Mighty Lord, remember us.
We are peaceful but we thrust
Swords into the world's deep side.
The gap to death is very wide.
Help us! Help us! Help us!
Come with flagellating flame,
And scorch the swine to Hell again.
We're a sweet and simple folk,
But we're bastards when we're broke.
And we're broke, we're broke, we're broke!

(*The PURITANS beat the floor with their hands as the ROYALISTS, led by NEWCASTLE and HYDE, swagger into view, singing. PRINCE RUPERT is with them.*)

ROYALISTS: We are fighting for the King.
He's on our side so we'll win.
They don't know that he is coming
To arrest them all this morning.
And they'll get no bloody warning!

PURITANS: They don't think that we know
That Charles is bringing the drums of snow.
But we smell his blood on doors,
And we lick his blood off floors.
It's the blood of royal whores;
And blood on blood, is what's in store.

(*The PURITANS are doing a dance on their haunches while the ROYALISTS are executing a more graceful dance above them. PYM and HOLLES stand, and PYM addresses the audience.*)

PYM: Mr Holles and I have to leave now. Or we'd have no heads to talk with. Our heads aren't important, but our talk is. See you – at Golgotha.

(*PYM and HOLLES exit while HYDE, NEWCASTLE and
the other PURITANS remain.*
*Off, a drum beats. Everyone freezes. CHARLES I enters, with
his personal Guard. Silence. No one bows to the KING.*)

CHARLES I: Don't let me stop you from dancing on air,
gentlemen. I always believe in gallows' rehearsals. Where
is Mr Pym? Where is Mr Holles?

HYDE: (*Coming forward.*) I am the Speaker. Kindly address
yourself to me.

CHARLES I: Where are they? (*Silence.*) Search them, Prince
Rupert.

RUPERT: Search them everywhere, sire?

CHARLES I: Everywhere.

RUPERT: (*Flashing his sword past NEWCASTLE's groin.*) Your
Highness, it is doubtful whether Mr Pym is hiding in my
Lord of Newcastle's codpiece. Lady Newcastle perhaps, but
not Mr Pym.

NEWCASTLE: Careful, Prince, careful!

CHARLES I: Where is P-P-Pym?

PURITANS: Beat, beat, beat the drum.
Steady with that gun.
Hate is on the run,
And Death is oh such fun!
Charlie's bared his bum;
So guess what is to come?

CHARLES I: I will not ask again! Now where are Pym and
Holles?

HYDE: I only see, I only hear, I only smell, I only taste what
this House tells me. I would I could tell your Majesty, but
I can't, and I shan't, and I won't. So please leave now.
It is unlawful for a monarch to burst into the House of
Commons.

CHARLES I: If I leave now without Pym and Holles, I will
have two million heads on the spikes of the grass for my
supper. Gentlemen, I warn you – not as your King, but
as your physical God in England – one thousand years of
death will storm out of the satanic pit for this, and England
will be haunted until the stars burn out.

(*Enter CROMWELL and PRINCE CHARLES from opposite directions.*)

CROMWELL: Have I missed the royal scream of defiance? Arrest me, Highness. I am one of the two million heads on the spikes of the grass.

PRINCE CHARLES: Why so serious, gentlemen? The result is the same. Everyone will die anyway. Painfully. Well, laugh! Go on; try it. It could become a habit. Just curl up the lips, and a smile comes. Open your mouths and laugh, and the sun comes. Then open yourselves, and hope comes – we hope.

CROMWELL: Boy, you should be the king – of a nursery.

CHARLES I: (*Trying to control his tears.*) Gentlemen, I am ashamed. The only thing this country has ever given me is t-tears. God forgive me, but I loathe and abominate…! (*CHARLES snatches a halberd from a Soldier, and he is about to hurl it at CROMWELL.*)

CROMWELL: Please do, Highness. (*Smiling.*) The honour would surely kill me.

CHARLES I: (*Now holding the point of the spear against his own cheek.*) This steel is quiet. Aquiver and quiet – waiting for the world's blood. (*He places the edge of the spear head against his mouth.*) It tastes sour like the apples this year. (*He has cut his mouth. He looks at the drop of blood on his finger.*) I have cut my mouth. I taste my blood. They will call this an omen. Perhaps it is. But all I will remember of today, is that my blood tastes as good as anything I have ever tasted – other than my tears. Oh I was forgetting: Death is declared! (*CHARLES exits with PRINCE RUPERT.*)

CROMWELL: (*To PRINCE CHARLES.*) Well, Laughing Boy, you had best go with your father.

PRINCE CHARLES: I've been thinking about you, Mr Cromwell.

CROMWELL: Try thinking about God. You'll find it's more profitable.

PRINCE CHARLES: I do, but I keep getting you both mixed up. And you don't really hate my father, do you? You just want to hate him – because you're frightened that without your hatred, you won't be anyone at all. Nothing but a blood smear on a dirty collar. I would like to like you, Mr Cromwell, if only you would let me – but you won't. And the loss is yours.

CROMWELL: (*Grabbing the PRINCE's arm.*) *We could ransom you, boy, for England's dear sake. Then there would be no war.*

(*PURITANS and ROYALISTS alike draw their swords on CROMWELL.*)

Oh don't worry, gentlemen, we won't. (*Releasing the PRINCE.*) *That would be too easy. And God is not easy. If only you understood that, boy. Your father thinks we want his death.*

PRINCE CHARLES: Don't you?

CROMWELL: Never! We want him to mature. That is all. And rule *through* the People.

PRINCE CHARLES: With Parliament manipulating the purse strings, of course?

CROMWELL: Of course.

PRINCE CHARLES: That will never happen. Thank God.

CROMWELL: No. Parliament must control the purse strings. And Charles must learn to accept that. I'll take you to him. Perhaps then *he* will ransom *me*.

PRINCE CHARLES: What would he get for you? A prayer book on fire?

(*PRINCE CHARLES exits, laughing. He is followed by CROMWELL. HOLLES and PYM rush onto the stage.*)

HOLLES: Is it war?

NEWCASTLE: War!

(*NEWCASTLE strikes PYM across the face and goes out.*)

HYDE: War!

(*HYDE turns over the Speaker's Chair and exits. MANCHESTER and ESSEX link arms and begin a patter number.*)

MANCHESTER / ESSEX: (*Singing together.*)
New games to play!
Swords out today!
But Death is the only pay
That we'll offer the soldiers!

PYM: Have I shrunk my insides for this foolery?

MANCHESTER / ESSEX: (*Singing together.*)
>So put death masks on,
>'Cause the sword and a worm,
>Blood and a song,
>Are all we'll give to our soldiers!
>(*CROMWELL re-enters and breaks the routine with his drawn sword.*)

CROMWELL: I will kill you both if you sneer at the soldiers. Without them, we are nothing. And even with them, we are not much.

LILBURNE: (*Singing.*)
>Out of the dark we come,
>Into the murk we go.
>Men have only the drum,
>And the hopes of the starving crow.
>One king is king today,
>Then come the drums of snow.
>A screech of the axe…
>(*During the song, CHARLES, PRINCE RUPERT, NEWCASTLE, HYDE and DIGBY re-enter, ready for war. The PURITANS form on the opposite side of the stage. A brief blackout coincides with the end of the song, during which there is the terrifying sound of an animal screeching in pain. The lights come up to reveal that the stage is strewn with dead bodies. All the PURITANS have gone. Only CHARLES and RUPERT remain, with DIGBY as the standard bearer.*)

CHARLES I: I did not realise that the dead smelt so sweet. Sweetness of rotting oranges. (*He picks up a blade of grass.*) This blade of grass bows under the dead a moment only. Now, once again, it challenges the wind. How much, Rupert?

RUPERT: How much what, Highness?

CHARLES I: Death – before I return in triumph.
(*Enter HENRIETTA, with her nose covered against the stench of the dead. PRINCE CHARLES is with her. When he sees the dead, he begins to laugh hysterically. With a single blow, CHARLES knocks his son down to the ground.*)

PRINCE CHARLES: Why hit me – when you mean everyone else?

CHARLES I: Your childhood is over. (*Helping PRINCE
CHARLES to his feet, and giving him his own sword.*)
Soon you'll be a throne-owner, a crown-wearer.
A manifestation of God.
But each year our royal power declines.
Once we were gigantic eagles.
Now we are hawk-owls.
And if you do not stop your laughing,
We will only be dead carrion birds.
Pin your emotions into your soft flesh,
But do not laugh with your pain.
Be silent. Watch. And learn.
Every moment may be the axe.

PRINCE CHARLES: No, father, no! I will laugh! I will not
be a tired and dreary king. Come, mother, you are safe
with me because I am only a boy. I haven't developed the
slyness and the coldness of my father.

CHARLES I: (*Holding his son at arms' length and gazing him
in the eyes.*) My son – this may be…the last time we…
(*PRINCE CHARLES rushes into his father's arms, weeping.
CHARLES pushes him away.*) I should hit you again because
there is no time for c-crying. What would you do with such
a son, Rupert?

RUPERT: I would hit him. But *you* will not hit him again.
After the initial gesture, you always stop the punishment.
That is why England is where she is today. Cromwell
would hit him. Cromwell's heart would bleed, but he
would hit him. I would hit him.

CHARLES I: You are a soldier – easy. My son, you are a
prince – fairly easy. Henrietta, you are a queen – harder.
But I am *the* King – with the responsibilities of God, and
the equipment of an exhausted man – almost impossible.

HENRIETTA: In everything you say and do, Charles, there
is always compromise. You hunt for beauty, but your
weakness only makes it pretty. So I will bring you an army
from France, to make you pretty again.

CHARLES I: Let us fight, Rupert. My dead Thomas, I would appreciate a visit from your ghost, with some good advice, if the Almighty will give you the time off.

(*CROMWELL marches into view with his Troops. Sir THOMAS FAIRFAX is beside him. They are stiff like toy soldiers.*

RUPERT and his Troops charge through Cromwell's Men – like flamboyant ballet dancers. Cromwell's Men are about to pursue, but LILBURNE steps between the ranks. The Soldiers on both sides freeze.)

LILBURNE: (*To the audience.*) I see no point in naming all these ridiculous battles, but there was an interesting one: today, actually, September twentieth, Sixteen Forty-Three. Look it up when you get home. It was a cock-up, of course. Literally. (*Shouting off.*) Well, come on, boys, bring on the fighting cocks!

EVERYONE: We want the fighting cocks! We want the fighting cocks!

LILBURNE: Well, there's nothing like a bit of *cock*-fighting, is there?

(*Both armies work themselves up into a blood fever, screaming: 'Let's have some blood! Blood! Blood!'.*)

FAIRFAX: Cromwell, this is no way to fight a war!

CROMWELL: Yes, Fairfax, God hates this. It is against life!

(*The shouting for 'blood' continues building to a climax.*

From opposite sides of the stage, two men, dressed as fighting cocks, leap into view, squawking. They have spurs tied to their ankles.

The Royalist Cock is in bright colours with silken wings whereas the Puritan Cock is dressed in black leather. Egged on by both Armies, the Cocks circle around one another. Then they attack each other.

CHARLES, and his entourage, throw feathers at the Fighting Cocks, as do CROMWELL and FAIRFAX. The first half of the fight should be farcical, accompanied by squawking and laughter.)

BOTH ARMIES: (*Singing.*)

Blood! Blood! Blood!

Very, very good

To taste and smell,
Because Heaven and Hell
Are understood
With lovely blood!

It's all so funny.

Blood's so runny.

It's so sweet.

Human meat
To suck and eat,
Is very good,
Is blood! Blood! Blood!

PYM: Highness, stop this! There can be peace.

CHARLES I: Yes, Mr Pym. With your head upon a spike!

(*By now the comedy has gone, and the drums throb feverishly. Finally the Puritan Cock knocks the Royalist Cock to the ground. Then the Puritan Cock proceeds to gouge at the wounded Royalist Cock's jugular.*

Then the Royalist Cock pecks at the Puritan Cock's eyes with his beak. But the Puritan Cock retaliates by lacerating the Royalist Cock with his spurs.

The ARMIES scream out their song.)

BOTH ARMIES: (*Singing.*)
Dying! Dying!
Bleeding! Bleeding!
Crying! Crying!
Needing! Needing!
Death! Death!

ROYALIST ARMY: Help us! Help us! Save the King!

PURITAN ARMY: Death! Death! Death! And yet again
– Death!

(*Although the Puritan Cock is now blind, it jabs its spurs into the Royalist Cock's face and breast.*

CHARLES rushes into the fight and stops it.)

CHARLES I: Mr Pym, let us talk! Let us hope that talk will bring hope.

PYM: (*Slumping to his knees.*) I am dying, Highness.

CHARLES I: Dying?

PYM: My entrails are grave-hungry. Come to us.

CHARLES I: What do you want? My h-head?

PYM: Never!

CHARLES I: My c-crown?

PYM: Never! We want you to be a *real* king. Rule the country *through* the country. That is all.

(PYM and CHARLES are standing opposite one another, with the dying Royalist Cock between them.

Flapping blindly, the badly-wounded Puritan Cock staggers to its feet. It cannot see. It stumbles towards the watching Puritan Army, tripping over CROMWELL, who tries to help the Puritan Cock recover. MANCHESTER draws his dagger.)

MANCHESTER: Let me slit its throat, Cromwell. It's not human!

CROMWELL: No! It's blind! It's dying! IT'S THE MAJORITY OF ENGLAND! For God's sake, man, enough is enough!

(CROMWELL releases the Puritan Cock. It flails out of his hands and blindly attacks the KING and PYM, who try to ward it off.)

LILBURNE: *(Fighting his way through the opposing Armies.)* It's the Hungry! It's me! *(Pointing at the audience.)* It's Them! But it's not any of you, gentlemen! Nor you, Mr Pym. Or you, Your Highness. It's Them! Out there! The Unknowns! The Outsiders!

CROMWELL: Lilburne, you sentimental fool! How dare you claim kinship with the People? They do not want a eunuch intellectual as their leader. *(To the audience.)* Do you? Do you!? You want a man of few words, but whose every word is a drop of fire. Don't you? You want order! Inspiration! Leadership! Discipline! So that the kingdom is safe to live in. You may not think you want it – but underneath you do. And by the living God, *I* am going to give it to you!

LILBURNE: No! *(To the audience.)* We want freedom of ideas, don't we? Freedom of speech! Freedom to be ourselves!

CHARLES I: They are not ready for freedom! *(To the audience.)* Are you? Are you?

LILBURNE: And we don't want to be preached at. We want to be left alone – to grow in our own way.

(*The Puritan Cock staggers to its feet. Then blindly it attacks the KING and PYM again. They knock it over. It gets up so they knock it over again.*)
That's it. Put the boot in! Knock us over a million times, we're just born to get up again. That's all we're born for – to get up again! Not even death can hold us down. We breed faster than the grave can rot our groins. And soon, very soon, we'll be so many – and you'll be so few – that we will eat you, gentlemen!

CROMWELL: Speak for yourself, Lilburne. You've no right to speak for England.

CHARLES I: Yes, they despise you. (*To the audience.*) Don't you? You always loathe those who are foolish enough to fight in your name. (*Crossing himself.*) Thank God.

PYM: (*Clutching his painful stomach.*) Peace! Please, let us have peace!

HOLLES: The People have nothing to do with anything. They're only here to die. I am fighting for England, *my* England, which, if the People behave themselves, I may allow them to live in.

PYM: (*Struggling with the wounded Puritan Cock.*) For God's sake, put him out of his misery!

LILBURNE: Yes, go on; kill him! He'll come back for more until you kill him. He's stupid, you see! He's trying to be a HUMAN BEING! (*As CHARLES and PYM struggle with the Puritan Cock, it pecks at them.*) He knows no better than to bite the hand that feeds him. Such bad taste.

CROMWELL: (*To a Soldier.*) Arrest that man. He breeds anarchy!

LILBURNE: That's it, my friend, betray the Liberty of Man before you've even found it! But if you hurt England, Oliver, as God is my eternal witness, I will hurt you!

CROMWELL: (*Pleading with LILBURNE sotto voce.*) Why can't you be silent? Despite your dangerous opinions, I know you are a good man. And I need good men.

LILBURNE: (*Laughing bitterly.*) I'm filth! (*Indicating the audience.*) Like They are! I talk – I screech about freedom – but I DO NOTHING! You watch me. When you kill that

fighting cock, I'll shout and I'll rave – but like everyone else – I'll *do* nothing!
(*In ritualistic unison, PYM and the KING kill the Cock. LILBURNE screams as if he is also being killed.*)
No! NOOOO! (*Laughing.*) But what's it matter? It's just another slit vein. Arrest me! I'm England! I'm a whore! Go on! Rape me! You do it with such style.
PYM: Charles, come back to England. We need you.
Parliament can pass the Laws, but only the King can make them beautiful. Please.
CHARLES I: I wish you would die, old man. You have bled me, and you are a bad physician.
(*Both Armies watch PYM, who is obviously in great pain as he is leaning against the slain Fighting Cocks.*)
PYM: Cromwell…Fairfax. Yes, Fairfax, not Cromwell. Come here…please. I am too weak to move.
FAIRFAX: (*Going to PYM.*) Don't talk, old friend. All you politicians talk too much. You only justify your injustice. Look at the dead. Look. Centuries of mass murder. Talking breeds murder. Pride and talking. Have you learnt nothing?
PYM: No, no! I have failed. I did not make a kingdom. I have ripped up one of the world's lungs, and stuck it with arrows. My wife…you know my wife. Hardly ever sees me. 'Put your stockings on properly. Brush your hair. People are looking at you. You are respected.' That's what she said. But I took no notice as I hankered after my stubborn God. Do you hear that, God? I gave up a human being for You! Are You worth it? Are You worth the death of a cockerel? Of a gnat? Are You worth the death of a stone?
CROMWELL: If you have to go into the dark, Pym,
Do not whine. Without God,
You would not have progressed this far.
PYM: Prove Him, Cromwell! Please, prove that God exists!
Just a bubble of proof before death pricks me. Please.
Already I hear the earth growling to climb into my veins.
So prove that everything is intended for good by God.
Prove it!

CROMWELL: Your gift was Prime Minister of England.
    Mine is God. The proof is me.
    I believe what you have done is right.
    I will bring what you have done to hope.
    That is proof enough for God.
    So it must be proof enough for you.
    Die in peace now. Come, Charles,
    You are only wasting time.
    Prepare for war.
RUPERT: I will cut you down, Oliver Cromwell. Your hair
    will be a tassel for my banner.
HYDE: (*To the KING.*) Highness, try peace!
PYM: Yes, try it, Charles, try it.
FAIRFAX: Talk, talk, talk.
PYM: Please!
CHARLES I: I am King of England, gentlemen – wherever
    that might be. And there is only one thing we share; the
    c-cake of G-God – and I happen to have the largest slice.
    W-W-W-War!
    (*CHARLES exits with his ARMY.*)
PYM: I wanted to see England… I wanted Justice… I
    wanted…
    (*PYM dies.*)
LILBURNE: But you didn't love. (*Closing PYM's eyes.*) Sleep
    now.
CROMWELL: He tried. He did that. That is more than
    enough in the eyes of the earth. Give him a king's funeral.
LILBURNE: No! No. No. NO! He's dead. That is sufficient
    funeral for any man. Leave him with the other dead. Let
    them listen to the worms' sermon together. They are equal
    now. It is enough.
CROMWELL: Death must have form. God has given
    everything form.
LILBURNE: You make me hate God, Cromwell. Don't hide
    behind Him. He will scorch you.
CROMWELL: Give Pym a King's funeral, and throw
    Lilburne in jail.

LILBURNE: (*To the audience, as PYM's body is carried out.*)
You notice that we always use the same soldiers for both
sides. Same faces, different gear. That's 'cause we're always
short of soldiers. See, they don't give a firkin as long as you
pay them, and we don't pay them.
(*LILBURNE is escorted off. CROMWELL and the other
Puritans follow. Only the dead Fighting Cocks remain.
Two looting SOLDIERS appear. They proceed to cut the dead
Cocks' throats, then they remove their masks, putting them on
their own heads.
Two WHORES enter. The WHORES and the SOLDIERS do
a song-and-dance number.*)
WHORES / SOLDIERS:
A pause between wars.
There are apples on the tree,
And lots of whores
To share breasts with me.
Sing goodies for you.
Sing goodies for me.
Let's sing as we do
The goodies we see.
(*Their dancing becomes raunchy. Soon they are lustily grappling
with one another on the ground.*)
FIRST WHORE: Rape! Rape!
SECOND WHORE: Please! Please!
FIRST SOLDIER: Lovely! Lovely!
SECOND WHORE: (*In a soixante-neuf position.*) Experiments
ahoy!
(*Enter FAIRFAX.*)
FAIRFAX: (*Raging.*) What is this?
FIRST WHORE: Goodie time.
FAIRFAX: Ladies!
SECOND SOLDIER: Oh, where?
FAIRFAX: Soldiers!
FIRST SOLDIER: (*Encouraging his WHORE.*) Show him your
potent potential, darling. If you follow my subtlety, sir.
FIRST WHORE: (*Winding her arms around FAIRFAX.*) You do
follow, don't you, handsome? Now, don't be bashful. I can
take anything. I've got the constitution of a whale on heat.

FAIRFAX: Yes there is something Leviathan about you. Perhaps it's your water-spumer.

SECOND WHORE: My name's Barley, 'cause I'm always home to the Raping Reaper.

FAIRFAX: I'll have you all on a charge! I want decency here!

FIRST WHORE: Well, everyone to his little knicker-knackers, is what I say.

(*CROMWELL enters.*)

CROMWELL: Soldiers, attention!

(*The SOLDIERS spring to attention.*)

FIRST WHORE: Now this one's a right little charmer who'd love it any which way; if he could get it. Underneath, y'see, all you Puritans are bobby-dazzlers, 'cause you bottle it up. God bless you.

CROMWELL: Soldiers, remove these pox-ridden whores!

(*The SOLDIERS chase after the WHORES, but they can't catch them.*)

SECOND WHORE: (*Playing with CROMWELL's sword and scabbard.*) Oh come on, Sexy Ironsides, give us a taste of your mettle.

CROMWELL: (*Breaking away.*) Because Charles Stuart allows *his* soldiers to indulge in debauchery, it does not mean that we will follow his depraved example. Whoring in future will be greeted with the whip!

FIRST WHORE: Oh lovely. I didn't know that you were such an inspired lover, Nolly.

(*CROMWELL grabs her and is about to hit her.*)

Yes, please. We'll both love it!

FAIRFAX: No violence, Oliver!

FIRST WHORE: No, hit me, hit me! Don't listen to him. Release yourself. Then we'll make it up tonight between the sheets, ducky.

(*CROMWELL releases her.*)

CROMWELL: Enough. You women, get down on your knees.

SECOND WHORE: Promises, promises.

CROMWELL: Now join with us in singing the twenty-third Psalm. It will cleanse your mildewed souls.

(*The WHORES begin to sing.*)

WHORES: There was a young strumpet
Called Annie,
Who inserted a trumpet
Right up her fanny...
(*This is drowned by the booming voices of CROMWELL and FAIRFAX who are singing the 23rd Psalm. Reluctantly the SOLDIERS join in, as do the WHORES. Then CROMWELL speaks above the singing.*)

CROMWELL: We have beaten the King three times. The fourth will be the last. We are fighting for Liberty. Wherever we go, they will say: 'Here are the Soldiers of God.' We will be the first soldiers in history who only fight for victorious Truth, and not for plunder and sexual gratification... (*As he pushes the WHORES off-stage.*) ...mark that, in particular!
(*CHARLES, RUPERT and DIGBY, holding the battered standard of the KING, enter from the other side of the stage.*)

CHARLES I: (*Sitting on the ground, exhausted.*) Interminable snow. I cannot run any more, Rupert. I need my wife. (*Removing his hat, in order to shake the snow off it.*) The weight of England...

RUPERT: The last battle is coming. I can feel its sting in the snow.

CROMWELL: (*To his TROOPS.*) You will be the greatest soldiers in Christendom because you will be the New Model Army. So you will obtain horses from anywhere, at any cost. Steal them, if necessary. God is very understanding. Parliament will pay your wages. I promise you on my body. You will be the first paid Army since Ancient Rome. You are free to believe in God in your own ways. But I want Charles. I want him.

RUPERT: (*To CHARLES.*) If only Cromwell was here, within the reach of my sword, I would...

CHARLES I: (*Overriding him.*) No more violence, Rupert. There must be other ways. More subtle ways...

CROMWELL: (*To his Troops.*) I want Charles Stuart alive. Or dead.

RUPERT: No, Charles, there is only the snow in our faces. The skyline, with skeletal trees, like witches' claws. And

me. And you. And our exhausted soldiers. Sweating and
thrusting. Heart-slitting. I would that I had Cromwell here.
I would kill him, and then England would glow. Kill him!

CHARLES I: No, Rupert, no! We have gone beyond the
Hero and the Villain. It has taken acres of blood to make
this apparent. (*He picks up a handful of imaginary snow.*) See,
when I squeeze this snow, the water drips...drips back
into the snow again. Blood is the same. Playing the Hero,
we squeeze blood into blood again. Nothing g-grows. Sing
something to pass the h-horror.

RUPERT: (*Singing.*)
There was a young man called Charlie,
Who drank cool blood from the barley.
The world's women and men were all his,
But he hadn't the energy left to kiss.
Sing winter is coming, heigh-de-ho.

CHARLES I: (*Singing.*)
And with it is coming...the drums of snow.
(*Speaking.*) Why can't we stop? Why can't we just exist
instead of...?

RUPERT: You have snow in your beard. Keep still. There
– it's gone now.

CHARLES I: My father slobbered every time he k-kissed me.
On his lips, I smelt the sweetness of young b-boys' lips...
and the acrid scent of Buckingham. But, nevertheless, my
father used to understand things. Secrets were transparent
to him. And he certainly wouldn't be foolish enough to sit
here in the snow – talking to himself.

RUPERT: What will you do, Charles, when the war is over?

CHARLES I: Chop off a few heads, imprison a great deal,
and flog the remainder. I am a gentle king. (*Shaking his fist
at the falling snow.*) God, You're not helping Your Anointed.
To let them defeat me is annoying, but to snow on me is
excessive.

CROMWELL: (*To his Troops.*) March! March! March!
(*CHARLES' exhausted Troops collapse into sleeping positions.
CROMWELL's Troops continue to march to the beating of a
drum. LILBURNE appears with a microphone. Both Armies
have large banners.*)

LILBURNE: (*To the audience.*) They've let me out of jail again – as cannon fodder – to watch the carve-up.

(*Drums throb as the light begins to fade.*)

On my left, in black breeches, we have the Round Heads, the Jesus Boys – otherwise known as 'You've not got a chance, Charlie, because God's on my side.' They're rough, tough, ready and a bit dull, but they're certainly heavy weights. And on my right, in every coloured codpiece in the book, we have the Cavalier Gents, Charlie's Laddies, otherwise known as 'For we are jolly good fellows and, what's more, we bloody well know it!' They're flashy and under-weight, but with first class sneaky intentions.

It's a thunder day here at Naesby. But, thank God, it's stopped snowing. The Jesus Boys, in their midnight knickers, have marched all day, and are tired and hungry, but still violent as hell. Whereas Charlie's Laddies are a touch sleepy, and won't bother to fight until sun-up. And now it's...sunset.

(*Cromwell's Army sit on their haunches, watching the sleeping Royalists. A Soldier beats a solitary drum. LILBURNE goes over to RUPERT, in his role as a reporter, with the microphone.*)

Have you anything to say to the coming generations, Prince Rupert, sir?

RUPERT: (*Yawning.*) Yes. We will slash their throats with the sun in their eyes at dawn.

LILBURNE: Charming. (*He crosses to FAIRFAX and CROMWELL with the mike.*) How's life here, gents? Ready for the do-or-die etcetera? (*To the audience.*) This was how the Gutter Press was born.

FAIRFAX: Just peace. That's all we want. Peace.

LILBURNE: Naturally. And you, Herr Cromwell, I'm sure you've a nice peaceful word or two that you would like to distil on this fine English evening. Pity about the rain.

CROMWELL: (*Grabbing the mike from LILBURNE.*) How perceptive you are. I would like to say... (*As he covers the mike with his hand.*) ...ATTENTION! CHARGE; AND ROUT THE ENEMY!

(As the sun sets, there is the stylised, iridescent Battle of Banners, with the black banners of the Puritans swirling above the multi-coloured Royalist banners.
RUPERT and CROMWELL engage in combat with their banners.
LILBURNE describes the action on his mike.)

LILBURNE: Now coming into the slope, Cromwell's Ironsides smash Heaven, or Hell, or both, out of Rupert's Dandies. It's a beautiful race here at Naesby. We thought the drizzle would stop the action, but no! There will be a lot of blood spilt here tonight, I'm pleased to tell you. Cromwell and Rupert are now engaged in mortal combat. It's a wonderful sight to see the whirl of Rupert's lance pitted against the cold stabbing of Cromwell's pike. A lovely parry there, Cromwell! No, Rupert has cut Cromwell's eye, and Olly is bleeding.

(Then two Puritans force RUPERT off-stage. On the opposite side, FAIRFAX is being surrounded by NEWCASTLE and his Troops.)

CROMWELL: *(Half blinded by blood and using his banner like a scythe.)* Rupert! Rupert, where the devil are you?

LILBURNE: 'Fraid Rupert the Bear has decided to run away. He's not stupid. Well, never argue if there are more than one of them. Just give 'em a quick kick in the crutch and run! Meanwhile, Cromwell is still on his benders. And now he's got that cut above his right eyebrow, is the ref going to stop the fight? If Rupert was here now, he'd land a couple more left hooks on that right eye, then another heroic villain would drip into death. Hooray! Or do I mean: 'boo'?

(CROMWELL sees that FAIRFAX is being defeated so CROMWELL forces himself to his feet.)

CROMWELL: *(To his Troops.)* Ironsides, form round General Fairfax – at the double!

(Four Troops obey.)

LILBURNE: Is Cromwell blind? Will he be able to save Fairfax? Will Rupert return, and kick Cromwell's crutch in? Find out in next week's episode.

CROMWELL: Ironsides, charge!

(*Cromwell's Men scythe down Newcastle's Men while NEWCASTLE escapes.*)

LILBURNE: (*Singing.*)

Beat, beat, beat the drums!

Here comes Death. Here it comes.

(*Speaking.*) Night falls. (*Blackout.*) But the moon stands up. (*Moonlight.*) Cromwell scythes through all resistance. Rupert escapes, losing his deposit. All the images are muddled. Nothing makes sense. And the Newcastle Gents are hacked to pieces by the mercy of Oliver Cromwell.

(*CHARLES is desolate as Cromwell's Soldiers thrust pikes into the dying and the dead. The Puritans sing as they kill.*)

PURITANS: Victory! Victory!

God is here!

Look and see

Eternity.

Have no fear;

God is here.

Victory! Victory!

CROMWELL: Cease this bestiality! Have mercy on the dying and the dead. Remember we join them soon. Begin the labour to LOVE – which is harder than death.

(*Two PURITANS push CHARLES into CROMWELL's arms. CROMWELL kisses the KING on both cheeks.*)

Welcome, Charles Stuart. Where is the King? If you find him, there may be hope. But *you* look like a man of blood to me.

LILBURNE: (*To the audience.*) A messy February, Sixteen Forty-Seven.

(*HOLLES appears, snapping his fingers. In response the Speaker's Chair is placed centre-stage, amongst the dead. HOLLES sits on the chair, using one of the dead as a footstool. He waves a handkerchief in front of his nose to deflect the stench of the corpses.*)

CROMWELL: (*To the Dead.*) ATTENTION!

(*The Dead spring to attention, and then stand guard.*)

LILBURNE: (*To the audience.*) I told you that we're always short of soldiers, so everyone has to turn coat. Even the

Dead. I know which side my bread is buttered on, don't you? You do? Good. Neither side. 'Cause there isn't any butter, and hardly any bread.

HOLLES: As your new First Minister, since the death of Mr Pym, I demand that you hand the King over to Parliament. (*Silence.*) The Army has no right to keep the King. (*Silence.*) I appeal to you, General Fairfax.

CHARLES I: Yes, Sir Thomas, you are obviously a reasonable man. So I am certain that some suitable arrangement for England can be negotiated.

LILBURNE: What about me? (*Indicating the audience.*) What about Them? They're who the argument should be about.

HOLLES: (*To the audience.*) They prefer their decisions made for them. Don't you? Don't you? You don't want to think now, do you? Do you? Of course, you don't. It would interrupt the routine. And that would never do. Government will always be *by* the Select Few *for* the Select Few. That is what Democracy means. So hand the King over, to the Select Few.

(*CROMWELL conducts his Troops like a military brass band.*)

SOLDIERS: We want our bloody pay,
And we want it today!
And we don't want telling what to say!
We want to worship Christ in our own way
Because we are individuals from today.

HOLLES: (*In horror.*) Individuals? We can't have that. This is a Democracy! It has nothing to do with Freedom! Now return His Majesty to Parliament!

CROMWELL: No, we think...

FAIRFAX: Yes, we think...

LILBURNE: (*To the audience.*) Well, that's a revolution, for a start.

CROMWELL: Yes, you tell him...

FAIRFAX: No, you tell him...

CROMWELL: You tell him, please...

FAIRFAX: No, after you...

CHARLES I: Manners? I don't believe it.

CROMWELL: All right, I'll tell him. We think…

FAIRFAX: Yes, we think…

LILBURNE: (*To the audience.*) Here we go again.

CHARLES I: Enough of this! May not I, as King of England, decide which set of rebels I will go with?
(*HENRIETTA and PRINCE CHARLES are escorted onto the stage by Soldiers.*)
My dearest wife…

CROMWELL: (*Barring the KING's way.*) Do not move. I advise you not to. For them.

PRINCE CHARLES: Try laughing, father. It would be an original experience all round.

CROMWELL: Charles Stuart, you are a prisoner of the Army.

HOLLES: Rebellion and sedition!

CHARLES I: Says one humorous traitor to the other.

CROMWELL: Soldiers, we march against Parliament!
(*The Soldiers advance against HOLLES who draws his sword. Then he changes his mind, and he slips a white handkerchief onto his sword.*)

HOLLES: We surrender. Immediately. Unfortunately.

CROMWELL: Purge the House of Commons and the House of Lords! (*To the audience.*) You, you and you – volunteer to be purged.

CHARLES I: Let us come to some agreement, Cromwell…

CROMWELL: Can we trust you?

CHARLES I: Can you trust G-God?

LILBURNE: Only on Sunday.

CROMWELL: Why must you blaspheme, Lilburne? God's Commandments are our only hope!

LILBURNE: What about love?

HOLLES: That's got nothing to do with politics.

PRINCE CHARLES: Has anything?

CROMWELL: By the Blood of Christ, yes! We, who rule England, may be wrong – although we are not! – but at least we take full responsibility when we rule.

LILBURNE: That's what Wentworth said.

CROMWELL: I want to build a New World!

LILBURNE: That's what I said.

CROMWELL: I want a progressive England. With equality. Freedom of religion. Toleration. But in order to achieve this, for the next ten years, the King and Parliament must rule jointly, but Parliament is to have total control over the Army, and Parliament must appoint all the Ministers of State. (*To FAIRFAX.*) Agreed?

FAIRFAX: Agreed.

LILBURNE: What about the Workers?

CHARLES I: (*Sotto voce.*) I would speak with you in private, Cromwell.

CROMWELL: Agreed?

FAIRFAX: Agreed.

HOLLES: I don't agree!

LILBURNE: You don't count. You're only the Prime Minister.

HOLLES: Throw Lilburne in jail!

LILBURNE: On my way, Holly. (*To CROMWELL.*) I'll be back, Olly. But watch out for Charley. He's dead slippery. Well, he's not the King for nothing.

(*LILBURNE exits between two Soldiers.*)

CROMWELL: (*To HOLLES.*) Leave us.

HOLLES: Cromwell…

CROMWELL: Shall we purge the House of Commons further, Fairfax?

(*HOLLES shrugs and exits with the rest of the Soldiers. FAIRFAX gives CROMWELL a nod of encouragement. CROMWELL is now alone with CHARLES, HENRIETTA and PRINCE CHARLES.*)

CHARLES I: When I was only a prince, I remember seeing you one day as we whirled through Huntingdon. You hurled your eyes at me – and I admired that. Even though you were covered in mud and p-pimples.

CROMWELL: I do not remember.

CHARLES I: Oh yes, behind your iron face, you remember. You shouted 'God save the P-Prince!'

CROMWELL: I do not remember.

CHARLES I: And you sat in the mud l-laughing. And my tutor said we should have you whipped for in-insolence. But I said 'no'. I liked you for your l-laughing.

PRINCE CHARLES: You've certainly changed, father.

CHARLES I: Silence, b-boy! (*To CROMWELL.*) Look into my face. Don't you remember me: minus beard, moustache and age? My hooded eyes.

CROMWELL: Why bring our youth into it, Charles?

CHARLES I: It is necessary that we know and understand one another.

CROMWELL: False King! You are using your childhood – *my* childhood – like you used England. But mine is private to me, sir. My days in grass – sky on my head – are mine, sir. MINE! I will not have you probing, or I will have your...

CHARLES I: ...Head, Mr Cromwell?

(*Pause.*)

CROMWELL: You know as well as I do that we have never met. Except conveniently in your imagination.

CHARLES I: You p-peasant!

CROMWELL: Wrong. We are no longer the Pauper and the Prince. Or even the Lieutenant General and the King. Because you are blood and I am blood. So all the fairy stories are over. And, God forgive us, we have both failed!

CHARLES I: Let us l-leave England, then, because we can never agree to your t-terms.

HENRIETTA: Yes, let us go, Mr Cromwell.

PRINCE CHARLES: Please.

CHARLES I: For mercy's sake, let us go!

CROMWELL: Do not beg. You are supposed to be the King. Silly, but the King. Do not beg.

CHARLES I: Let me g-go now.

CROMWELL: That is all your friend, Strafford, asked – of you. And your considered response was to give us his head. So will you not betray me who is your sworn enemy? Will you not raise a French army against me?

CHARLES I: Never! I swear by...

CROMWELL: Yes?

CHARLES I: ...By my-myself.

CROMWELL: You dare not swear by God. (*Pause.*) If only...

CHARLES I: Yes?

CROMWELL: If only you were truthful, Charles Stuart. I want to believe you. I am sick of blood...on my knuckles...

in my dreams. (*Pause.*) I am a fool. (*Indicating HENRIETTA and PRINCE CHARLES.*) They can go. You must stay. But do not conspire with Scotland or France, or, by the living God, there will be no mercy a second time.

(*CROMWELL exits. CHARLES puts his arms around HENRIETTA. Then he places his forefinger on her lips to prevent her from speaking.*)

CHARLES I: (*To PRINCE CHARLES.*) Treasure your mother, Charles. Teach her laughter. You are right; it is worth a kingdom.

PRINCE CHARLES: I will cry later.

HENRIETTA: (*To CHARLES.*) My love, Our Lord Jesus Christ will not desert you as long as you believe.

(*PRINCE CHARLES and HENRIETTA leave.
Dusk. CHARLES is alone.*)

CHARLES I: Christ has left me that I might taste wormwood and the loneliness of spirit. To show me that I am not a God. But He will come back in the morning and crown me. (*Smiling.*) Of course, I'll help God by helping myself to escape – with the Scottish Ambassador.

(*ARGYLL, the Scottish Ambassador, materialises out of the shadows. CHARLES moves towards him, but he is interrupted by the returning CROMWELL and two Soldiers.*)

CROMWELL: Traitor!

(*ARGYLL exits.*)

I trusted you, Charles Stuart, boyhood playmate, and you betrayed me.

CHARLES I: Rupert was right: Hero and V-Villain.

CROMWELL: But which is which?

(*Enter BRADSHAW.*)

BRADSHAW: (*To the audience.*) You've nearly forgotten me, haven't you? Sneaky human, third class, remember. So are we ready to begin?

(*Enter LILBURNE.*)

LILBURNE: Are we ever ready?

CHARLES I: For what, pray? Yes, *pray* – it might help you.

CROMWELL: You tell him, Sir Thomas.

FAIRFAX: No, you tell him, Mr Cromwell.

BRADSHAW: I'll tell him. I hate him – so I'm unbiased. Are you ready, Charles Stuart, for your trial – which begins now?
(*CHARLES laughs.*
Off-stage the drums begin to beat. The Speaker's Chair is placed in the centre, facing the audience.
Out of the darkness, the whole casts appears, save for HENRIETTA and PRINCE CHARLES. Puritan Soldiers keep the Crowd back with their pikes.)
It is essential that posterity should see the Justice of our proceedings.
(*The Soldiers crash the butts of their pikes on the ground. The drums stop.*
CHARLES is led to the Speaker's Chair.)

CHARLES I: (*Breaking away from his captors.*) No, a moment, please!

BRADSHAW: You have no leave to go!

CHARLES I: Yet I *will* g-go, for a m-moment. So follow, spaniels.
(*The Guards follow CHARLES off.*)

BRADSHAW: Stop him!

CROMWELL: No; a moment. Give him that. We will take much more from him.

FAIRFAX: He will ask by what authority we try a King.

CROMWELL: By the authority of England, invested in the name of the Commons in Parliament.

FAIRFAX: He will say it is illegal. *He* is England.

CROMWELL: *Was* England. Guard, return him.
(*CHARLES re-enters in a black cloak. He holds a silver-headed cane. He sits on the Speaker's Chair.*
From the back of the audience, we hear LILBURNE's voice.)

LILBURNE: Oliver Cromwell is a traitor to England, and should be axed head from shoulders!
(*Soldiers level their muskets at the audience.*)

BRADSHAW: If there is another murmur from the mob, my soldiers will shoot. We are not short of people in England but we are short of shot. Therefore, I assure you, our shot-shooting will prove to be excellently fatal.

LILBURNE: Oliver Cromwell is the Beast, and the potential
Tyrant of England!

BRADSHAW: Soldiers, take aim!

CROMWELL: Hold your fire!

LILBURNE: (*To the King.*) Charlie, why did you behave so
stupidly? Don't you know that the English always need a
king? We're not brave or mature enough to lose our pomp
and circumstance. And we love to be told what to do!
(*To the audience.*) Don't we?

CROMWELL: Cut off the exits!

LILBURNE: Olly, it's me! Me!

CROMWELL: I do not know you.

LILBURNE: Me! The People! Us! And we want Freedom
from the lot of you!

CROMWELL: Irresponsible clod! How dare you offer
freedom to the People? We are not ready for you, Lilburne.
Neither the People, nor Parliament, are ready for you.

LILBURNE: (*Appealing to the audience.*) Tell them that we
are! Now don't be embarrassed. Stand up for yourselves
and tell him! What happens in here is nothing to what
will happen to you when you all get outside – when the
soldiers, the executives and the spies pour into your lives
– into your wives! (*Pointing at CROMWELL.*) Pull down this
despotic shadow while there is still time. Pull Cromwell
down!

BRADSHAW: Arrest him!

CROMWELL: No. We are a democracy. Let him rave on.
(*Sotto voce to BRADSHAW.*) Simply arrest all those who *listen*
to him. Leave the choice to him. Well, Mr Lilburne?

LILBURNE: Don't worry, Olly, I'll find a way – if it takes me
a thousand years. I'll still find a way.
(*LILBURNE exits through the audience.*)

BRADSHAW: Charles Stuart, I charge you with Treason,
Tyranny, and the Murder of England. How do you answer
me?

CHARLES I: By what authority do you try your King?

BRADSHAW: By the authority of the Commons in
Parliament and all the Good People of England.

CHARLES I: (*Laughing.*) But P-Parliament has no authority *without* the K-King – and the King – to my royal knowledge – has not given you the authority to *try* the King.

BRADSHAW: Do you plead guilty, or not guilty, to our heinous charges?

CHARLES I: I plead nothing! You are a rebel regime. Your only authority is f-force. But force does not make you right.

BRADSHAW: No, but we're not complaining.

CHARLES I: I am Eng-England, gentlemen. I am the Son of the Son of G-God!

CROMWELL: That was yesterday.

BRADSHAW: I recommend you answer our charges, Charles Stuart, because our right to try you lies in the Will of the People whom you have wantonly trampled upon, even though they elected you King…

CHARLES I: Elected? Never has a k-king been elected in England. I am King by direct inheritance from my f-father, James the First, who was King before me. This court is not only totally incapable of attempting the trial of a king, it is not even fit to try an ordinary man, let alone a d-dog or a stone!

BRADSHAW: You must answer our charges, sir, or we will be forced to condemn you out of hand, for all the English blood that you have spilled. You, Charles Stuart, declared war upon England – *as a man.* We do not attempt to try and kill a king. But we will try and we will kill Charles Stuart if he is guilty of the crimes that we charge him with.

CHARLES I: (*To CROMWELL.*) B-Beast, when I am gone, anarchy will rout the land. Then you will be the most hated m-man that England has ever spawned from her w-womb!

CROMWELL: No, I will bring peace. Even if I have to shackle every man to the earth! There will be peace. There will be security. Safety, and, above all, belief. BELIEF! All of which you should have bestowed upon us from your largesse, but you were a lying, selfish fool.

CHARLES I: Silence!

(*CHARLES raps his silver-headed cane on the ground. The silver head rolls across the floor until it comes to rest at CROMWELL's feet.*)

Pick it up, and g-give it to me!

CROMWELL: We are men. Equal. Now. You must pick it up yourself.

CHARLES I: I said p-p-pick it up! I c-command you!

(*CROMWELL shakes his head. CHARLES leaves his chair and picks up the silver head. As he does so, a Soldier spits full in the KING's face.*)

SOLDIER: My son died for you! And you're not God, so there will be no Easter Day!

CHARLES I: May God forgive you for you know not what you d-do!

(*The Soldier is about to kick the KING but CROMWELL prevents him. FAIRFAX forces the Soldier back into line. CROMWELL goes to help CHARLES to his feet but CHARLES shakes him off. CHARLES is trying to control his tears.*)

CROMWELL: There is still time, Charles Stuart. So what do you plead?

CHARLES I: Learn to cry, Beast, and perhaps you will begin to b-be human.

CROMWELL: What do you plead?

CHARLES I: (*Through his tears.*) You are all so ridiculous!

CROMWELL: For the last time, what do you plead?

CHARLES I: R-Ridiculous!

CROMWELL: Sentence him.

CHARLES I: (*Prodding CROMWELL with his cane.*) Are you G-God? Is that it? Is that the point I've been m-missing? Am I your Son? Are you my F-Father which art in Heaven? Who are you? Or *what* are you that you do not give your K-King a quarter of the justice that you would give a s-stone?

(*A beat.*)

CROMWELL: (*Fighting for words.*) I am necessary. That is all.

BRADSHAW: Charles Stuart, on this day, January Twenty-Seventh, in the year of Our Lord, Sixteen Forty-Nine, the People of England find you guilty of Treason, Tyranny and Murder in the sight of Christ...

CHARLES I: What will you do when I am g-gone? Will you rule any b-better? Will you offer mankind anything other than more d-death?

BRADSHAW: Guilty also of Blasphemy and corrupting the Principles of God...

CHARLES I: I know you, C-Cromwell. Please have m-mercy on England. Have mercy on her soul...

BRADSHAW: And worst of all, we find you guilty of turning our civilisation into a whirlpool of blood.

CHARLES I: A m-moment! A m-mo-moment!

CROMWELL: Too late.

CHARLES I: May I not de-defend myself against these charges? May I n-not speak?

BRADSHAW: We have given you ample opportunity to plead, sir, but you have denied our authority – so how can you possibly defend yourself in a Court that you do not recognise?

CHARLES I: If you carry out this impious Act, no one's head is safe. Everything will become ar-arbitrary Law. Law of force without J-Justice. The most frightening state in the condition of man – An-An-Anarchy!

BRADSHAW: Charles Stuart, you will be taken on a said day to a said place, where your head will be severed without ceremony from your body.

CHARLES I: (*His stutter makes him almost inarticulate.*) M-may I sp-speak? May I n-not def-defend...?

CROMWELL: No. You are dead.

CHARLES I: P-Please, I m-must d-d-defend the King-King-Kingdom! P-Please!

CROMWELL: In the eyes of the Law, after the sentence is spoken, you no longer exist.

CHARLES I: (*The effort to speak seems to tear him apart.*) Pppplllease....

BRADSHAW: The dead do not stutter.

CHARLES I: PPPPLLLEEASE!!!

(*CHARLES is dragged off. LILBURNE reappears. CROMWELL stands emotionless.*)

LILBURNE: (*Singing.*)

Chop his head off, Olly.

You know you won't be sorry.
His blood streaks down your arms.
His hair is matted in your palms.
(*CROMWELL stands emotionless.*)
(*Speaking.*) The dark Beast roars from below.
You played upon the drums of snow.
You made the evil darkness grow.
Not us, but only you, you know.
You're right, and wrong as well.
You're Lucifer and Christ, Cromwell.
(*CROMWELL exits.*
An executioner's block is brought onto the stage. The Crowd hiss.
A drum beats – like a stuttering heartbeat.
Enter the masked EXECUTIONER – who looks like CROMWELL.
CHARLES enters with DIGBY.)

CHARLES I: January is a cold time to die. If I wear this extra cloak, I will not shake with cold. The mob must not think that I shake with fear because I do not.
(*The drum stops.*)
My impediment has left me 'til the end of time. Strange to die perfect. This is my second wedding day. Today I marry Christ. Cut deep, Cromwell. You have made a messy job of England. Oblige me with a clean, headless pair of shoulders.
(*The EXECUTIONER rubs his finger along the blade.*)
Hurt not the axe, so that it may hurt me swiftly.
(*CHARLES examines the block.*)
Have you not a higher block for me, Cromwell? I have never lowered my head this far before.
(*To the audience.*) Thank you, England, for being definite about one thing at least – my death. Even though you will never be free, I still love you for what you could have been.
(*He lowers his head on the block.*)
Stay, Cromwell, for the sign.
(*He holds out his arms as the sign.*)
Now!

(*As the axe descends, the Crowd pushes forward so the audience cannot see the blow.*

A screeching animal cry erupts from the Crowd as the axe strikes home. The Crowd converge on the KING's body, enveloping it. The EXECUTIONER removes his mask and holds it up as a substitute for the KING's head. The EXECUTIONER is not Cromwell.)

EXECUTIONER: Behold!
The King of England's head!
The King of England's dead!
God save...who?
(*The Crowd falls to its knees. CROMWELL cradles CHARLES in the manner of the Pieta while he sews the KING's head back on.*)

LILBURNE: (*To the audience.*) We've sewn Charlie's head back on. 'Fact it's more firmly on now than when he was alive. He used to be so absent-minded. The rest you know because you're living it. Mediocre, isn't it?
(*Singing.*)
We're preparing for the night.
Hush, my friends, nothing's right.
You will not sleep deep tonight
Or sleep any other night.

CROMWELL: (*Cradling CHARLES.*) Your Majesty – am I right? Are we right? Ask Christ whether we are right because we are the ones who will have to live with the dregs.
(*The CROWD slithers over the stage like a giant python.*)

CROWD: (*Sing.*) His head's, his head's a nice old head.
He was nice alive but he's better dead.
He didn't die on the job in bed.
I'm doing the job for him instead.
So come on, darling, let's get wed.
No, better still, go straight to bed.
We'll save our wedding 'til we're dead,
'Cause that's what life is, when all's said.

CROMWELL: Help us!
(*A breathless SOLDIER enters.*)

SOLDIER: Prince Rupert has gathered an army against you.

CROMWELL: (*Getting to his feet and drawing his sword.*) Good.
That at least is definite. Further retrogression. Thank You,
God, for Your boundless horror.

LILBURNE: (*Singing, in the failing light.*)
O, listen to the drums of snow.
Into, into dark we go.
All that's left for us to do
Is to watch the darkness grow.
The future's all left up to you.

Dare anyone of you say 'no'
To us buried under snow?
O, light Love's fires before you!
Don't listen to the drums of snow
Because in Charles' eyes dead lilies grow.

We listened, and we fear you will,
And if you do, you'll have to kill
Our endless dead again
Because we'll rise up and shame
You with our futile pain.

You see, we made the darkness grow.
We played upon the drums of snow.
We thought God always loved the dead
From everything Christ Jesus said,
But now in dark – we really know.
(*By the close of the song, it is almost dark. Blackout.*)

The End.

RICHELIEU

Characters

HENRI IV, the King of France

QUEEN MOTHER, Marie de Medici

LOUIS, heir to the throne

ANNE OF AUSTRIA, Louis' wife

GASTON, Louis' brother

MARIE DE ROHAN, Gaston's mistress

PRINCE CONDÉ, Louis' cousin

MONTPENSIER, a nobleman

RICHELIEU, the Bishop of Luçon

MOTHER of Richelieu

FATHER JOSEPH, a Capuchin monk

LUYENS, a huntsman

CINQ MARS, a beau

DE CHALAIS, a gallant

FANÇAN, a pamphleteer

CAPTAIN OF THE MUSKETEERS

THE ABBOT

THE DOCTOR

The Court, The Mob, Troops, Musketeeers,
Monks, Messengers, Huguenots, Children etc.

Richelieu was broadcast by the BBC on 13 September 1976, with the following cast:

MARIE DE MEDICI, Maxine Audley
LOUIS XIII, Michael Deacon
GASTON, Denis Lill
ANNE OF AUSTRIA, Catherine Griller
FATHER JOSEPH, John Hollis
CARDINAL RICHELIEU, Alfred Burke
CAPTAIN OF THE MUSKETEERS, Jack Holloway
DOCTOR / PRIEST, Ray Llewellyn
CINQ MARS, Peter Craze

Produced and directed by Michael Rolfe

PART ONE

RICHELIEU and LOUIS are discovered in pools of light. RICHELIEU is in his bishop's cope. LOUIS is dressed as the heir to the French throne.

They are watching the murder of Louis' father, KING HENRI IV, by Ravillac, in the form of a macabre dance. This is enacted in silhouette in front of giant mirrors that throw distorted shadows across the murder.

Most of the action of the play takes place on a bare stage. Mirrors, banners and puppets can be used at the director's discretion.

Ritualistically Ravillac stabs the KING on a small pyramid of writhing bodies. The bodies comprise the nucleus of the MOB. Their rhythmical movement provides a virile counterpoint to the decadent Puppet Court.

As the KING dies, LOUIS lets out a cry of desolation. The MOB, on their bellies, crawl away from the dead KING singing.

MOB: We are the blood of the world's dead.
    In despair we ooze from the King's head.
    The King has been stabbed to Eternity
    While we're left to rut in poverty,
    So our only hope is Anarchy
    And Anarchy.
    (*Henri's widow, Marie de Medici, known as the QUEEN MOTHER, with the PRINCE CONDÉ, emerge from behind the distorting mirrors. Frenziedly they try to pull the dead KING's body apart.*)
QUEEN MOTHER: (*Declaiming.*) Now that Henri, my fleur-de-lys, has been trampled into the dust, I, Marie de Medici, the Queen Mother, claim the paradise of France as mine.
MOB: (*Singing.*) All you offer in the way of birth
    To the rest of the self-butchering earth
    Is the decadence of nobility,
    Impotence and futility.
    That's why our only hope is Anarchy
    And more Anarchy!

CONDÉ: (*Declaiming.*) Now that that well-intentioned fool of a King is frying in Hell, I, the Prince Condé, am the foremost aristocrat in the realm, so I claim the dancing palaces of France as mine.

(*The MOB swarm between the QUEEN MOTHER and CONDÉ like foraging ants, seething over the dead KING's body.*)

MOB: (*Singing.*) We need guidance in the fog.
Man is reduced to a two-legged dog.
Our King is dead. Our freedom's gone.
We're the first blood in the storm
Of Anarchy and Anarchy
And yet more Anarchy!

LOUIS: (*Fighting to control his pronounced stutter.*) Now that my dear father is slain, I, Louis the Thirteenth, powerless and in-in-inarticulate, demand...Lo-Lo-Love!

(*The MOB become the parody of a funeral cortège.*)

MOB: (*Singing.*) Our time is coming, then we will
Raise up the Dead, and then we'll kill
These monsters who have gouged our lives,
Maimed our children, ploughed our wives,
And we'll them bring Anarchy.
Endless, barbarous Anarchy!

(*Light fades on the funeral cortège.*
RICHELIEU, in his bishop's garb, is being helped into armour by his DOCTOR. RICHELIEU is trying to conceal that he is in pain.)

RICHELIEU: Not so clumsy, Doctor. You're ripping the holy silk.

DOCTOR: Forgive me, my lord, but a bishop clambering into armour is somewhat unorthodox.

RICHELIEU: I was a soldier long before my mother stuffed a crucifix in my codpiece. (*To the DOCTOR.*) Enough!

(*RICHELIEU hurls his armour away and swishes his sword in an arc.*) I'll carve my way through those effete courtiers. Then I will dedicate my sword – and my mitre – to the Queen Mother.

(*RICHELIEU lurches, clutching his stomach.*)

DOCTOR: The only way I can alleviate the pain, my lord, is by bleeding you again.

RICHELIEU: Every time I see you, Doctor, I lose half a kilo of my blood. (*In pain.*) God Almighty, why does Your Son and the Holy Ghost always have to play tennis with my intestines?

DOCTOR: Let me prepare a potion, my lord.

RICHELIEU: No, no, I prefer the agony I have to another of your experiments. Now leave me.

(*The DOCTOR exits.*)

Dear Christ, I have tried to pray. (*Kneeling.*) And I *am* still trying, even though I had no intention of becoming a priest. But my mother insisted on keeping the Bishopric of Luçon in the family – and I was the only son who was available. Despite the fact that I was doing splendidly in the Military Academy. And ever since I have continually tried to offer You – me. But now I cannot find You anywhere. Although for the last seven years, in Your Name, I have mewed up my mind here in Luçon, striving to make it a centre of Christian charity. Yet it all seems meaningless because outside these abbey walls, France is haemorrhaging her life's blood. I want to serve You. God knows, I do. But can't You see that You leave me no choice but to join the world – in order to save it from itself?

(*Light dims on RICHELIEU.*

The macabre funeral cortège reappears and winds around the stage. The MOB hums a discordant Requiem. The QUEEN MOTHER brings up the rear, sobbing and beating her breast. LOUIS watches.)

LOUIS: (*To the QUEEN MOTHER who ignores him.*) Mother! Listen to m-me! I'm so bewildered. F-formless. (*To the passing cortège.*) Father, you should have taught me the mystique of kingship. I don't understand the principles of government. (*Stuttering badly.*) I can't even f-force the words out of my m-mouth! I wish I could ex-express what I feel, but I can't...

(*The cortège exits. LUYENS, a handsome hunter, enters, carrying a wren in a cage. He has a hooded hawk on his wrist.*)

I did not send for you.

LUYENS: No, Your Majesty, but I *was* sent.

LOUIS: My mother.

> (*LUYENS nods.*)

To spy on me, I presume.

> (*LOUIS pulls on a hunting glove, then takes the hawk from LUYENS.*)

Put the cage down.

> (*LUYENS obeys. LOUIS gestures at the hawk on his wrist.*)

Shall I loose the wren from its cage, and then unmask the ex-executioner?

LUYENS: If it pleases Your Highness.

LOUIS: Nothing pleases me! Who are you?

LUYENS: Merely a hunter, sire.

LOUIS: What do you hunt? My peace of mind? My mother's body?

LUYENS: I don't understand you, sire.

LOUIS: I think you do, Luyens.

LUYENS: How did you know my name, my lord?

LOUIS: In France, sirrah, it is necessary to know everything in order to stay alive.

LUYENS: Would you prefer me to leave, my lord?

LOUIS: (*Addressing the wren in the cage.*) My pretty, were you snared with lime? Or merely deceived like the rest of us?
> (*LOUIS takes the wren out its cage, and puts the bird inside his shirt.*) When father was alive, my mother used to smother me like this. She needed me then because *he* didn't need her.

LUYENS: The wren will die, Majesty.

LOUIS: True.

> (*LOUIS pulls the wren out from inside his shirt and throws it off-stage. Then he removes the hawk's hood and hurls the hawk after the wren.*)

LUYENS: For pity's sake, my liege!

LOUIS: Rend her, my brave hawk. She is my m-mother! And *you* are my father! (*Turning away from the killing fest.*) So quick. Yet so infinitely k-kind. It's not like that for *us*, though, Luyens, because we stuff ourselves on death, purely for the experience. We won't rest until the whole world has gangrene.

LUYENS: Shall I call the hawk back, sire?

LOUIS: No, my brother will shoot it on his travels. Killing is one of Gaston's specialities.

(*The lights dim on LOUIS and LUYENS.*

RICHELIEU is spotlit, with his sword in one hand and his mitre in the other. Three masks are illuminated on a table.)

RICHELIEU: I must learn to crawl in order to rise. I must bend my pride like a bow in pretended humility. Then when the time is propitious, I will swish the arrows into my enemies. In the interim, I must never write down what can be spoken, and I must never speak unless pressed. Even with one's friends. And the fewer of those the safer. I will hone my brain to cut through my emotions like a knife through a sweating pear, until I am nothing but pure intellect. Yes, I will be the mirror-image of what the State will become – impartial, unified and inexorable. Thus I bequeath my humanity to the Four Horsemen of the Apocalypse.

(*Richelieu's MOTHER, a proud, gaunt woman in her seventies, enters. RICHELIEU is so engrossed in his thoughts that he doesn't see her. She touches him. He flinches.*)

MOTHER: Obsessed with your destiny as usual, my son?

RICHELIEU: Mother.

MOTHER: I am right, though, am I not?

RICHELIEU: Pad, pad, pad! My life seems to have been punctuated by your slithering shoes. Why do you always look at me that way?

MOTHER: Your prayers are barren, aren't they, Armand?

RICHELIEU: Prayers are never enough, mother. Action is what is needed. (*He touches his robe.*) Now excuse me, I must change.

MOTHER: Why is there no rest for any of us?

RICHELIEU: Because we've run out of time. Or hadn't you noticed?

MOTHER: I deserve a little civility, Armand.

RICHELIEU: Why are you blinking like that? Aren't you well?

MOTHER: Are *you*, my son?

RICHELIEU: (*Coughing.*) My robe is always so tight across my chest. In desperation this morning I slit one of the seams, but to little avail.

MOTHER: Your sister. She…she…

RICHELIEU: Is Nicole ill again?

MOTHER: Worse.

RICHELIEU: In what way?

MOTHER: Despite all your protestations, you always wanted the Bishopric of Luçon. Oh you pretended you were doing it for me but you were aware of the advantages.

RICHELIEU: (*Coughing.*) What is the matter with Nicole?

MOTHER: She thinks she is made of glass. And that if anyone touches her…she will break.

RICHELIEU: Like France.

MOTHER: My God, how could I have given birth to such an unfeeling creature? Oh I can comprehend a man binding himself to concepts like honour, loyalty and devotion, but to chain your ambition to the chaos that is France is lunatic hubris. Armand, what are you doing to *you*?

RICHELIEU: I promise I'll pray…

MOTHER: …To yourself! (*Touching his sleeve.*) Please!

RICHELIEU: Too late, mother!

MOTHER: No. If you wanted, you could change. Your sister is in hell, but she still wants you to go to her and bless her. (*Ironically.*) Yes, God help her, she wants *you* to bless *her*.

RICHELIEU: My blessing is worth nothing until France is secure.

MOTHER: I beg you, my son…

RICHELIEU: (*Shaking his head.*) Too late, mother. I have given my humanity away.

(*RICHELIEU exits. His MOTHER follows.*)

MOTHER: No, it will still shadow you. We will all shadow you. Especially your sister.

(*LOUIS and LUYENS are spotlit.*)

LOUIS: Are you alone, Luyens?

LUYENS: My lord?

LOUIS: Inside your skull?

LUYENS: I don't understand.

LOUIS: *I* am. Will you be m-m-my…m-my…?

LUYENS: What, sire?

LOUIS: Fr-fr-friend! Very soon my mother will have no recourse but to relinquish her power, then I will be a real k-king. So I repeat – will you be my f-f-friend?

LUYENS: Of course, my liege.

LOUIS: Hold me.

LUYENS: Sire…?

LOUIS: Hold me!

    (*Tentatively LUYENS embraces LOUIS.*)

    (*Laughing.*) Tighter! Kingship is not so easily crushed.

    (*LUYENS breaks away.*)

LUYENS: I like you, Your Majesty. Truthfully I do.

LOUIS: Never tell me the truth, or I will begin to believe you. Then I will become a very bad statesman. Like my mother.

    (*Trumpets. Dazzling light shimmers on the QUEEN MOTHER who is seated on the throne. She is talking to Father JOSEPH, the éminence grise. JOSEPH is a burly man in a grey monk's robe. GASTON, Louis' fop of a brother, is flirting with the nubile MARIE DE ROHAN.*

    From the encroaching shadows, the MOB whisper over and over: 'Condé is coming!'.)

    (*Stepping into the light.*) Mother, it seems that Condé, your royal l-l-lover, has come here to Blois in person, so you had better re-paint your m-mouth.

QUEEN MOTHER: Must you always reduce life to the stud-farm, Louis? (*Smiling.*) But then I suppose you *are* your father's son.

LOUIS: Don't soil father's name, you…you… (*Stuttering badly.*) …yyyyyou…!

QUEEN MOTHER: Yes?

LOUIS: But why not? When you have already soiled his kingdom. *M-m-my* kingdom!

QUEEN MOTHER: You may be old enough to rule, dear, but, as yet you do not have the regal disposition to be a credible king.

LOUIS: It is my r-r-right, mother!

QUEEN MOTHER: What's more, *I* will be the first to inform you if, and when, your readiness occurs.

LOUIS: Everything that father created, you have debased. You are auctioning France off to the highest bidder!

GASTON: Now, now, brother, don't provoke Mother. She'll burst her confines.

LOUIS: Have you no feelings, Gaston? He was *your* father, too.

GASTON: But he always favoured you, Louis.

LOUIS: No. I just loved him. That is all.

QUEEN MOTHER: But you didn't have to *sleep* with him! Or have his brutish face breaking into your dreams. I'm sorry, Louis, if I offend your delicate nature, but your father made me less of a mother than I wished to be.

LOUIS: How can you lie to yourself? While my poor father was alive, nightly you rollicked with every rampant centipede in France under this very roof.

QUEEN MOTHER: When *your* father *bought* me at *my* father's auction, I was an innocent! And I was capable of such inordinate love.

LOUIS: Then why did you turn father's funeral into a libidinous festival, with silver on your eyebrows and vermilion on your mouth? You were so lewd that the only time you cried, was with l-l-laughter! And that was only when you saw my father, f-f-freezing in that vault, with his skin embossed with icy scales!

JOSEPH: (*To the QUEEN MOTHER and LOUIS.*) Your Royal Highness, Your Majesty, you must both stop this!

LOUIS: Father Joseph is right, mother. (*Indicating the MOB who are still whispering: 'Condé is coming'.*) So throw open the gates to B-Bluebeard. Well, we've nothing left to bribe your bestial lover with – save your honeyed loins.

QUEEN MOTHER: Enough!

LOUIS: (*Smiling.*) That will be the night.

QUEEN MOTHER: (*Returning his smile.*) So be it, my son. (*To Father JOSEPH.*) Your acolyte is moderately delectable you say?

JOSEPH: More important, madam, my acolyte is willing to sacrifice himself for France.

QUEEN MOTHER: How chivalrous.

LOUIS: Mother, Condé will soon be here. We must act now, whatever the consequences.

JOSEPH: And my protégé is also devious, cunning, and very reliable.

QUEEN MOTHER: He sounds refreshingly unhealthy. But can your friend prevent the Prince Condé from ransacking Paris?

JOSEPH: Yes. If anyone can.

LOUIS: Mother, give me control of the Army, and *I* will do it for you. I'll run France, I'll...

GASTON: (*Overriding him.*) Run France, brother? You don't even make a profit on your brothels.

LOUIS: I've never seen a b-b-brothel!

(*MARIE DE ROHAN undulates towards LOUIS.*)

MARIE: So it's true that your bedroom gymnastics are limited to garlic breath and wishful thinking.

LOUIS: How dare you insult your k-k-king?

MARIE: I have seen the way you look at me, Your Highness.

JOSEPH: Scour your mouth with brine, my Lady de Rohan. What chance have we of avoiding civil war if you all don't control your lascivious appetites and face reality?

QUEEN MOTHER: Oh come now, Father Joseph, you know the only object of my apparently-convoluted policies is Peace. What is more, I will sacrifice everything – and everyone – to achieve Peace.

LOUIS: Including your laundryman, Condé, at the back gate?

QUEEN MOTHER: Silence!

LOUIS: Give me my throne, and I will hack C-Condé down myself!

JOSEPH: Sire, your mother is right about the problem. It's only her solution that is wrong. That's why Spain and Austria are waiting for us to fully expose our self-inflicted wounds before they pounce upon us. They know that we are being eaten alive from within – by the Huguenots – at present led by Prince Condé. But most all by everyone in this chamber!

GASTON: Priest, you're overstepping your sack-cloth and ashes.

JOSEPH: It is you, Prince Gaston – not I – who have
crammed your pockets with the State's gold. And we need
that gold now to bribe Condé to skulk back to his castle.
But you have spent it all. Indeed, between you, you have
sold off the realm, acre by acre, so you can dance from
ballroom to bedroom, and back again. Well, now Condé is
coming, and the games are over. Anarchy is swaying over
the kingdom like a rapacious dragon.

MARIE: I wouldn't mind *you* swaying over me sometime,
holy beard and all.

JOSEPH: Christ rot your soul, you harlot! (*To GASTON.*) I
advise you to watch her. Watch each other. All of you!
Because there is only one man who can help you now.
And he is devoid of compassion. He has never known
love. But he possesses an intellect more voracious than all
your groins grinding together. And, by the crucified eyes of
Christ, you need him. We need him! I feel God is about to
revenge Himself on your cupidity, lechery and wilfulness.
So I prophesy – yes, now I prophesy – that France will be
sucked under the sea, or flamed into desert, if you do not
accept *this* man!
(*RICHELIEU, still dressed as a bishop, but moving with
the vigour of a soldier, sweeps into view. With a flourish
RICHELIEU kneels before the QUEEN MOTHER.*)

RICHELIEU: I, Armand, Jean du Plessis de Richelieu,
Bishop of Luçon, do hereby swear perpetual allegiance
to my Queen and country, and I promise that I will save
France from her approaching enemies, so help me, God.

LOUIS: Priest, remember that you have dedicated your life to
my *m-mother* – because *I* certainly will.
(*LOUIS exits. LUYENS is about to follow.*)

QUEEN MOTHER: Luyens. Watch everything my son does.
And report.

LUYENS: Your Majesty…

QUEEN MOTHER: Or return to the forest.
(*LUYENS bows and exits. The QUEEN MOTHER turns to
RICHELIEU.*)

Bishop, you have made an enemy of my son but I enjoyed your entrance. You move like an athlete. Why?

RICHELIEU: Before priesthood, Your Majesty, I was a soldier.

QUEEN MOTHER: Why should I trust a soldier-turned-cleric?

MARIE: (*Pouting.*) Yes, why, Bishop?

(*RICHELIEU studies MARIE.*)

RICHELIEU: A priest – like myself – is a perfect servant to the State because he has no personal ambition. Or sensual ties to his neighbours. And his reward is in Heaven.

MARIE: (*Amused.*) Like Adam, before his fig leaf.

RICHELIEU: I am immune to bribery, corruption and seduction, my lady. I suffer so there will be no second crucifixion.

QUEEN MOTHER: Are you always so serious, sir?

RICHELIEU: Only in public, Your Majesty.

(*The noise of CONDÉ's approach becomes louder and more insistent. The MOB chants: 'Condé for KING!'*
LOUIS and LUYENS reappear, armed.)

LOUIS: So what do you propose we do now, mother? Condé is at the gates of Paris, backed by the Huguenots *and* the mob, and you have nothing left to b-b-bribe Condé with. Your last ball cleaned out what was left of the Treasury.

RICHELIEU: (*To the QUEEN MOTHER.*) Let me speak to Prince Condé, Majesty.

LOUIS: I am the King. Speak to m-m-me, priest!

QUEEN MOTHER: I wish to have conference with the bishop. Alone.

LOUIS: Whore!

(*QUEEN MOTHER rises from her throne and slaps LOUIS across the face.*)

QUEEN MOTHER: You insolent whelp!

LOUIS: Yes, hit me, mother, hit me. They're all used to it.

QUEEN MOTHER: (*Lowering her hand and whispering at LOUIS.*) If only you knew what I have had to suffer.

LOUIS: (*Indicating the 'Condé' chant.*) You mean while you were saying your prayers between Bluebeard's legs.

QUEEN MOTHER: Louis, we only *used* one another – in our battle to control France.

LOUIS: You *both* used m-me!

GASTON: Now don't cry, Louis, you'll ruin your ruffles.

QUEEN MOTHER: (*Touching LOUIS' cheek.*) My poor darling, don't you understand? I did what I *had* to, in order to protect you – because I love you.

LOUIS: (*Rushing into his mother's arms.*) Mother, oh mother. (*Turning on the Court.*) No need to stare! But that's all you're capable of, isn't it? Sycophancy, whispering and scheming. It's true that my father was a loveless man, but he did everything he could to rebuild France. He tried so hard. And for what? For you to throw it all away! (*Breaking away from his mother.*) Would to Christ I could trust you?

QUEEN MOTHER: You can, my son. Now leave me with the Bishop.

LOUIS: Mother!

QUEEN MOTHER: Leave us!

LOUIS: Very well. (*To LUYENS.*) We will make our own preparations.

(*Exit LOUIS and LUYENS.*)

GASTON: (*To QUEEN MOTHER.*) Richelieu can't help us, mother.

QUEEN MOTHER: (*To MARIE.*) Oh for God's sake, take Gaston back to bed. We'll all feel better.

MARIE: (*Winking at RICHELIEU.*) I do believe I've found fresher fish to fry.

GASTON: Were you *ever* a virgin, Marie?

MARIE: Yes; inside my mother.

(*GASTON follows MARIE off, laughing. Father JOSEPH indicates the sound of marching feet.*)

JOSEPH: (*To QUEEN MOTHER.*) You had best act swiftly, Majesty. The Prince is here. (*To RICHELIEU.*) You are only God's claw, Armand. Remember our bond.

RICHELIEU: Will you ever let me forget, Father?

(*Exit Father JOSEPH.*)

QUEEN MOTHER: I don't like that monk. He's too much of a zealot. And he never laughs.

RICHELIEU: The Prince will be in the Palace within moments.

QUEEN MOTHER: (*Patting the throne.*) Sit here. It will suit you.

RICHELIEU: (*Shaking his head.*) Only Kings and Popes decorate thrones.

QUEEN MOTHER: Cardinals have been known to. Your eyes. I like them. Clear – (*Smiling.*) – and treacherous.
(*The rapidly approaching MOB shouts 'Condé for KING!'.*)

RICHELIEU: For Christ's sake, madam!

QUEEN MOTHER: Don't you mean for *your* sake, Armand? (*Now close to him.*) Mm…exquisite perfume.

RICHELIEU: Your Majesty, I advise you to invite the Prince Condé to come to Paris – officially. And then…

QUEEN MOTHER: (*Placing a silencing finger over his lips.*) Understand one thing. I need peace. At any price. France is too poor to be anything other than peaceful. The slightest puff of wind and we'll be up to our petticoats in civil war.

RICHELIEU: (*Indicating the marching.*) If you won't listen to my advice, madam, I can do nothing to save France.

QUEEN MOTHER: Help me to ensure Peace, and I will share France with you.

RICHELIEU: Your Majesty…

QUEEN MOTHER: I require total obedience.

RICHELIEU: Naturally.

QUEEN MOTHER: Soul and body.

RICHELIEU: My soul is Christ's.

QUEEN MOTHER: (*Smiling.*) And the other?
(*RICHELIEU kisses the QUEEN MOTHER's hand.*)
Now what were you saying about your strategy?

RICHELIEU: Nothing. Only you must trust my instinct and wit.

QUEEN MOTHER: Why should I trust you?

RICHELIEU: Because now *you* must trust your instinct.
(*LOUIS and LUYENS re-enter. The MOB's insistent shouting for 'Condé' is now very close.*)

LOUIS: Condé's in the Palace and our musketeers are cheering him on. (*Drawing his sword.*) This is your last chance, mother!
(*Enter GASTON.*)
GASTON: (*Indicating LOUIS' drawn sword.*) You're not going to be boring and actually fight, are you?
LOUIS: I shall sluice Bluebeard's blood into the gutters!
RICHELIEU: No!
LOUIS: (*To LUYENS.*) Dispose of this malapert priest.
(*LUYENS draws his sword.*)
QUEEN MOTHER: Enough, Louis! With your usual infantile fervour, you have shown that the only realm you can rule, is your nursery. So go to it.
LOUIS: (*Indicating RICHELIEU, to LUYENS.*) KILL HIM!
RICHELIEU: (*Smiling.*) Please, Highness. Sainthood has always appealed.
(*The cries of 'Condé for KING!' are deafening. The blue-bearded CONDÉ enters, followed by Musketeers. RICHELIEU steps forward.*)
Welcome to Blois, Prince Condé.
(*LOUIS is about to attack CONDÉ but RICHELIEU whispers in LOUIS' ear.*)
Trust me, sire. I will tame him.
LOUIS: Yes, for my *m-m-mother*, priest.
(*CONDÉ silences the MOB's shouting with an imperious gesture.*)
CONDÉ: (*Sneering.*) Greetings, Louis.
LOUIS: You whoremaster! Down on your knees to your K-King!
CONDÉ: (*To the QUEEN MOTHER.*) You should keep him on a leash, Marie. Even a stuttering pussykins can bite.
(*CONDÉ kisses the QUEEN MOTHER's hand intimately and whispers.*) I'm glad your skin is still as soft.
QUEEN MOTHER: (*Whispering.*) My lord, why have you come here?
CONDÉ: Because you are incapable of decision, my sweet. And, above all, France needs decisiveness.
RICHELIEU: (*To the QUEEN MOTHER as he leads her to one side.*) Your Majesty, this is no place for emotion. Your

silence will gain you everything. (*Turning to CONDÉ.*) The Queen is indisposed.

CONDÉ: I refuse to parley with one of God's bitches!

LOUIS: (*To CONDÉ.*) How dare you presume to rebuke even the meanest of *my* n-nation?

CONDÉ: (*Laughing.*) France isn't a nation, Louis. Everyone in this godforsaken country has, and always will, live only for themselves. That's the reason we're forever split into warring factions. And that's the way we like it. Huguenots, Burgundians, rogue war-lords and a few million peasants – all at each other's throats. Besides, unification is the dream of the tyrant. So we must be realistic and live with what we have, and improve where we can – because we dare not mutilate our beloved France in pursuit of a despotic nightmare.

RICHELIEU: (*Under his breath to CONDÉ.*) I think it would be wiser if you listened to *me*, my Prince.

(*RICHELIEU leads CONDÉ to one side. They speak sotto voce.*)

CONDÉ: Your skirts offend me, priest.

RICHELIEU: But I agree with everything that you have just uttered, Highness.

CONDÉ: You agree…?

RICHELIEU: (*Nodding.*) What's more, I will be your most faithful servant. No, listen to me, my Prince. The Queen is incapable of logic, and Louis is hysterical, so I advise…

CONDÉ: Advise!?

RICHELIEU: Yes, I advise you to enter Paris – officially, and in full regalia – but *without* your troops. Oh I know your objections. But although you have the People behind you at the moment, they will change horses in the blink of an eye if they think the Monarchy is truly being threatened. So it would be more profitable if you insinuated your way back into the Court. (*Smiling.*) And…into the Queen. Then, within days, you will have the Mob *and* the Monarchy in the princely palms of your hands. And within the week, she will give you the throne. (*Glancing in the QUEEN MOTHER's direction.*) Her mouth is offering you everything now.

QUEEN MOTHER: (*Moving towards them.*) I would be
   honoured, Lord Bishop, if you would now share with *us*
   any treaty that you may have devised with the Prince.
RICHELIEU: (*To CONDÉ, under his breath.*) Smile, my Prince.
CONDÉ: I have not agreed...
RICHELIEU: (*Aloud to the QUEEN MOTHER.*) His Highness
   wishes to join you in Paris – as your honoured guest, Your
   Majesty.
CONDÉ: (*Under his breath to RICHELIEU.*) Dare I trust you?
RICHELIEU: Dare you instigate a civil war that could spiral
   into a revolution?
CONDÉ: I'll play your game, priest, but I promise you that
   if I fall, I will ensure that *you* will be the first to join me on
   the headsman's block.
LOUIS: (*To RICHELIEU and CONDÉ.*) So the t-treachery is
   agreed between you.
QUEEN MOTHER: (*To RICHELIEU.*) Remember, bishop,
   you are *my* hawk.
CONDÉ: Then I must congratulate you on your aviary,
   Marie. Now if Your Majesty will excuse me, I must make
   my preparations to enter Paris – officially. (*Smiling and
   bowing to the QUEEN MOTHER.*) But without my army.
QUEEN MOTHER: (*Sotto voce to CONDÉ.*) My dearest.
CONDÉ: (*Also sotto voce.*) And if it's convenient – which I'm
   sure it is – I will call upon you come midnight, my sweet,
   and pay my profound respects to your exquisiteness.
   (*Elaborately CONDÉ kisses her hand.*)
QUEEN MOTHER: You make me so very happy.
   (*LOUIS is about to speak when he is silenced by a trumpet fanfare.
   CONDÉ exits smiling, accompanied by his MUSKETEERS.*)
LOUIS: You betrayed us, cleric.
QUEEN MOTHER: Silence, Louis. Instead why don't you
   do something useful for once, and go and de-flower your
   virgin bride? Well, I understand that for over a month, ever
   since she first arrived, Anne of Austria has been panting for
   the merest glimpse of your inert groin.
LOUIS: You spout nothing but filth, mother!
QUEEN MOTHER: And despite your perverse
   squeamishness, Louis, you still have to get Anne with child.

It's the only way we can continue to ensure peace with
Austria.

LOUIS: No! I told you that my marrying Anne was madness.

QUEEN MOTHER: That is as nothing compared to an
all-out war with Austria! But you are too consumed by
your new favourite, Luyens, to see that. Which is why *I*
am sitting on *your* throne. Now close your gaping mouth
and take my arm. (*To RICHELIEU, as she descends from the
throne.*) For your sake, bishop, I trust your solution to the
Prince-Condé-conundrum is as comprehensive as it seems.

RICHELIEU: It is, Your Majesty.

QUEEN MOTHER: Then attend me in my boudoir at dusk.
And don't be late. Remember, falling is so much easier
than rising.

(*The QUEEN MOTHER, LOUIS and the Court exit. Only
RICHELIEU and Father JOSEPH remain.*)

JOSEPH: Well?

RICHELIEU: Arrest Condé immediately.

JOSEPH: You're going to break your word to him?

RICHELIEU: Necessity compels me to.

JOSEPH: And the Queen Mother? Who – I can tell from her
walk – intends to stretch your resources.

RICHELIEU: She will wait. They all do.

JOSEPH: And when she discovers that you have imprisoned
Condé?

RICHELIEU: Arrest him discreetly. Then she won't discover
until much later.

JOSEPH: You ought to have been a tradesman.

(*Father JOSEPH exits.*)

RICHELIEU: (*Kneeling.*) Christ Jesus, the nets are out now.
And what there is left of France is mine for the taking
because *I* am a real fisher of men. Yet I'm disturbed by
this De Rohan girl. Green eyes and a moist mouth. But
once I straddle her, I'll be like everyone else. Vulnerable.
And itching for more. So, Lord, chastity does have its
compensations. Already I feel the soldier's pike slitting my
holy silk. And during Mass, I confess I think of nothing
but the State and the economy of France. Oh King of
Thorns, why does everything I do lack harmony? Only

You can chime me like the great iron bell I wish to be. But You are never there, are You? Well, if You exist – for once – bid Your Light strike. Give Your Silence sound. And do it now! (*A long pause. RICHELIEU stands.*) Nothing. But then nothing is the norm. Well...thank the Virgin, there is always the soldier.

(*RICHELIEU is about to leave when he is surrounded by the MOB. They level sharpened stakes at him. FANÇAN, a burly pamphleteer, holds a knife at RICHELIEU's throat.*)

FANÇAN: Who did it, priest?

RICHELIEU: (*Shouting.*) Musketeers!

FANÇAN: I'm afraid they're otherwise detained, trying to suppress a little riot that I started down by the Seine. So don't call out again or we'll rip you apart. Now – *who* did it?

RICHELIEU: Did what?

FANÇAN: Ordered Prince Condé's arrest.

(*The MOB choruses the word 'arrest' like hissing snakes.*)

So who is the arsehole who's responsible? The Queen Mum? That pimp, Gaston? The whore, de Rohan? Or our imbecilic, stuttering King?

RICHELIEU: Enough!

(*RICHELIEU moves to unsheathe his sword – which he realises he is not wearing.*)

FANÇAN: See that, mates? Went for his sword, he did. (*To RICHELIEU.*) You're a real believer in the Crucifixion, you are.

RICHELIEU: What's your name, fellow?

FANÇAN: Fançan.

RICHELIEU: Now, Fançan...

FANÇAN: (*Interrupting.*) Shut up when I'm speaking! (*Suddenly realising.*) Of course! It was *you* who arrested him, wasn't it?

RICHELIEU: Sometimes I wonder if there is any purpose in unifying France into a nation when it is entirely composed of illiterate scum.

FANÇAN: (*Turning to the MOB.*) Scum! You hear that, mates? (*To RICHELIEU.*) Priest, hasn't it got through to you yet? *We're* what it's about. We're what *you* should be fighting for.

RICHELIEU: Treason! France is a *regal idea* – to be built on *your* backs. Can't you hear France, crying out to be saved?

FANÇAN: It's not France that's jibbering, priest. It's the Rich. And they are pissing their silk pantaloons because of *us*. But then fear is a new sensation for your lot, isn't it? Mind, you've got every right to be scared shitless, 'cause, believe me, nothing's ever going to be the same here again. It's coming, see! It's coming!

RICHELIEU: What? The plague? To wipe you out.

FANÇAN: No. Blood! *Your* blood. On your altars, in your wine, in your sperm. When the Revolution comes – as it will – and soon – none of your class will escape. Your clerical finery won't help you then. Nor your Christ. 'Cause we don't give a tosser's fig about *Him*! See, your Christ dumped us long ago, and the coming Revolution will ensure that we will dump Him forever.

RICHELIEU: God curse your soul, you blasphemous hedgehog! (*To the MOB.*) Down on your knees, all of you! I am the vengeful essence of Christ here on earth. I feel His Iridescent Brightness searing through my veins. I will blast your souls with His Holy Fire.

(*The MOB cowers to its knees.*)

So humble yourselves before the Lord of Hosts, or I will hurl a lightning through your lives and transfix you to the Gates of Hell!

(*FANÇAN crosses himself and kneels.*)

Now pray for forgiveness, you entrails of Satan. Before the sky opens its abyss and sucks your seditious souls into the sun. Do some of you still sweat with pride and blasphemy? By the living death of God, I will call a scourge of angels down and flame your offal into ash! (*Raising his arms to invoke his curse.*) Lord Jesus Christ, bequeath these sinners to the Four Horsemen of the Apocalypse if ever again they have the profane temerity to raise their claws against the Lord's anointed nobility of France. This Curse is written in the Book of Death, and is your heritage until the Second Coming of the Light, when all will be judged, and even Death will die. Now, you leprous filth, home to your hovels

where you will live the rest of your miserable days in the
knowledge that *kneeling* is your only destiny!
(*The MOB crawls out. Only FANÇAN and RICHELIEU
remain. FANÇAN gets to his feet.*)
FANÇAN: (*Grinning.*) The bleeding shame is, you didn't
believe a single word of that. But then nor did I. But I
didn't want to show you up, did I?
RICHELIEU: (*Calling out.*) Captain!
(*The CAPTAIN of the Musketeers enters.*)
FANÇAN: (*To RICHELIEU.*) Listen, I can be of great
assistance to you – your Eminence.
CAPTAIN: (*Indicating FANÇAN.*) Do you want him shot, my
lord?
RICHELIEU: Depends. (*Taking FANÇAN to one side.*) What
can you offer?
FANÇAN: Unlimited propaganda.
RICHELIEU: Interesting. (*To the CAPTAIN.*) Have him
flogged.
FANÇAN: What?
RICHELIEU: Then give him a good meal. (*To FANÇAN.*)
Then we'll talk.
FANÇAN: Thanks very much. Nothing I like more than a bit
of flagellation on an empty gut. But I'm sure the wages'll
improve. (*Sotto voce to RICHELIEU.*) I won't tell the gentry
who was responsible for Condé's arrest. (*Grinning.*) Least
– not unless you force me to.
(*RICHELIEU signals to the CAPTAIN to remove FANÇAN. As
they leave, Father JOSEPH returns. FANÇAN bows mockingly
to JOSEPH and exits.*)
JOSEPH: All is as it should be.
RICHELIEU: Good, because I've found a possible
mouthpiece to manipulate the gutter.
JOSEPH: Fançan?
RICHELIEU: You know him?
JOSEPH: Pimp, pervert, and penis of the People.
RICHELIEU: (*Smiling.*) He sounds perfect.
JOSEPH: However could I have allowed the Church to
become embroiled with you?

RICHELIEU: You needed a front – so *you* could be 'holy' behind. (*Looking off.*) Mm…I see Condé's on his way to the Bastille. It certainly improves the landscape.

JOSEPH: The Prince is not going to thank you for this.

RICHELIEU: In whose name did you have Condé arrested?

JOSEPH: In Louis' name, of course. It would have been dangerous to have had him arrested in the Queen Mother's name.

RICHELIEU: Then Condé will need *me* as a friend, won't he?

JOSEPH: Good God!

(*Enter CONDÉ under guard. He sees RICHELIEU and breaks away from his captors to confront him.*)

RICHELIEU: My dear Prince, I cannot begin to express my disbelieving horror at what has happened to you.

CONDÉ: You crapulous crozier!

RICHELIEU: I assure you at this very moment Gaston's motives are being thoroughly investigated.

CONDÉ: Gaston?

RICHELIEU: I thought you knew. Gaston is responsible for your arrest, but being a congenital coward, he used Louis' name.

JOSEPH: (*Crossing himself.*) Resurrection in Purgatory!

CONDÉ: (*To RICHELIEU, indicating his chains.*) It was Gaston that did this to me then, and not you.

RICHELIEU: Yes, and, what is more, I am truly shocked that you could possibly believe that one of God's ministers could have betrayed you. But don't worry, my Prince, salvation is at hand. The Queen has granted me an audience. Within the hour, I guarantee that you will be released and publicly exonerated. Then Gaston will take your place in the Bastille. (*Whispering to CONDÉ.*) The Court is already behind you. And Marie de Rohan told me that she is certain – and I quote her exactly – that you will prove to be the most permanently-erect King in Christendom.

(*A MUSKETEER steps between them.*)

MUSKETEER: Intimacy is forbidden with the prisoner, Lord Bishop. Come, Highness. The Bastille awaits you.

CONDÉ: (*To RICHELIEU.*) I shall reward your loyalty. This
I swear.

RICHELIEU: Your Highness is too kind.

(*Exit CONDÉ and the MUSKETEERS.*)

JOSEPH: What did you promise him?

RICHELIEU: (*Smiling.*) Thirty solitary years in a cell. After
which, if he survives and gains his freedom, Condé will
prove to be a compliant asset to the Throne. Old age does
remarkable things for a man. Ambition wanes whilst one's
paunch and chins grow. Impending death always assures a
healthy respect for reality.

(*LOUIS enters with LUYENS.*)

LOUIS: (*To LUYENS.*) One down. Two to g-go.

(*RICHELIEU kneels before LOUIS.*)

RICHELIEU: I wish to serve only you, Your Majesty.

LOUIS: Then why are you still wearing my mother's
g-garter, sirrah? Although I do congratulate you on
Condé's relocation.

RICHELIEU: I merely anticipated *your* desires, my King.

(*A MESSENGER enters, and approaches the kneeling
RICHELIEU.*)

MESSENGER: (*To LOUIS.*) I have something for the Lord
Bishop, Your Majesty.

LOUIS: Then give it to him.

(*The MESSENGER gives RICHELIEU a letter.*)

RICHELIEU: Your pardon, sire.

(*LOUIS dismisses the MESSENGER with a curt nod. Then
he indicates that RICHELIEU may stand apart to read the
letter.*)

LOUIS: (*Noting Father JOSEPH's concern.*) You may join your
altar, Father Joseph.

(*Father JOSEPH joins RICHELIEU.*)

Luyens, this is our opportunity to e-e-eliminate them all!

LUYENS: I don't understand.

LOUIS: I know. That is why I love you. The question is: will
you k-kill for me?

LUYENS: Who?

LOUIS: (*Indicating RICHELIEU.*) A caterpillar that aches to
pillage my mother's pollen.

(*RICHELIEU rocks with horror at what he has read. He bows to LOUIS, and is about to leave.*)
Not so fast, cleric. We did not give you leave.
RICHELIEU: Forgive me, sire...
LOUIS: (*With a smile.*) Bad news?
RICHELIEU: My mother.
LOUIS: (*Still smiling.*) Is she dead?
(*RICHELEU's face is a blank.*)
Now don't pretend what you don't feel, Richelieu. You used your mother like you're using *mine!*
RICHELIEU: No!
LOUIS: Which is appropriate as mine is as d-dead as yours.
RICHELIEU: It's not the same, sire. (*Crumpling the letter in his hand.*) They shovelled earth into her mouth, and I was not there. I have never been there... Already I can hardly remember her face. All I can see is an old woman, her features like crumpled paper, with pleading eyes. Yet however much she pleaded, I...
JOSEPH: Armand...
RICHELIEU: I needed her blessing! Any kind of blessing.
LOUIS: Don't we all? (*To RICHELIEU and Father JOSEPH.*) Leave us.
(*As RICHELIEU and Father JOSEPH exit, the beautiful but nervous 25-year-old ANNE OF AUSTRIA, Louis' wife, enters. Father JOSEPH bows to ANNE, but RICHELIEU is too preoccupied with his own thoughts to notice.*
ANNE hovers, wanting to attract LOUIS' attention. LOUIS puts his arm around LUYENS' shoulder.)
LUYENS: So our bishop is human.
LOUIS: Luyens, I want you to kill – and now. (*Placing a silencing finger over LUYENS' lips.*) Don't speak his name. Just kill. Then it will no longer matter that my mother is a whore.
LUYENS: (*Aware of ANNE.*) Your Majesty...
LOUIS: (*Oblivious.*) Or that I tear butterflies to rags to see how they are made. Under every wing...a corpse. Or that my wife means no more to me than a discarded brooch.
(*ANNE steps forward.*)
ANNE: Your Majesty.

LOUIS: (*Kissing her hand.*) Madam.

ANNE: Louis, why do you always avoid me?

LOUIS: You mistake me, madam.

ANNE: You don't even smile when you see me. True, my
nurse warned me that...

LOUIS: (*Overriding her.*) Then you had best go play with your
nurse, madam.

ANNE: I do not deserve this abuse, sir.

LOUIS: My m-mother invited you to France, not me.

ANNE: But it's a whole month since our wedding. (*Touching his
lace collar.*) And no one but me cares that you are dressed
in tatters. Always neglected. My poor love, you're just like
me.

LOUIS: I don't understand you.

ANNE: Untouched. Unpossessed.

LOUIS: I once...kissed a woman. In a rose garden.

ANNE: (*Whispering.*) Then why won't you kiss me, my love?
(*LOUIS turns away. ANNE indicates LUYENS.*)
Does *he* always have to listen to everything we say? Can't
we ever be alone?

LOUIS: (*In his own world.*) She denies it now, of course.

ANNE: I'm so lonely, Louis!

LOUIS: It was my m-mother who kissed me in the rose
garden.

LUYENS: Your Majesty, allow me to leave.

LOUIS: No.

ANNE: Louis, I beg you, please, tonight...
(*She touches him.*)

LOUIS: I am in-incapable!

ANNE: Every evening I scatter rose petals on my pillow but
you never visit me.

LOUIS: I cannot! Dear Christ, I... Luyens, help me!

ANNE: (*Realising.*) Are you and he...?

LOUIS: No! I told you; I am incapable – with anyone. I wish
to God it could be otherwise. (*To LUYENS.*) Come, we've
some k-killing to do.

ANNE: I only want a little warmth. A hint of kindness. Is that
too much to ask?

LOUIS: The audience is at an end, madam.

ANNE: Please don't make me hate you, Louis.

LOUIS: Leave us.

(*ANNE exits.*)

Are you ready, Luyens?

(*Enter CONDÉ, with GASTON, followed by some of the MOB who are dressed as CLOWNS, and who are quietly chanting CONDÉ's name.*)

CONDÉ: (*To GASTON.*) You really expect me to believe that it was Richelieu? (*To the CLOWNS.*) Keep your distance, my good fellows. I will inform you if I need you.

LOUIS: (*Approaching CONDÉ.*) Who ordered your release?

CONDÉ: Initially I believed it was Richelieu, until your brother informed me that it was *he* who secured my freedom.

LOUIS: You can certainly rely on my brother, sir.

(*LOUIS and LUYENS exit.*)

GASTON: (*Escorting CONDÉ into the shadows.*) Now I have freed you, Prince, how do you propose that we advance one another?

CONDÉ: France is still in my pocket, Gaston.

GASTON: So I understand was my mother.

CONDÉ: I'm sure she still *is.*

GASTON: No, my mother seems to have developed a penchant for more clerical vestments.

(*RICHELIEU enters talking with a MESSENGER.*)

Talking of which.

RICHELIEU: (*To the MESSENGER.*) Inform the Queen that matters of State have temporarily detained me.

(*The MESSENGER exits. CONDÉ steps out of the shadows.*)

How in the name of Hell…? (*Calling off.*) Musketeers!

CONDÉ: (*Calling off.*) Musketeers, to me!

FANÇAN: (*Who is the leading Clown, removes his clown's mask and addresses RICHELIEU.*) Oh thanks for the flogging, Bishop. It's tuned up my muscles nicely.

CONDÉ: (*To RICHELIEU.*) You whoreson mitre! (*Shouting off.*) Musketeers, to me! At the double!

(*Enter the CAPTAIN of the Musketeers with two MUSKETEERS.*)

RICHELIEU: Captain, there's been a conspiracy.

CONDÉ: This villain is a nefarious liar, Captain.

RICHELIEU: On the contrary, Captain, against the express orders of His Majesty, this traitor has bribed his way out of the Bastille.

CONDÉ: More damnable lies! This priest is the traitor, Captain! In the name of the Queen, shoot him. D'you hear me? Shoot…!

CAPTAIN: Certainly, Highness.

(*The CAPTAIN shoots CONDÉ who crumples to his knees.*)

CONDÉ: Not me, you fool, the Bishop…!

(*CONDÉ dies.*)

GASTON: (*Dumbfounded.*) But he is…was…the Prince Royal.

RICHELIEU: Captain, on whose orders did you execute him?

(*Enter the QUEEN MOTHER.*)

QUEEN MOTHER: *I* ordered Condé's release!

RICHELIEU: Madam, does the King…? (*Correcting himself.*) I mean, does His Highness know?

(*The QUEEN MOTHER kneels by CONDÉ's body.*)

QUEEN MOTHER: He was very good to me. (*Touching CONDÉ's blood-stained chest.*) Weren't you, my dear? (*Looking at the blood on her hand.*) It's never the colour I imagine it to be.

RICHELIEU: But why did you release him?

QUEEN MOTHER: Because I was certain that if I did, someone would kill him. And that was imperative for France. Well, Condé was too capriciously volatile to live. (*Stroking her cheek with CONDÉ's lifeless hand.*) This once stroked me…by itself.

GASTON: Have you no shame, mother?

RICHELIEU: (*To the CAPTAIN.*) Who ordered you to do this?

CAPTAIN: Initiative, sir.

QUEEN MOTHER: Well done, Captain. I know you will appreciate a prolonged death.

(*Drums and trumpets resound. Enter LOUIS in his royal robes, complete with crown. For the first time he looks regal. LUYENS follows in appropriate finery.*)

RICHELIEU: (*Going down on his knees, in a resonant voice.*) The traitor, Condé, is dead. God save the King!
(*The CLOWNS and FANÇAN fall to their knees, crying 'God save the KING!'.*)

LOUIS: Congratulations, Mother, the timing of your late lover's release was perfect. (*To the CAPTAIN of the Musketeers.*) And – thank you, Captain; long life and promotion for you are now assured.

QUEEN MOTHER: It was you!

LOUIS: On your knees, Mother.

QUEEN MOTHER: How dare you…?

LOUIS: Silence, woman! You are to retire to Blois forthwith, until we decree otherwise.

QUEEN MOTHER: Louis, I am your mother!

LOUIS: In name. But rarely in l-love.

QUEEN MOTHER: Everything I have done has been for you, and to stabilise the Kingdom. (*Indicating CONDÉ.*) I sacrificed this good man's life so that you could be secure upon your throne. So that your father's death…

LOUIS: Don't defile his name!

QUEEN MOTHER: …Would not prove to be your fate also.

LOUIS: Escort my mother to her palace at Blois, Captain.

RICHELIEU: Your Majesty, please allow me to intercede. You are our anointed King, but you still need guidance, and your mother…

LOUIS: (*Overriding him.*) Oh forgive me, Bishop, I was forgetting *your* services. You had best retire to your bishopric in Luçon before I have your head on a spike! (*Indicating CONDÉ's body, to the Musketeers.*) And throw this – to the circus maximus.
(*The MUSKETEERS toss CONDÉ's body to the CLOWNS who throw the corpse backwards and forwards between them like a rugger ball. Simultaneously they spin the QUEEN MOTHER and RICHELIEU around like tops. The CLOWNS sing as they transform the stage into a carnival with fireworks and coloured streamers.*
In a golden light, LOUIS stands on a high vantage point, viewing the proceedings.)

CLOWNS: (*Singing.*)
> We're free! We're free! We're bloody free!
> Free from Condé's tyranny!
> Free to murder! Free to dance!
> Justice now has come to France!
> We're free! We're free! We're bloody free!
> Free from false servility.
> So long live France and King Louis!
> Justice, Hope and Stability!

> (*As the song ends, CONDÉ's body is thrown off-stage. The QUEEN MOTHER is spun off, followed by the CLOWNS and FANÇAN who surge into the shadows.*)

LOUIS: Freedom!

> (*The light snaps off LOUIS and LUYENS.*
> *RICHELIEU is spotlit as he spins slowly to his knees, with his back to the audience.*
> *He seems weighed down by the passing years. This is accompanied by the sound of amplified heartbeats, and punctuated by the accelerated ticking of a clock.*
> *RICHELIEU is now a ball of purple. Abruptly the ticking and the heartbeats stop. Slowly RICHELIEU uncoils to his feet. He looks at least twenty years older, greyer and haggard. Only his eyes burn.*
> *A WOMAN materialises on the edge of the shadows. RICHELIEU cannot see her face. She moves towards him. It is MARIE DE ROHAN. They meet.*
> *Behind them, the Puppet Court appears, controlled by their strings. Their movements are angular and grotesque. RICHELIEU is not aware of them.*)

RICHELIEU: Who sent you?

MARIE: You don't look at all well, Armand.

RICHELIEU: After ten years in exile, it's hardly surprising.

MARIE: Longer.

RICHELIEU: Certainly seems so.

MARIE: The Queen Mother returned to Paris yesterday.

RICHELIEU: The Queen... How?

MARIE: (*Shivering.*) It's bone-chillingly damp here.

RICHELIEU: I get so little news. The last I heard from Father
Joseph was that Louis had antagonised the Huguenots

again. With no tangible way to crush them. So the Queen has returned to Paris. She won't last.

MARIE: She will. Now Luyens is dead.

RICHELIEU: Well, it is good to know that the poltroon who all but owned France for the last ten years, is now only a tenant in his own grave by permission of the worms.

MARIE: Yes, and the gravediggers played dice on the poltroon's coffin.

RICHELIEU: There's dew on your sleeve. We had best go in.

MARIE: Since I first saw you all those years ago, you have haunted me.

RICHELIEU: (*Chafing his hands together.*) Skin flakes off – like candle grease.

MARIE: (*Moving closer to him.*) You are the only man who has ever made me shiver with anticipation. Oh I'm fully aware that I'm flouting etiquette, but once a Huguenot, always…

RICHELIEU: (*Interrupting her.*) Of course! Your brother, the Duc de Rohan, sent you, didn't he? Because he wants me to join the Huguenots against Louis.

MARIE: No, the Queen Mother sent me. She needs you. (*Uncurling her fingers.*) I want you. And you definitely want me. We both know that.

(*MARIE touches RICHELIEU's cheek. He flinches. MARIE smiles.*)

RICHELIEU: It is time for Compline.

MARIE: You can't bear to be touched, can you? Have you ever had a woman, Armand?

RICHELIEU: God is not always good.

MARIE: What's that supposed to mean?

RICHELIEU: He is not always here.

MARIE: How can a man with your vocation say such things?

RICHELIEU: Often there is nothing. Only my need.

MARIE: For me!

RICHELIEU: For France. My terrified France.

MARIE: If only you would let me, Armand, I could so easily love you.

RICHELIEU: Strange.

MARIE: What?

RICHELIEU: To love. Anything. Marie – tell Her Majesty that my services will cost more than a pair of exquisite nipples. Even though they advance before the most beautiful woman in France.

MARIE: I could have redeemed you – *from* yourself. But now… Oh God help us both.

(MARIE moves back towards the motionless Puppet Court. RICHELIEU stands, isolated. His face is a death mask.

The QUEEN MOTHER, who also has puppet strings, is in the centre of the Puppet Court. MARIE whispers something in the QUEEN MOTHER's ear, then MARIE leaves.

LOUIS is spotlit on his throne.)

LOUIS: Parliament is in session!

(The QUEEN MOTHER, Father JOSEPH, GASTON and Queen ANNE snap their puppet strings. With MARIE de Rohan, they form a semi-circle around LOUIS. Musketeers stand either side of the KING. Their banners, decorated with the fleur-de-lys, form a pyramid over LOUIS' throne. The Puppet Court, silhouetted against the cyclorama, sways backwards and forwards as if the Court is being blown about in the wind of the ensuing debate.)

QUEEN MOTHER: Richelieu must be recalled!

LOUIS: Mother, you are already breaking the terms of our ag-agreement. But rest assured, you will never rule France again with the swish of your skirts. I, and I alone, will decide what is for the betterment of my realm.

ANNE: You mean the Pope will, dear.

LOUIS: Anne, I warn you!

QUEEN MOTHER: Louis, you have treated Richelieu abominably.

LOUIS: Mother, do you wish to retire again to your palace at Blois? Or would you prefer to join Richelieu in his fen-ridden bishopric at Luçon?

GASTON: Oh come now, Louis, you can't send Mother back to the country.

LOUIS: For the safety of France, I can do anything, brother. Since the death of my beloved Luyens, I have learned the meaning of anguish. But I know all your thoughts: 'Now the King's friend is dead, we will be able to manipulate

Louis once again.' Yes, and even you, my wife, have started
to stir the pools of intrigue.

ANNE: You wrong me, Your Majesty.

LOUIS: No, Anne. You are all trying to out-plot each other,
hoping to possess my mind, and thus regain your rabid
influence over my blighted kingdom.

QUEEN MOTHER: That is why we need Richelieu, my son.
He is the only man who can lever France out of the pit that
is being dug for us by the Spanish and the Huguenots.

JOSEPH: It's true, my liege. Remember who saved us from
Condé's rebellion? It was Richelieu. And who tricked
Condé into incarcerating himself in the Bastille? Again it
was Richelieu. And who...?

LOUIS: (*Interrupting.*) ...Is more than capable of betraying his
own soul for the sake of his malefic ambition! But enough
of this. I have more serious matters to attend to. Taxation,
for instance. Our Exchequer is rat-ridden. The musketeers
are on half pay, while certain members of our royal
household are proving to be outrageously expensive.

GASTON: Now, brother, be fair. I've been cleared of those
charges.

LOUIS: It does not alter the bill.

QUEEN MOTHER: Richelieu is a genius with money.

LOUIS: For God's sake, mother! You have only returned to
Court these seven days, yet in that little time your every
word has pleaded for that spindly bag of bones. Why? Are
you and Richelieu lovers? (*Pause.*) I see; so you *are* lovers.

QUEEN MOTHER: Even though you are the Anointed
King, Louis, such impertinence is unforgivable.

GASTON: But you have visited your precious cleric in the
interim years, Mother, have you not?

QUEEN MOTHER: No! But Richelieu must be recalled
before France withers off the vine, and all we're left with
are the shrivelled skins of our beloved country.

LOUIS: Can't I ever be free of Richelieu? He's here, all
around me. He's the f-fetid air I breathe!

GASTON: Then chop his head off, brother. We've not had a
decent execution for months.

LOUIS: No! We need…

QUEEN MOTHER: Richelieu!

(*The MOB bounces onto the stage with rattles and banners like football fans, led by FANÇAN. As they sing out their demands, FANÇAN conducts them.*)

SONG: We want Richelieu. We want him today!

We want Richelieu! We want our own way!

He'll help the King to help the Court help us!

He'll prick the scabs and squeeze out all the pus!

So bring him back and then we'll all rejoice

'Course we're the Voice of God, so you've no choice!

Richelieu! Richelieu! Richelieu!

(*The song is deafening.*)

GASTON: I'm sure Richelieu paid that scurrilous pamphleteer to do this. (*To LOUIS.*) Have Fançan arrested.

QUEEN MOTHER: And have the pride of our musketeers torn apart by filth? That's why you'll never make a politician, Gaston. The art of sound government is to induce someone else to dirty his curls for you. Fortunately, like most religious vermin, Richelieu can't tell the difference between the Church and a Paris sewer.

LOUIS: Silence, woman. For pity's sake, I'm t-trying to think!

MARIE: Why don't we tax a few peasants to fill in the time?

(*TWO MESSENGERS run in from opposite sides. They collide in the middle, landing on their backsides. The MOB cheers. Father JOSEPH appears on the edge of the shadows.*)

FANÇAN: That's what's known as a brief summary of our current foreign and home policies.

FIRST MESSENGER: Majesty, the Duc de Rohan, with his Huguenots, is destroying all the villages along the coast.

LOUIS: By the living Christ, is there no end to his perfidy?

JOSEPH: No, Majesty, and soon every Huguenot in our midst will rally to de Rohan's banner.

LOUIS: (*To SECOND MESSENGER.*) So what's *your* bad news, sirrah?

SECOND MESSENGER: Sire, the Pope is now in league with the Hapsburg House of Spain *and* Austria, and His Holiness has sent his troops against Your Majesty in the Vatelline!

LOUIS: Whichever way I turn, the wolves converge.

QUEEN MOTHER: That's why we need Richelieu.

(*FANÇAN and the MOB take up the 'Richelieu' chant again.*)

GASTON: I advise against it.

ANNE: Gaston is right, my love. Richelieu is just a self-seeking mountebank.

LOUIS: (*To Father JOSEPH.*) What is your opinion, Reverend Father?

JOSEPH: It is important that you make your own decision, sire. If you invite Richelieu back this time, you must realise that it is not a mere man you are inviting to Paris. You will be receiving into your midst an intellectual stone that will grind your bones down in order that a state may be born out of your marrow.

LOUIS: What kind of advice is that?

JOSEPH: No advice at all, sire.

LOUIS: L-Lucifer has set fire to my coast and my mountains in the name of the P-Pope and the Huguenots. So what choice have I but to employ Lucifer's son to save us? Father, tell Richelieu that he may sit on my council.

(*Father JOSEPH pushes through the MOB that continues to whisper: 'Richelieu!'. JOSEPH confronts the isolated figure of RICHELIEU.*)

JOSEPH: So what is your answer, Armand?

RICHELIEU: I am too ill, Father.

JOSEPH: This is a unique opportunity for you to fulfil your destiny, and for the Church to flower in France again.

RICHELIEU: (*Shaking his head.*) Give the King my blessing. He will need it.

JOSEPH: This is the third offer that you have refused.

RICHELIEU: Have you forgotten everything you taught me? 'Be patient and wait for the right time, Armand.' You taught me because *you* were incapable of learning yourself. Well, *I* have learned to wait, Joseph. And my time is not yet come.

JOSEPH: You're wrong, my friend. The King is desperate.

RICHELIEU: But he's not desperate enough to countenance the measures I have in mind.

JOSEPH: In God's Name, man!

RICHELIEU: Our Lord has nothing to do with it. The only way we can prevent Spain from invading us, and also ensure that the Huguenots do not eat us alive from within, is to make the Throne unassailable. Yes, we must make the King's power absolute and infinite. So that no one; not even his wife, brother, or, God help us, his mother, can ever again believe themselves to be above the Rule of Law. Above the *King's* Law.

JOSEPH: (*Laughing and sitting on a bench under a dappled branch.*) You have been vegetating in this garden too long, Armand. Oh yes, bird song is bewitching, it's true, but their singing doesn't necessarily lead to political wisdom. Nature makes things seem easier than they are.

RICHELIEU: (*Listening to a cuckoo calling.*) I doubt that.

JOSEPH: Well, there is nothing 'easy' about the present anarchic convulsions that are torturing the *English* monarchy.

RICHELIEU: What relevance has that to France?

JOSEPH: Charles the First of England is more than living up to your most despotic regal expectations, Armand. Indeed Charles has gone further, and now rules by Divine Right. He refuses to be answerable to either his Parliament or his subjects, so he has set himself beyond the Law in all respects. Yet even as we speak, the English Parliament is refusing to grant Charles all the monies that he needs for his various designs. The English Commons object to the capriciousness of his favourite minister, the Duke of Buckingham...

RICHELIEU: (*Interrupting.*) And the nub of your argument?

JOSEPH: By controlling King Charles' exchequer, the English Parliament will control the King. And very soon they will force Charles to sacrifice Buckingham. If he refuses, then the King may well not survive himself.

RICHELIEU: So?

JOSEPH: So – what chance would *you* have, my friend, if *our* Parliament – with or without the tacit support of the

nobility – decided to challenge *your* Buckingham-like
authority in the same manner?

RICHELIEU: (*Smiling.*) France is not England, Joseph
– thank God. Unlike its powerful English counterpart,
our Parliament is weak and dissipated. True, we have
Huguenot thorns embedded in our thighs and Spanish
lances levelled at our bowels, but we don't have a rich
Puritan merchant class pulling the strings of the King's
purse – like Charles has. No, only the English could
produce those embittered, puritanical zealots of the
Anti-Christ – who may very soon crucify their own King.
The beauty of France is that she is split, from Brittany
to the Vatelline, with innumerable envious factions. The
Burgundians snarl at the Huguenots, the Huguenots sneer
at the Gascons, the Church whines at the Nobility, and
the Nobility jousts with the King. So wherever you turn,
there is no semblance of political unity, no love of King
or country. (*Indicating the cuckoo close by.*) We're a land of
cuckoos, piping pretty noises as our wings knock our
neighbours' mottled eggs into the rushing stream. I see I
bewilder you, Father.

JOSEPH: Yes…your every word proves that you are a
dreamer.

RICHELIEU: On the contrary. It is the eternal chaos within
France, with its accompanying narrowness of vision, that
gives me genuine hope for a prosperous future.

JOSEPH: Hope?

RICHELIEU: Indeed. For the first time in our swamp of a
history, there is a serious chance that the King – with my
help – can transform this rebellious mass of humanity, into
a unified nation. So leadership embracing the Law is what
I will offer the King – because that is what all men crave
in time of fear. And, by the Stigmata, there will *be* fear
throughout the realm until everyone accepts that the King's
Law is absolute. And I will bring this about – whatever the
cost to me – or to my friends. So tell His Majesty that when
he deems it fit to crown me…with a Cardinal's hat – in
return, I will crown him…with France.

(Father JOSEPH shakes his head at RICHELIEU's hubris. The QUEEN MOTHER appears in the garden.)

QUEEN MOTHER: *(To JOSEPH.)* Leave us.

JOSEPH: *(To RICHELIEU.)* One day you will misjudge the time, my friend.

(Father JOSEPH leaves.)

QUEEN MOTHER: Have you missed me, Armand?

RICHELIEU: Your Majesty.

QUEEN MOTHER: Your apple trees need pruning.

RICHELIEU: Madam, why are you here?

QUEEN MOTHER: You received my last letter.

RICHELIEU: And you mine.

QUEEN MOTHER: That's why I've come – to bring you yourself.

RICHELIEU: Myself?

QUEEN MOTHER: Yes – Cardinal. *My* Cardinal.

RICHELIEU: *(After a pause.)* I am beyond words.

QUEEN MOTHER: How unusual. Now – gratitude.

(She moves towards him, touching his lower lip with her finger. He flinches.)

RICHELIEU: Ten years ago perhaps. But now celibacy is more than just a hobby.

QUEEN MOTHER: *(Laughing.)* Really?

(She kisses him on the mouth. In spite of himself, he responds. Her hands surge over his body as she kisses him again. He breaks away, stunned, trying to wipe the kiss from his mouth.)

RICHELIEU: Christ forgive you!

QUEEN MOTHER: *(Amused.)* He generally does. *(Moistening her lips.)* So there is still a rank goat behind the crucifix. I thought I smelt him.

RICHELIEU: Have you no pride?

QUEEN MOTHER: Certainly not. My son is incapable of ruling, so *I* have to! And, like you, I will impose God's Will any way I can.

RICHELIEU: For France?

QUEEN MOTHER: In order to survive.

RICHELIEU: Tell the King that I have recovered, madam, and that I am entirely at his command.

QUEEN MOTHER: No, you are at *mine*, my goat!

(*RICHELIEU and the QUEEN MOTHER exit in opposite directions.*

A triumphant organ is heard. A stained-glass window glows against the sky. The shadow of a vast crucifix extends its arms across the stage. A boys' choir is heard singing in Latin.

The shadowy Puppet Court dangles in Notre-Dame Cathedral. LOUIS, the QUEEN MOTHER, ANNE, MARIE, GASTON enter. Everyone but LOUIS kneels as RICHELIEU enters in his Cardinal's red robes. RICHELIEU kneels before LOUIS who, in turn, places a Cardinal's hat on RICHELIEU's head. Then RICHELIEU rises, and LOUIS kneels. RICHELIEU blesses LOUIS.

Above them, the shadow of the crucifix grows more intense like a black claw.

The stage is filled with blank white light. The Puppet Court is jerked from view. RICHELIEU, LOUIS, the QUEEN MOTHER and GASTON remain. Their faces seem to be made of paper.)

Well? What are we to do concerning the relentless advance of His Holiness into the neutral territory of the Vatelline?

GASTON: Ignore him.

LOUIS: (*To RICHELIEU.*) And *your* 'humble' opinion – Your 'Eminence'?

RICHELIEU: Drive the Pope *out* of the Vatelline.

LOUIS: But he is God's F-F-Forefinger!

RICHELIEU: Then I am God's Boot! Oh don't pretend that you're surprised, my Liege. You only made me into a Cardinal because you know that it's much easier for me to romp through excrement in a red robe. So inform His Holiness that if he does not retreat peaceably and immediately, we will send the Danes in against him, to forcibly assist in His Holiness' removal from the Vatelline.

QUEEN MOTHER: Are my ears failing me? As a newly-appointed cardinal, are you seriously suggesting that we use Danish Protestants to attack the very Catholic Pope, who elevated you to your present sacred position?

RICHELIEU: (*Smiling and nodding.*) You have to concede, it is original.

QUEEN MOTHER: Armand!

RICHELIEU: The hypocrisy on all your faces is gut-griping. We have a choice between remaining the most holy but impotent country in Christendom, or grabbing this God-given opportunity and triumphantly surviving. You think the Pope has scruples? Or Spain? Or Austria? No! And nor should we. It's only fear that makes you screech like virgins who have smelt the stallion. (*Crossing himself.*) That was just a metaphor – in the heat. So, Your Majesty, forthwith, we must make treaties with every Protestant country that is willing. Then we will *pay* all those friendly Protestant countries to *attack* the Pope.

LOUIS: How, in the name of the Virgin, can I explain this to the Holy Roman Church?

RICHELIEU: We can always disclaim responsibility if things go wrong, sire. And, in the interim, the war with the Pope will strengthen us financially. So gird up your regal loins and be an imperious King, my liege, and not a impotent angel.

LOUIS: Who concurs with His Eminence's 'peaceful' policy?

GASTON: Not me. It's far too strenuous.

LOUIS: Not even you, Mother?

QUEEN MOTHER: Absolutely not!

LOUIS: Then His Eminence must be right. (*Shouting off.*) Soldiers of France, go and humble His Holiness.

RICHELIEU: (*To GASTON.*) And, my Prince, your military genius would be a decided asset in this war, so why don't you lead the Army in *person*?

GASTON: How can I? I don't even know what a raised sword looks like. Except from a very great distance.

LOUIS: (*Takes his own sword out of its scabbard.*) Oh there's nothing remarkable about a naked blade, brother. Until it's sheathed in another man's b-belly. (*LOUIS makes as if to stab GASTON who cowers behind his mother. LOUIS winks, then proffers his sword to GASTON.*) No, please, brother, take my sword to the front with you. With my fraternal blessing.

GASTON: (*Swishing the sword.*) If I must, I must. Well, I
suppose it is my duty to inspire our Cavalry with my
military charisma.

(*Puppet Soldiers, on strings, march past, accompanied by a
solitary drum. The effect is absurd. GASTON, now with puppet
strings attached to him, leads his Puppet Troops off. They salute
LOUIS as they pass.*)

RICHELIEU: Gaston will either win us a resounding victory,
or he'll be blown to pieces. With luck, he'll accomplish
them both simultaneously.

QUEEN MOTHER: Careful, my perfumed goat. (*Indicating
LOUIS.*) It is my son that you are manipulating, and my
love could so easily turn.

(*The QUEEN MOTHER exits.*)

LOUIS: (*To RICHELIEU.*) Don't my troops look splendid?

RICHELIEU: 'Look' being the operative word, sire. We have
yet to blood them in a proper war. Don't worry, we will.
But don't commit any of our strategy to paper.

LOUIS: But surely...?

RICHELIEU: When the Pope accuses us of violating our
treaties – as he will – we will simply say: 'Sorry, Holiness,
but one of our generals became so over-excited that he
attacked instead of defending. And, as I'm sure Your
Holiness knows, it was really the fault of the Danes. As
always.' Naturally we will then decorate the 'over-excited'
general after the battle. Presupposing that we win, of
course.

LOUIS: B-b-brilliant!

RICHELIEU: Hardly surprising, sire – as it was *your* idea.

LOUIS: Oh come now, it was *your* idea.

RICHELIEU: Forgive me, Majesty, but I distinctly heard *you*
suggest it.

LOUIS: (*Laughing.*) You have a devious sense of humour,
Eminence.

RICHELIEU: I've always been willing to learn from my
betters, sire. And who could be better to learn from than
the son of the Son of God? So will you allow me to sit on
your right?

LOUIS: You'd best ask my mother.

RICHELIEU: She is not my all-powerful King, my Liege, as far as I know.

(*LOUIS rubs his temples.*)

Are you ill, sire?

LOUIS: Always. But then you are a sufferer yourself, aren't you?

RICHELIEU: Since birth Majesty. But *my* pain is immaterial whereas yours… Speaking of which, have you attended the Queen, your wife, in private recently?

LOUIS: No, we…do not have much in common. Why do you ask?

RICHELIEU: You should visit her, sire. And often.

LOUIS: In matters of state, Cardinal, I will overlook the occasional lapse in etiquette, but this does not mean that I will…

RICHELIEU: (*Interrupting.*) The Queen *is* a pre-eminent matter of State, sire.

LOUIS: You p-presume…

RICHELIEU: (*Relentless.*) As is Marie de Rohan.

LOUIS: She is insignificant.

RICHELIEU: Does that also apply to your brother?

LOUIS: Are you su-suggesting…?

RICHELIEU: Anne must give you an heir, sire, before the Kingdom evaporates between your knees. There are already rumours, passage talk, and bedchamber whispers of insurrection.

LOUIS: You really expect me to believe that my wife and my b-brother are…?

RICHELIEU: (*Overriding him.*) It is imperative that Her Majesty give you an heir forthwith, in order to stabilise the realm. It does not matter how you do it, as long as you do it.

LOUIS: Christ's Spleen! I will not tolerate a spinster priest dribbling over my marriage bed.

RICHELIEU: You are France, Louis. You have no privacy.

(*LOUIS is about to strike RICHELIEU.*)

LOUIS: You v-v-vile…!

(*RICHELIEU kneels.*)

RICHELIEU: If striking me will help you to do what is necessary, I will not take offence.

LOUIS: (*Lowering his hand.*) You are presumptuous, Eminence.

RICHELIEU: No, only practical. Besides, it is better you bruise my cheek than that you ignore your country's needs. (*RICHELIEU is about to stand but LOUIS prevents him.*)

LOUIS: Stay. Humility becomes you. You are a disturbing man. Given time, I think I will grow to hate you. But I will consider your advice. Attend me in the morning.

RICHELIEU: May I say one more thing, Majesty?

LOUIS: If you must.

RICHELIEU: I have only one all-embracing desire; to traduce the nobility, break the Huguenots, restrain the Pope, confound the Spanish, and exalt my King. Which is why my mother embroidered my cradle with the motto: 'Armand for the King'. Good night, sire.

LOUIS: If only it was a 'good' night.

(*LOUIS exits. RICHELIEU stands. He is also about to leave when Father JOSEPH appears from the shadows and taps the Cardinal on the shoulder. RICHELIEU gasps.*)

JOSEPH: So young and yet so guilty.

RICHELIEU: It's been a long day.

JOSEPH: Well, embrace me then.

(*RICHELIEU flinches. JOSEPH laughs.*)

I know how you loathe being touched. I shouldn't tease you.

RICHELIEU: Joseph, what I'm about to tell you may well shock you.

JOSEPH: I doubt it.

RICHELIEU: France is pleading for an enlightened dictatorship. She must not be disappointed.

JOSEPH: Go on.

RICHELIEU: I want you to create the finest network of spies that has ever existed. I *have* shocked you.

JOSEPH: No, you only talk of what *I* have already begun.

RICHELIEU: I don't think you follow me.

JOSEPH: I'm ahead of you. Already I have created a spy system that is so intricate and so ruthless that it even frightens me.

RICHELIEU: You amaze me.

JOSEPH: What other way is there? Satan always abuses the freedoms of the Poor. So – for the greater glory of God upon earth, and in order to safe guard Law and Order, I have given instructions that the Poor are to be watched.

RICHELIEU: And the Rich?

JOSEPH: Even more so. I have only one problem: I know whom *I* serve. But I have never been exactly sure who *your* master is.

RICHELIEU: God, of course. Reflected in the eyes of men. But fortunately God is eternal, so He can afford to wait. Whereas Man, poor worm, is now or not at all. Have your spies uncovered anything of import yet?

JOSEPH: Yes. The Duke of Buckingham is trying to persuade his fickle master, Charles the First, that it would be in England's interest to militarily assist the rebellious Huguenots. So the Duke wants to bring his navy to their ants' nest at La Rochelle. He knows that once the Huguenots openly revolt, then we will have a civil war on our hands.

RICHELIEU: Hm.

JOSEPH: Have you nothing to say but 'hm'?

RICHELIEU: What else have you gleaned?

JOSEPH: Gaston is back in the palace.

RICHELIEU: Impossible!

JOSEPH: He told me to tell you that leading the Cavalry wasn't really his style. Added to which, Marie de Rohan, your favourite widow, because *you* are unavailable, has…

RICHELIEU: (*Interrupting.*) Careful!

JOSEPH: She has taken a new lover.

RICHELIEU: Who?

JOSEPH: De Chalais.

RICHELIEU: He is one of the most politically unreliable hot-bloods in the kingdom.

JOSEPH: What's more, she intends to use him.

RICHELIEU: I'm sure she does.

JOSEPH: But she still wants you.

RICHELIEU: Does she now?

JOSEPH: Yes. Dead.

RICHELIEU: Oh.

(*RICHELIEU glances around nervously.*)

JOSEPH: (*Smiling.*) Don't worry. I have *you* watched, too.

RICHELIEU: You dare to…

JOSEPH: (*Overriding him.*) To ensure that you only make love to France, Armand. De Rohan is a succubus. You must forget her. Your sperm, genitals, mouth, eyes, lungs, heart, mind and soul must be wedded forever to France. Through France, you may be privileged to kiss the festering wound in Christ's Side. But only through France. So work and pray. Then die. There is nothing else for you.

(*Father JOSEPH exits.*

Against the blood-red sky, French Soldiers in green and gold struggle with the Pope's Troops in black and crimson. The battle is highly stylised. Pikes are pushed into bodies that drift to the ground like autumn leaves. Then the bodies rise up and thrust pikes into their attackers. Neither side gains the upper hand. Withering cries erupt from their mouths. It is the Vatelline; the Inferno.

Then it becomes a battle of silent shadows in slow motion.

RICHELIEU watches, withdrawn into himself.

GASTON enters with ANNE. They are not aware of RICHELIEU – or he of them.)

ANNE: No, Gaston, it is too dangerous.

GASTON: So is everything in the Louvre.

ANNE: But if it recoils against us?

GASTON: It won't. The Cardinal is too self-absorbed, and Louis is just a fool.

ANNE: I wish you would not insult my husband.

GASTON: Is he?

ANNE: (*Touching her brow.*) It's so close out here. Even the leaves are sweating. (*Moving away from him.*) I had best go in.

GASTON: Look at me, Anne.

ANNE: It's absurd my wearing a taffeta dress on a day like this. I must change…

(*Gently he restrains her.*)

GASTON: Do you love him?

ANNE: Please, Gaston, don't complicate matters.

GASTON: Has he ever satisfied you?

ANNE: We are man and wife, if that is what you mean. Not often. But we are.

GASTON: Yes. Well, I should go inside if I were you. It's becoming more oppressive, believe me.

(*GASTON exits.*)

ANNE: I didn't mean to offend you, Gaston.

(*LOUIS enters.*)

LOUIS: Why would he think you had?

ANNE: Your Majesty. Louis…I have some wonderful news.

LOUIS: I visited your apartments, madam, but your ladies-in-waiting had no knowledge as to your whereabouts. Why is that?

ANNE: I went for a walk and…Gaston suddenly materialised beside me.

LOUIS: Do you see him of-often?

ANNE: Why do you ask?

LOUIS: Is the De Rohan creature still your confidante? Don't avert your eyes, madam.

ANNE: Louis, please…

LOUIS: Well?

ANNE: Three months ago, for a very little time, Louis, you and I became one. Remember?

LOUIS: What has that to do with my questions?

ANNE: I'm going to have our child.

LOUIS: Ag-again?

ANNE: This time I won't lose it. At least I pray to God I won't! My love, aren't you pleased?

LOUIS: Is it m-m-mine?

ANNE: Louis!

LOUIS: Or is it my b-brother's?

(*She tries to touch him.*)

No, you smell of him!

ANNE: (*Cold.*) Whose do you wish it to be, sir?

LOUIS: Forgive me, my dear, please forgive me. If only…

ANNE: Yes?

LOUIS: If only I could believe...anyone.

ANNE: There's always His Eminence.

LOUIS: Anyway, you're bound to mis-miscarry. You're nothing but a three-month receptacle.

(*ANNE fights back her tears.*)

Now don't misunderstand me, madam. I don't care if it *is* Gaston's. Indeed if he has successfully dammed your twelve-week flood, I'll give him Bordeaux.

ANNE: Have you ever considered that the weakness might be *yours*, Louis?

LOUIS: M-many times. (*Pause.*) Anne, help me.

ANNE: God made you so badly, my love. And for a lady's chamber, He scarcely made you at all.

LOUIS: Help me, Anne, help me!

ANNE: The seed you shiver into me has no roots.

LOUIS: Please! (*LOUIS pulls her to her knees. Then he kneels opposite her, and kisses her. She responds voraciously.*) Be gentle.

ANNE: (*Breaking away from him.*) No, stay where you belong – on your knees. You may please God, but you bore me! (*ANNE is about to exit when she is confronted by the QUEEN MOTHER. LOUIS stands.*)

QUEEN MOTHER: Everywhere I go, in every corridor, I hear them sniggering as I pass, whispering: 'The Cardinal's leching after that whore, De Rohan.'

ANNE: Yes, and *she* wants him – dead, too!

QUEEN MOTHER: Richelieu's activities must be curtailed, Louis, or I will have a gargantuan sulk. And you know what terrible excesses that will lead to.

LOUIS: Oh for the Virgin's sake, just bed him, Mother!

QUEEN MOTHER: Louis!

LOUIS: Well, if it weren't for your c-c-cock-sure Cardinal, we wouldn't be mired in the Vatelline now, would we? And we wouldn't be fighting the Pope, and the Huguenots wouldn't be rebelling, and the Duke of Buckingham wouldn't be preparing to invade us! God in Hell, I de-detest the man!

QUEEN MOTHER: My poor son.

(*The women try to embrace LOUIS simultaneously.*)

ANNE: My poor husband.

LOUIS: Oh for the chilly confines of a monastery.

(*LOUIS fights his way out of their embraces and runs off, pursued by the women.*

RICHELIEU is alone in the last of the embattled sunset. The ticking of a gigantic clock punctuates RICHELIEU's hectic amplified heartbeats.

Led by FANÇAN, the MOB, with animals' heads on, crawl around the perimeter of the stage.)

RICHELIEU: Pope, King, Queen, Prince, Buckingham, Huguenots, Austria, Spain and England are all playing into my hands. France begins to be born. But why, Christ, why, can't I shut her face out of my sleep? In my dreams, her tongue probes my mouth.

(*One of the animals, with a boy's voice, sings.*)

SONG: Cardinal Richelieu's come to town.

He scratches the pox beneath his gown.

He pokes the Queen to steal the crown.

Then humps the King to keep him down.

And if he could, to the sound of a psalm,

Under the shadow of Notre-Dame,

He would take us all down and drown

Us in the Seine, so he could wear the crown.

(*RICHELIEU covers his ears.*)

RICHELIEU: Voices. No, they must exist *outside* my brain. Yet insanity scratches when we are least aware.

(*FANÇAN begins the next verse as the animals converge on RICHELIEU.*)

SONG: We've more than, more than had our fill

Being ground to chaff in the Cardinal's mill.

Day in, day out, he employs his skill

To corrupt the Church against Christ's Will.

Then he crucifies Christ upon the hill.

There is no end to the blood he'll spill.

The Cardinal will go on killing us until

There's no one left in France for him to kill.

RICHELIEU: I've the best brain in France but my reasoning's disintegrating. So what must all the others

suffer, trying to make sense out of their daily despair? But
I'll make things easier for them. In Your Beneficent Name,
Christ, I will ensure that even treasonous *thoughts* and
seditious singing are punishable by prison.
(*The animals and FANÇAN cower off into the shadows. Father
JOSEPH enters.*)

JOSEPH: Buckingham is sailing for La Rochelle!

RICHELIEU: Good.

JOSEPH: He's sailing against *us,* Armand.

RICHELIEU: Naturally.

JOSEPH: Can't you understand what is happening?

RICHELIEU: Perfectly. While we're establishing a dynamic
Monarchy, Charles the First is blundering towards Civil
War.

JOSEPH: Oh for God's sake!

RICHELIEU: Simultaneously Charles is being manipulated
by Buckingham into waging a wasteful war against us.
Whereas *we* need a war, in order to survive.

JOSEPH: Why do we need a war?

RICHELIEU: Because once I announce that England
is invading us, the spendthrift nobility, the avaricious
bourgeoisie and even the grasping peasantry will be forced
– out of sheer patriotism – to pour all their gold into the
King's coffers. And, in turn, this enforced 'generosity'
will help to transform this unfocused country of ours into
becoming a unified nation.

JOSEPH: But Buckingham intends to exploit the Huguenots,
who are the enemy *within!*

RICHELIEU: Then I sincerely hope that Buckingham
succeeds.

JOSEPH: What?

RICHELIEU: Yes – until the Huguenots have irrevocably
committed themselves to total rebellion, we cannot utterly
destroy them. But once they have openly joined with
Protestant England against Catholic France, why, then,
the rest of our countrymen will rise up in the name of
their glorious King, and drive both the English and the
Huguenots back into the sea.

JOSEPH: Armand, we will never successfully besiege La Rochelle. Especially if Buckingham's navy slips into the harbour and relieves them.

RICHELIEU: We'll blockade the harbour.

JOSEPH: How?

RICHELIEU: I'll have wrecks chained to the ocean bed that will rip huge holes in the hulls of Buckingham's ships. If some of his vessels survive, our engineers will repel him with a dike of masonry that will span the mouth of the harbour. As for the Huguenots, we'll besiege them and starve them out. Then I'll feed their treacherous bodies to the foam. This I swear.

JOSEPH: Oh by the by, Marie's lover, De Chalais, is already sharpening his knife to gouge out your throat.

(FANÇAN, in a rat mask, enters.)

RICHELIEU: *(As FANÇAN removes his mask.)* How did you pass my guards, Fançan?

FANÇAN: For a snippet of gold, one can always see the Spider. Besides, I felt that you needed me. Well, propaganda can do anything. Whatever you want said, I'll publish it. Whoever you want dead, I'll arrange it.

RICHELIEU: You revolt me.

FANÇAN: The feeling's mutual. But I'm vermin and I look it. *(Putting his rat mask back on.)* You just don't look it.

RICHELIEU: Prepare the minds of the rabble for war.

FANÇAN: And my wages?

RICHELIEU: There's a remote possibility that you'll still be alive at the end of the week. You may kiss my ring.

FANÇAN: *(Doing so.)* As I've said – for a price – I'll do anything.

(FANÇAN exits. LOUIS enters from the opposite direction.)

LOUIS: My bitch has mis-miscarried again.

RICHELIEU: Your Majesty, allow me to express my…

LOUIS: *(Overriding him.)* I have informed Gaston that he is to marry the lucrative Madame de Montpensier forthwith. We must have an heir at all costs.

RICHELIEU: We need a navy more.

LOUIS: N-navy? But we've never had one.

RICHELIEU: That's why we must build one. To besiege La
Rochelle. Then we must conscript soldiers for our Army,
and stop relying on mercenaries.

LOUIS: At last; war with England and the Huguenots!

RICHELIEU: Yes, sire, but not before we're fully prepared.
I refuse to become involved with death without being
certain that our enemies receive the largest helpings.

LOUIS: I'm looking forward to k-killing. Then no one will be
safe. Not even…

RICHELIEU: Me, Highness?

LOUIS: Who knows?

(*LOUIS exits. RICHELIEU slumps to his knees before Father
JOSEPH.*)

RICHELIEU: Help me.

JOSEPH: This is an about turn, my son. But I will try.

RICHELIEU: Last night as I drifted into the dark, I felt a
weight, like a coffin full of sand, pressing down on my
body. Then out of the coffin came a Shadow. Its formless
lips were bleeding. I awoke, glowing with terror. Then
I looked in the mirror. There were these…sores, oozing
pus, around my beard. It was only then I realised that it
was Christ who had kissed me because the Shadow had
wounds in His side, and in His hands and His feet. Like
Doubting Thomas, I wanted to thrust my fingers into His
Wounds. I needed a sign to prove that I am right in what
I'm doing. Or, in truth, am I leading France towards a
second Golgotha?

JOSEPH: Our Lord Jesus Christ is also the Resurrection and
the Life, my son.

RICHELIEU: I know, but *I* always see Him broken on the
cross at Calvary.

JOSEPH: The pity is, Armand, you view everything,
including the Saviour of the World, through the distorted
spy-glass of yourself. Yes, my son, you have chosen despair
and sterility as the rack on which you can exquisitely
wrench yourself apart. You have even convinced yourself
that your anguished body is the map of humanity
– because pain to you is the norm. So, for all our sakes, I

pray that Our Lord will soon dry up all your sores and heal your heart. Because if He does not, you will make us all suffer, as you suffer. Won't you, my son?

RICHELIEU: Father... Father...what must I do to be well?

JOSEPH: Make France great again. And then pray for mercy on your immortal soul.

(*Father JOSEPH exits as DE CHALAIS, a handsome youth in his finery, enters. They exchange silent salutations. DE CHALAIS looms over the kneeling RICHELIEU.*)

RICHELIEU: (*Without looking up.*) Ah my dear De Chalais, I have been hearing so much about you.

DE CHALAIS: (*Drawing his knife.*) Come where it's quiet, Eminence.

RICHELIEU: (*Standing.*) With pleasure. I trust Marie has been rewarding you satisfactorily with her erogenous favours.

(*RICHELIEU coughs. Musketeers enter and seize DE CHALAIS. MARIE DE ROHAN enters as DE CHALAIS struggles.*)

I see you are in good health, madam.

DE CHALAIS: Your Eminence, I beg you to have mercy on me.

RICHELIEU: You'll have to be satisfied with Justice.

DE CHALAIS: Marie, please help me!

RICHELIEU: Remove him.

(*DE CHALAIS is dragged off. RICHELIEU turns to MARIE.*)

Retire to your estates, Marie. While you still can.

(*He tries to pass her but she prevents him, flaunting her body.*)

Let me pass.

MARIE: Release him.

RICHELIEU: He will be released soon enough – when his head is in a bucket.

MARIE: You dare not slit another vein of the Blood Royal.

RICHELIEU: It is the King's Law.

MARIE: Wasn't Condé's death enough for you?

RICHELIEU: As long as there is conspiracy in the land, nothing is enough.

MARIE: But, Armand, De Chalais is only a youth.

RICHELIEU: In the interests of the State, the individual does not exist. You've always known that. And before your

youth dies, he will sign a confession, implicating *all* who
have plotted my demise. So, again, Marie, I urge you to
retire while you are able.

MARIE: Oh you don't know De Chalais, my dear. He is not
like you. He believes in honour. So he will never confess,
because *I* am his altar. I carry his soul – here.
(*She indicates her décolletage. RICHELIEU averts his eyes. But
by continually moving into his vision, she makes him look at
her sinuous body. Then she begins to remove her clothes, starting
with her bodice.*)

RICHELIEU: I promise you that I will have him racked limb
from limb until he tells me *all* the names.

MARIE: You're sweating to possess me, my love. Admit it.

RICHELIEU: I am not a voyeur where another man's pain
is concerned. But I will personally watch De Chalais howl
until he confesses everything.

MARIE: (*Moving very close to him.*) Touch me, my sweet. Like
you do every night in your dreams. Ar...mand. The truth
is, you are jealous of my lover.

RICHELIEU: And when the names bleed from De Chalais'
mouth, I will have *all* their owners racked before they die.

MARIE: Free him, and I will ease you...deeply...into me.
Then there will be no more cruel Christs, or icicles in your
brain. There will be just you and me.
(*She exposes her breasts. Tentatively his hands move towards
her breasts. Then his hands freeze into claws, inches away from
her nipples.*)

RICHELIEU: Cover yourself, before I summon the world in
to see you as the whore you would like to be.
(*He walks past her. She starts to dress herself, calling after
him.*)

MARIE: (*Laughing.*) Yes, I *am* a whore!
(*He turns.*)
But at least I *know* I am. And I'm proud I am. I would even
sleep with *you*, if it would make you human! But you are
not a man, Armand. You are a dead THING! (*Pause.*) Why
don't you bed me? The world already thinks you have.
And it's absurd to be accused of sins that you have never
enjoyed. So why not be what you are inside that anaemic

shell – a rapacious lecher? Snuffle and fang my body. I'll play any games you like. I'll grovel before you, then you can torture me, and we'll hump in churchyards, on the altars, up against the crucifix – because we can never commit so great a blasphemy as is your life!

(*MARIE moves to embrace RICHELIEU as the Puppet Court enters, led by LOUIS. GASTON, the QUEEN MOTHER and ANNE follow.*)

QUEEN MOTHER: To heel, Cardinal.

MARIE: (*In a mocking imitation of RICHELIEU's walk and speech.*) 'Yes, madam. No, madam'. (*She imitates RICHELIEU's cough.*) 'I'm so ridiculously humble, madam.' (*The Puppet Court laugh.*)

LOUIS: You should strut the st-stage, M-Marie.

MARIE: I do, sire. (*Without considering the consequences, she imitates the King's stutter.*) We must have w-war! Beget me an Heir, Anne, with G-Gaston!

LOUIS: T-Treason!

RICHELIEU: Banish her.

LOUIS: I will.

MARIE: (*Devastated.*) Your Majesty…

LOUIS: Go and strut among the yew trees on your estates.

MARIE: (*To RICHELIEU.*) I'll come back to watch you die, Armand. That I promise.

ANNE: (*To MARIE.*) My dear friend, I will do everything in my power to bring you back to Court.

(*ANNE exits with MARIE as Father JOSEPH enters.*)

RICHELIEU: Are the troops ready?

JOSEPH: Hardly. But the Huguenots' uprising is widespread, and Buckingham…

(*The CAPTAIN of the Musketeers enters.*)

CAPTAIN: Sire, we need more men inside the Vatelline if we're to have any chance of keeping the Pope at bay.

JOSEPH: No, sire, we require those very men on the coast, or the Huguenots will slash our arteries.

LOUIS: Then split our troops between the two fronts.

RICHELIEU: No!

QUEEN MOTHER: Your insolence is insufferable.

RICHELIEU: Your Majesty, we need more time! So we
must inform the Pope that we have already beaten the
Huguenots at La Rochelle, and, as a result, the Huguenots
have now agreed to help us smash the Pope.

LOUIS: What?

JOSEPH: (*Smiling.*) Brilliant.

RICHELIEU: Then His Holiness will sign a peace treaty
with us out of fear. Simultaneously we will inform the
Huguenots that we have beaten the Pope in the Vatelline,
and that the Pope has now agreed to help us smash the
Huguenots. Then the Huguenots will also sign a treaty with
us because they are frightened.

LOUIS: Why all these fallacious treaties?

RICHELIEU: They're devices to buy us invaluable time so
we can complete our war preparations – in peace. Within
a fortnight, we will besiege La Rochelle. Then when we
have subdued the Huguenots, we will crush the Pope in the
Vatelline. And then...

LOUIS: The rest of Europe?

RICHELIEU: Your Majesty...

LOUIS: Cardinal, look to yourself because I am not as
naive as I seem. Soon I won't need anyone to assist me
in anything. I have savoured enough pain around me to
know that *you* are merely temporary, sir. Where as *I* am
f-f-forever! (*To JOSEPH.*) Come, Father. We will whip the
peasants into an army.
(*Father JOSEPH and LOUIS exit. The QUEEN MOTHER is
about to follow when she hears the tolling of a funeral bell. Led
by FANÇAN, the animals crawl into view, beating drums. DE
CHALAIS, who has been tortured, is dragged in by Musketeers.
A Musketeer hands RICHELIEU the confession that has been
signed by DE CHALAIS.*)

DE CHALAIS: France is ruled by excrement in a red robe!

RICHELIEU: (*Reading the confession.*) Excellent. Your
confession is all-embracing.

QUEEN MOTHER: (*Crossing herself.*) God have mercy on our
souls.

RICHELIEU: (*To the Musketeers.*) Execute him.

(*DE CHALAIS is led off to the accompaniment of drums. The Puppet Court, in black, files in silently. GASTON stands nervously with ANNE. RICHELIEU shows GASTON the confession.*)
Amusing, isn't it?

GASTON: (*Fierce whisper.*) I beg you not to show this to the King.

RICHELIEU: It will depend.

(*The Puppet Court hiss in horror. The animals laugh. The drumming increases. There is the hacking sound of the axe.*)

QUEEN MOTHER: (*Vomiting.*) The beginning of the end.

RICHELIEU: (*In response to the hacking sounds.*) Inefficient. There has to be a better way.

(*Off, DE CHALAIS screams out.*)

DE CHALAIS: (*Off.*) Mother of God, finish it!

(*Silence.*)

FANÇAN: (*To the animals.*) That's one less to oppress us, brothers! Well, what are you waiting for? Let's collect our souvenirs.

(*FANÇAN leads the animals, who are still beating the drums, in the direction of the execution. The white-faced Puppet Court file past RICHELIEU and exit.*)

ANNE: (*Passing RICHELIEU.*) Who's next? Me? The King? Who, Cardinal?

(*RICHELIEU is alone with the QUEEN MOTHER.*)

QUEEN MOTHER: I'm frightened, Armand.

RICHELIEU: I know.

QUEEN MOTHER: (*Now a defeated old woman.*) You won't desert me, will you? (*RICHELIEU turns away.*) Please!

RICHELIEU: Why will no one ever leave me to myself?

QUEEN MOTHER: Because you have intruded on us all! (*She tries to embrace him but he shakes her off.*) It's that whore, Marie, isn't it?

RICHELIEU: (*Shaking his head.*) I love…

QUEEN MOTHER: Yes!

RICHELIEU: …No one.

QUEEN MOTHER: (*Forcing her body against his.*) Sweet Heavens, please prove that I am here! You owe me that. By Christ, you owe me that!

RICHELIEU: (*Moving away from her.*) If you touch me again, so help me, I will vomit in your face.

QUEEN MOTHER: (*Pleading.*) Armand, for pity's sake. I loved you because you were incorruptible. And when we kissed in your orchard, I...

RICHELIEU: (*Cutting her.*) That was in another world.

QUEEN MOTHER: Yes, you climbed over my breasts and between my legs, to take my son from me! So you could enslave France to your will. And now you spew my love into my face. Well, have my hate then! Because, by God's Eternal Grace, I'll have your sex hacked off, and forced down your dying throat.

RICHELIEU: Marie, I did not mean to...

QUEEN MOTHER: (*Overriding him.*) God help you, you did!

(*The QUEEN MOTHER exits. RICHELIEU falls to his knees.*)

RICHELIEU: Christ, what is this thing they jibber of? This...love. I am – outside. Eyes stare in at me. Ice.

(*Behind RICHELIEU, in the sulphurous dusk, the MOB enters, forming an armoured pyramid. LOUIS, in his golden armour and carrying a golden sword, climbs to the top of the pyramid. Siege ladders converge in the smoke of war. MEN climb into the fire amid withering death cries. There are bodies made of sacking everywhere.*)

I am...ICE!

(*RICHELIEU's cry echoes over the growing inferno. Blackout.*)

PART TWO

La Rochelle.

The sky is filled with sulphurous smoke. Black and red shadows flicker. Death is everywhere. Starvation. Animals mewing. Cries of children and old men. Everything is amplified.

Huguenot Leaders crawl into view with chains around their necks. They are led by the smiling GASTON, like dogs on a leash.

LOUIS XIII, his golden crown and armour glinting in the smoky light, appears with his sword suspended above the defeated Huguenots' necks. LOUIS is backed by his Musketeers.

On the shadowy perimeter, the QUEEN MOTHER, ANNE and the Puppet Court are chanting: 'God save Louis the Thirteenth, King and Conqueror!'

Down-stage centre RICHELIEU stands with his arms outstretched. He is wearing his crimson cardinal's robe over a suit of silver armour. He is bareheaded and glorying in the victory like a triumphant vampire.

RICHELIEU: La Rochelle is ours! The Duke of Buckingham is murdered. Gustavus Adolphus, the Protestant King of Sweden, is carving *our* initials on the Pope and on his crumbling Holy Roman Empire. Christ be praised, King Louis is in his glory, and, at last, France is triumphant!
(*The Huguenots crawl forward like panting dogs.*)
GASTON: (*Eating grapes and tossing some to the Huguenots.*) Well, snuffle 'em down, you whining curs.
ELDEST HUGUENOT: (*His eyes burning and his bones razors.*) You have starved us into defeat, Prince, but we are not dogs!
(*GASTON is about to kick the ELDEST HUGUENOT. RICHELIEU restrains GASTON with his levelled sword. GASTON draws his sword in response. Before they can fight, LOUIS steps between them, and addresses the Huguenots.*)
LOUIS: You Huguenots are seditious believers in the Anti-Christ, and therefore you are all blasphemers and traitors, so your collective doom is assured.

(*The HUGUENOTS sing.*)

HUGUENOTS: O Black God! O Grey Christ!
Shine mercy from Your Burning Eyes.
We do not ask for love or light,
But save us from the sword of night!
Save our children! Save our old!
Save them from the killing cold.
O Grey Christ! O Black God!
Spare us from Your Lightning Rod!

QUEEN MOTHER: Your seditious walls are to be razed to the ground!

GASTON: Yes, and after we've disembowelled you, we will spike your treacherous heads on the Gates of Paris! (*To LOUIS.*) And, what's more, the Parisians will love you for it, brother. They've not had a decent holiday since De Chalais was beheaded.

LOUIS: (*To the HUGUENOTS.*) And if any of you manage to survive, you will become Catholics. Incense will smoke your skies, beads notch your fingers, and the Mass will haunt all of your dreams. This I swear!

RICHELIEU: No!

HUGUENOTS: Save us, Cardinal, save us!

RICHELIEU: No.

LOUIS: (*To RICHELIEU under his breath.*) You have successfully prevented Buckingham from relieving the siege here, Richelieu, but it does not mean that you can counter my orders.

RICHELIEU: Your Majesty...

LOUIS: (*Relentless.*) The Huguenot leaders will die, and the remainder will embrace the One Faith, or they will be mutilated on the strappado!

RICHELIEU: Yes, slaughter, maim, rape and crucify! It is your privilege, sire; it is your kingdom. So none but Christ will say you nay.

(*RICHELIEU moves to leave but LOUIS clutches RICHELIEU's sleeve.*)

LOUIS: Why do you humiliate me?

RICHELIEU: You humiliate yourself, sire.

LOUIS: (*Striking RICHELIEU across the face.*) By the
Holy Stigmata! (*LOUIS is about to strike him again when
RICHELIEU turns the other cheek. LOUIS lowers his hand.*)
No, I will not indulge you, priest. You will only luxuriate
in the pain. (*Under his breath.*) Why are you deliberately
chipping at my sanity?

RICHELIEU: Control yourself, sire – I beg you.

LOUIS: Each day you twist and change. Why?

RICHELIEU: Because I want you to consider the
consequences of instigating a massacre, and then brutally
enforcing mass conversions to our Catholic Faith.

LOUIS: Sometimes I feel as if I am nothing more than an
extension of your will. I would to Heaven I could kneel
into these stones, and transfigure myself through prayer.
I'd give anything to forget my wife, my mother, my
brother, you – and even France – for one moment of true
friendship. I still miss Luyens. Oh I'm well aware that you
hated one another, Eminence. And I know Luyens abused
his power. But he did love me. After his fashion.

RICHELIEU: Everyone is waiting, my King, to hear your
considered royal wisdom.

LOUIS: Yes, yes. So what do you require of me?

RICHELIEU: Less swingeing passion and more statecraft.

LOUIS: Then, in God's name, why did you continually urge
me to humble these Protestant rebels if now you want me
to spare them?

RICHELIEU: Because I want you to show them…

LOUIS: (*Finishing RICHELIEU's thought in disbelief.*) …Mercy?!
(*The Puppet Court, QUEEN MOTHER, ANNE and GASTON
screech in chorus like demented parrots.*)

COURT: MERCY???!!!

RICHELIEU: Well…something like it.

LOUIS: France is not secure enough to allow such a foolhardy
gesture.

RICHELIEU: On the contrary: by allowing the Huguenots
freedom of worship, and by not beheading their leaders,
you will be regarded by them as a surprisingly benevolent
but truly just monarch.

LOUIS: Yes, but benevolence and justice at a time like this will be perceived by the rest of Europe as signs of our internal we-weakness!

RICHELIEU: Not if we raze the walls of La Rochelle to the ground first. Then we will tear down the walls of every other Huguenot stronghold throughout your kingdom. Indeed we must also ensure that there are *no* walled cities left in France of any persuasion.

LOUIS: There is wisdom in that, certainly, but...

RICHELIEU: (*Overriding him.*) And to further concentrate all the minds of Europe on the growing greatness of France, we should make Spain think that we are about to attack her, too.

LOUIS: That is pure lunacy! Well, we cannot even *defend* ourselves if Spain attacks us!

RICHELIEU: (*Smiling.*) True, but Spain is still uncertain of that. And she will grow even more fearful when we threaten to use our new allies, 'the grateful and patriotic' Huguenots, against her. This will ensure that the Hapsburg Dynasty will think twice before it calls Your Majesty weak. Furthermore, the time is rapidly approaching when you will carve your royal insignia on the flaccid belly of the Holy Roman Empire. By then we will have trained our zealous Huguenots into becoming patriotic warriors. And they will be the first lances that we will hurl into Spain's tumescent groin.

LOUIS: (*Laughing.*) Ah! So it's all expedience. For a moment I thought you were advocating that we should be genuinely merciful to the Huguenots.

RICHELIEU: I'd rarely go that far. Mercy is fashionable in current chivalry, but in political reality, it is generally detrimental to the State. So let us sprinkle a little – what shall we call it? – judicious Compassion on the defeated Huguenots. Then we will thank the Virgin for *your* continuous inspiration because now your people will know that war is merely the road to ultimate peace.

(*RICHELIEU exits.*)

LOUIS: (*Turning to the HUGUENOTS.*) The Almighty has just spoken to me in a vision.

GASTON: How magnanimous of Him.

LOUIS: (*To the HUGUENOTS.*) And the Lord said: 'Have mercy on My Miserable Sinners.' So I will be merciful to you erstwhile traitors, and once again, I will make you citizens of France, to glorify the Almighty's Name.

HUGUENOTS: God save the King! Louis the Merciful! May he reign forever!

QUEEN MOTHER: (*To LOUIS.*) Has Richelieu persuaded you to make this absurd speech?

LOUIS: (*To the HUGUENOTS.*) I give everyone their freedom. Now go in peace. Go in peace!
(*Chanting 'God Save The KING', the HUGUENOTS exit. LOUIS cries out in pain, reels backwards and collapses on the ground. The QUEEN MOTHER kneels and cradles her son in her arms. ANNE hovers. The Puppet Court gather round. GASTON yawns.*)

QUEEN MOTHER: Leave us!
(*The Puppet Court leave with GASTON who is laughing. ANNE remains.*)
And you, too, lady.
(*ANNE exits. LOUIS stirs.*)
My little boy.

LOUIS: I'm dying, Mother.

QUEEN MOTHER: Nonsense, dear. You merely swooned again because you continually allow those quacks to bleed you.

LOUIS: Bleeding is good for me.

QUEEN MOTHER: No, having all those leeches habitually sliming over your body is doing you irreparable harm. And the myriads of poisonous medicines that you daily imbibe are making things even worse.

LOUIS: I have endured two hundred kinds of restorative elixirs, and two hundred and seven purges, and I'm still dying.

QUEEN MOTHER: It's that damnable Cardinal!

LOUIS: No!

QUEEN MOTHER: Can't you see? The only thing that you both have in common is your infinite capacity for suffering unnecessary pain.

LOUIS: Richelieu is nowhere near as ill as I am! We've compared our number of bleedings and purgations, and I am well in the forefront of the race. So there is no question that in the realm of suffering: *I* am still King!

QUEEN MOTHER: (*Stroking his forehead.*) Oh my pathetic baby boy.

LOUIS: Yes, yes, keep stroking my brow, mother. It's almost worth my anguish to have you to myself.

QUEEN MOTHER: I know I often seem cruel, my dear. Even heartless. I don't want to be. But unfortunately in France, when one is the Queen Mother, one has to have distended claws in order to survive.

LOUIS: Even if it means conspiring against your own son?

QUEEN MOTHER: Sometimes. Where does it hurt, dearest?

LOUIS: Everywhere. Inside my head. My veins. In the marrow of my bones. (*As she continues to stroke him.*) That's wonderful, mother. At least I have lived long enough to see my kingdom lurch towards change.

QUEEN MOTHER: (*Ironically.*) Yes, his ineffable Eminence has certainly ensured that.

LOUIS: We are *all* changing, mother. We have no alternative. And *you*, too, must learn to conform to the New Order. You will have to grow with the rest of France. Even though it might prove a te-tedious experience for you. (*Producing a lozenge from the pouch on his belt.*) Would you like one of these restorative lozenges? I have been assured that they're very g-good for the bl-blood.

QUEEN MOTHER: No! Now listen to me, my son. This Cardinal of yours…

LOUIS: (*Interrupting her.*) And *yours*, mother!

QUEEN MOTHER: He is no longer mine! Can't you see that the insidious monster is manipulating you?

LOUIS: (*Shaking his head.*) It merely *seems* so, mother. And it is only for a little while.

QUEEN MOTHER: Oh my dear, it is because of Richelieu that we are drifting into an all-out war with Spain. It is because of him that Gustavus Adolphus, the Protestant swine of Sweden, is now hacking his way through the Holy Roman Empire. What is worse, *we* are *paying* Adolphus to do it. All for the greater glory of the Cardinal!

LOUIS: No, mother. Richelieu and I have done these things *together* in order that the House of Bourbon will finally dominate the whole of Europe. We have an Army now. Half a Navy. The Arts blossom. And under Richelieu's inspired guidance, we are creating an Academy for Literary excellence. Even as we speak, our foremost scholars are compiling the first French dictionary. Within the year, we will open the Jardin des Plantes. And all because King and Cardinal are one! There is no change, no reform that we cannot implement together – because unity, under the seal of the King, is everything.

QUEEN MOTHER: My child. You're being deceived by his clerical conjuring tricks. Richelieu is nothing but a political lecher, humping his way to power over De Rohan, your wife…

LOUIS: With Anne? He would not dare! (*Unsure.*) Surely he would not dare…

QUEEN MOTHER: (*Smiling.*) Well, *you* are the best authority on your wife's aberrant deviations, my dear. At least you should be.

LOUIS: I know Richelieu. Above all things, he has respect for my crown. For what is m-mine! No, mother, such an act would be ab-abhorrent to him.

QUEEN MOTHER: Yes, of course, you're absolutely right, dear. And to prove your unswerving trust in his fidelity, why don't you extend His Eminence's power even further?

LOUIS: No, he has more than enough.

QUEEN MOTHER: But, my darling son, you have just affirmed that France has never been so prosperous, or so sublimely happy, as it is under the stimulating tutelage of our compassionate Cardinal. Well, no one is ever coerced, or spied on, are they? And now that he's banned all duelling on pain of death, the executioner is chopping off heads faster than our Louvre's chef is breaking eggs for his omelettes. As for the contented populace, every day they pour out their life-savings into the countless jolly little wars that your peace-loving Cardinal has so jocundly embarked upon. Indeed it can be said that never has France been so jubilant as she is now – as she capers to every rustle of his red robe. So why not complete the circle, my son, and appoint Richelieu as your Regent? Or better still – your Heir?

LOUIS: Never, never! I can scarcely bear his corrupting flesh near me. He treats me like a flowered doll, and he reprimands me as if I am his son.

QUEEN MOTHER: Oh come now, Louis, you are being excessively ungenerous. How can you possibly besmirch Richelieu's name, when you have just proclaimed that *he* made France, not you.

LOUIS: No, *I* made my c-country into a n-nation! I just used him. If I raised my hand against him, he would splinter against my throne like a gl-glass sword! Yet it is true that he controls my every movement, every thought. By the terror of the Holy Ghost, I ab-ab-abhor him!

QUEEN MOTHER: Oh you shouldn't, my dear. He is the greatest statesman since Creation.

LOUIS: Sometimes I want to see him rotting in an alien grave.

QUEEN MOTHER: Give the command, my liege, and the King's thought will be made flesh upon the instant.

LOUIS: Then chop his b-b-bastard head off!

(*RICHELIEU appears, swathed in scarlet. The QUEEN MOTHER and LOUIS back away nervously.*)

RICHELIEU: (*Smiling.*) Good evening, Your Majesties.

LOUIS: (*Flustered.*) Oh Your Eminence.

RICHELIEU: (*Continuing to smile.*) I sensed I was being discussed, sire.

LOUIS: N-no!

QUEEN MOTHER: Oh no!

RICHELIEU: Your eyes say otherwise.

QUEEN MOTHER: How did you happen to stumble upon the secret entrance to my bed chamber, Your Eminence?

LOUIS: Mother, you are too modest.

RICHELIEU: Before God, I swear, sire, I have never...with your mother. Never! I have too much respect.

QUEEN MOTHER: You have none, sir. To insult me to my face! Though, by my womb, I would have had you racked, had you dared!

RICHELIEU: Well, I'm glad we are agreed upon something.

QUEEN MOTHER: You globe of dung! You presume to jibe at me. You impotent snuffler! It is you who have turned Man against God, and God against Man – and all for your own dung-hill elevation!

RICHELIEU: Madam, allow me to defend myself.

QUEEN MOTHER: Oh Armand, I would have given you anything for a little understanding...a little gratitude.

RICHELIEU: It were better you were silent, madam.

QUEEN MOTHER: Louis! You heard him. You hear this sewer priest – to me, to your own mother.

RICHELIEU: (*To LOUIS.*) Sire, you force me to offer you a choice.

LOUIS: *You* are in no position to offer *me* anything, sir.

RICHELIEU: The choice is me – or Anarchy and Chaos. And you know it, Majesty. For if I fall from grace, France will surely follow.

QUEEN MOTHER: How dare you play at being God? When you are worth less than the leeches that bleed you. You have murdered and pillaged France, sir cleric. Yet you grow richer than the King with every dart you hurl into his kingdom. You are a Catholic Cardinal who splatters Catholic blood across a map to satisfy – what? The ignominious desire to manipulate your betters. You've even taxed the Clergy while simultaneously manoeuvring your own relations into positions far above them. And, worse, I hear that you have made your blasphemous brother into a Cardinal, too. Oh Louis, for Christ's Immaculate Sake, hang, draw and quarter this rabid traitor!

RICHELIEU: Thank you, madam.

QUEEN MOTHER: For what, you jakes' priest?

RICHELIEU: I have rarely been praised so highly.

QUEEN MOTHER: You bilious filth!

RICHELIEU: Oh lady, you disturb me. You are the Queen
Mother, yet you behave like a scavenging gypsy, forever
shovelling garbage into your belly. You only prove that
Mankind is incapable of change.

QUEEN MOTHER: Louis, I demand that you execute this
traitor!

RICHELIEU: Listen, madam. No, no, you will heed me! It
hurts me profoundly to hear such bestiality seeping out
of royal lips. Christ Jesus, where is the hope, when only
Man's sophisticated manners change, and not his heart?
Has History taught us nothing but how to compound evil?
Because you, madam, are a predatory owl, gouging at
my throat out of frustrated spite. Yet, God knows, I wish
to serve you, as I wish to serve your son, the King. But
I can serve neither – unless you chain up the beast that
growls behind your ribs. I'm too tired to indulge your
hysteria. Too ill! I demand the birth of civility. Of charity.
Of compassion. Above all, I insist that Intellect takes
precedence over Instinct. (*To LOUIS.*) We are the beginning
of a New Age, sire. Yes! And we, the Enlightened Ones,
must set a beneficent example to our peers. If we are to
survive the birth pangs of our royal civilisation; strategy
and subtlety must be our swords, the King's all-embracing
Law our armour, and constructive imagination our banner
of the future.

LOUIS: Enough, sir, enough! I am not a child to be
catechised.

QUEEN MOTHER: (*Flailing her fists at RICHELIEU.*) In
God's name, my son, rip this creature's tongue out, thrust
white-hot brands into his eyes, and castrate his cramped
virginity!

RICHELIEU: Yes, strike me, lady, again and again! Go to it.
Such savagery becomes a Queen.

QUEEN MOTHER: You lascivious lump of Hell!
(*RICHELIEU buckles to his knees under the blows.*)

RICHELIEU: As you will, madam. (*Resigned and broken.*) As
you will.

QUEEN MOTHER: Grovelling on your knees won't help you!

RICHELIEU: Your point is taken. Obviously I have failed. Compromise in politics, as in life, is the only way that we can contrive a tolerable future. But you cannot see this. (*To LOUIS.*) So I beg you to accept my resignation as your Premier Minister, Lord King.

QUEEN MOTHER: Yes, Louis, accept it, accept it!

RICHELIEU: Please, sire. My body is a well of pain. Let me go hence in peace.

QUEEN MOTHER: I am growing old, my son. I don't ask much of you, but I beg you to cast this incubus into the outer darkness!

LOUIS: (*Almost inarticulate with angry tears.*) Do this! Do that! Say this! Say that! Execute that man! Declare war! Enforce the Law! Hate, kill, maim, torture and crucify! God save the King! Oh sweet Luyens, when we began to climb to where I am, I never thought… To where…I am? (*Screaming.*) WHERE AM I?? (*Breaking down.*) In the name of all that's Holy, where the Hell am I?

QUEEN MOTHER: You are the King, and, as such, you must save your realm from this serpent with the crimson halo!

RICHELIEU: As I love you both, as I love France, sire, let me go.

LOUIS: Aaah! Satan everywhere!! Richelieu, I know you now for what you are. Your mastery is ended. Find a tomb and take up house! And you, mother, l-leave me!
(*LOUIS exits, close to breakdown.*)

QUEEN MOTHER: (*Screaming like a fishwife.*) The bloody Cardinal is finished! The Monster's reign is over! (*Reflective.*) And *I* have…destroyed him.
(*The Puppet Court emerges, waving torches and coloured bunting. Church bells ring out in jubilation. ANNE and GASTON enter hand in hand. Everyone is laughing.*
The Puppet Court sing as they dance around the prostrate RICHELIEU.)

SONG: This is the fall
Of the Cardinal.
Once he ruled all,

But now he must crawl.
So God damn the soul
Of the Cardinal.

(*RICHELIEU tries to get to his feet.*)

RICHELIEU: Can't breathe…

GASTON: (*Pushing RICHELIEU onto his knees.*) That will soon
be remedied forever!

(*The MOB, dressed as CLOWNS, enters, leading a black
Bear on the end of a paper-chain. Across the Bear's chest is
written 'Executioner'. The Bear is followed by two beautiful
CHILDREN, dressed as the KING and the QUEEN, complete
with paper crowns and ceremonial robes made out of painted
sacking. The Puppet Court applauds them.
Finally, to the tinny sound of a child's drum, an EFFIGY of
the Cardinal enters. His head is a luminous pumpkin. The
Cardinal's EFFIGY is fourteen feet tall, extremely thin, dressed
in blood-red cloth, and is on stilts. The CLOWNS sing as they
kick and punch the real RICHELIEU who is now coughing
badly.*)

SONG: This is the fall
Of the Cardinal.
Hear the bells toll.
See his head roll.
God damn the soul
Of the Cardinal!

EFFIGY: (*To the CHILD KING and his CHILD QUEEN, in a
high, squeaky voice.*) I am France!

CHILD KING: (*In an even squeakier voice.*) Yes, sir, no, sir,
three bags full, sir. Please be kind to me and her, sir.

EFFIGY: Never! I am France. Me – or Revolution and
Anarchy. Choose!

(*Everyone laughs.*)

FANÇAN: (*Taking off his clown's mask.*) To the point!

CHILD KING: (*To the Bear who is straining and rearing on the
end of its chain.*) Mother, kill the Cardinal!

(*With a great roar, the Bear breaks his paper-chain and lumbers
towards the EFFIGY of Richelieu. Then the Bear proceeds to
tear and rend the EFFIGY – until the EFFIGY's head rolls*)

off, still crying; 'I am France!' The EFFIGY disintegrates into a crumpled heap of red rags and firewood.)

CHILD QUEEN: Come out, Satan!

(The heap of red rags stirs, and then a LITTLE GIRL crawls out of the heap of rags. Everyone laughs and cheers, throwing streamers.)

GASTON: I always knew there was something very odd about the Cardinal. *(Putting his arm around the GIRL.)* Come and amuse me in my boudoir, darling Eminence.

(GASTON exits with the GIRL, followed by the dancing Puppet Court. The CLOWNS, except for FANÇAN, dance off in the opposite direction, jumping over the crumpled red cloth, and also over RICHELIEU, who is still on his knees. The Bear performs somersaults. Everyone is singing.)

SONG: This is the fall
Of the Cardinal.
Under the swirl,
He's only a girl!
So God damn the soul
Of the Cardinal!

FANÇAN: *(To RICHELIEU.)* I've always told you that you should've retired while the going was good. But don't worry; I'll still see that your fingers and toes are sold off for a fair price. As religious relics.

(FANÇAN exits. ANNE and the QUEEN MOTHER are left staring at the broken RICHELIEU.)

ANNE: I almost pity you, priest.

QUEEN MOTHER: That's what he's playing for. Aren't you? But his fall cannot be great enough for me. I once loved him, Anne. I know it defies all reason, but what I felt for this spiky tangle of heartlessness was far beyond our ridiculous lives of powdered ruffs and snuff boxes. Because once he had the potential to be a fully-equipped man, and that's a rarity.

ANNE: This cannot be necessary, madam.

QUEEN MOTHER: Is anything really necessary? *(To RICHELIEU.)* You fool, Armand, you arrant fool! Now we will have to rule without you. Perhaps not so adventurously, but with much greater serenity. You see, we're sick to the soul of all your facile masks. We refuse to kiss your feet, simply to satisfy the Inferno in your skull. Oh it's true, there are times when we need someone like you to tell us how to live, and how to die. But we abhor being *watched* while we do it! And that's all you ever did, with your infernal spying and your mania for manipulation. And I gave you *me*, and you…you just… Even if I damn my own soul to Hell and back, as God is my eternal witness, I will have your head in the morning! (*The QUEEN MOTHER and ANNE exit.*)

RICHELIEU: When will you learn? When will anyone ever learn?
(*RICHELIEU is alone. Shadows flicker on the perimeter of things. RICHELIEU stumbles to his feet, coughing. Then he subsides on the tattered robes of the EFFIGY Cardinal. Father JOSEPH enters, breathless and distraught.*)

JOSEPH: Armand, you've the pallor of a corpse.

RICHELIEU: How appropriate. Within the month, I will also have the disposition. So…what is the news on the life-side of the grave?

JOSEPH: The Queen Mother is plotting with Anne and Gaston.

RICHELIEU: So where is the news?

JOSEPH: After your demise, they intend that the King will join you on his angel's wings. Then his overly-solicitous wife will be free to marry Gaston.

RICHELIEU: God grant their wedding bed an heir, then.

JOSEPH: They will obliterate all your life's work. You must fight, Armand, and save us from ourselves.

RICHELIEU: I'm finished, Joseph.

JOSEPH: Gustavus Adolphus…

RICHELIEU: (*Overriding him.*) Unimportant.

JOSEPH: (*Using the EFFIGY's tattered robe in lieu of a map.*) …Is scything his way through Austria.

RICHELIEU: So?

JOSEPH: Adolphus acknowledges that *you* have financed his success, so he is now offering you the opportunity of dividing up Europe with him; half to Sweden, half to France.

RICHELIEU: What?

JOSEPH: With a little diplomatic persuasion, my informants indicate that Adolphus will 'give' you everything to the left bank of the Rhine.

RICHELIEU: The ancient borders of Gaul! France's rightful inheritance. When? When will he do this thing?

JOSEPH: By the autumn. But only if he can bargain with you personally, Armand.

RICHELIEU: Hm. Tell him – yes. We will come to terms. (*Pause.*) But why should I bother to play the cockscomb? It's impossible. Thank him for his magnanimity, but tell him 'no'. You seem relieved, Joseph?

JOSEPH: I am.

RICHELIEU: Why?

JOSEPH: Whatever the prize, Our Saviour does not approve of Catholics assisting Protestants to gobble up Catholics.

RICHELIEU: The Lord of Hosts has nothing to do with my decision.

JOSEPH: No?

RICHELIEU: (*Smiling.*) No. The truth is, we have neither the military equipment nor sufficient men to successfully occupy so great a territory as Adolphus offers us. And even if we had the necessary resources, I have been eclipsed by two nipples and a stutter.

JOSEPH: Eminence, you are indulging yourself again – at France's expense. Be the statesman you were born to be. Seek the King out this instant. I know it is not yet dawn; but what other alternative is there?

RICHELIEU: A long overdue rest in the charnel house.

JOSEPH: Where you will only come face to face with the Shadow of your despair. But this time Christ will not kiss you on the mouth. He will turn His Back on you while Lucifer leads you through the purgatorial whirlwind into the fires of Hell. My son, you must go to the King this instant. Crawl round his footstool if needs be in a hair shirt, with ashes on your arms and face – but go now! As you have always prophesied, without you, France will be at the mercy of the Four Horsemen of the Apocalypse.

RICHELIEU: (*Panting.*) I am so breathless. My lungs are cloaked with phlegm. To have the chance of dividing Europe in half... What a beginning! (*Coughing.*) The Red Robe is too heavy. I feel as if I'm clad in iron, daubed in blood. Marie de Medici was right; I *am* running out of masks.

(*The CAPTAIN of the Musketeers enters.*)

CAPTAIN: Your Eminence.

RICHELIEU: Am I under arrest?

CAPTAIN: Your Eminence is to come with me. Immediately.

RICHELIEU: Don't fret your heart, Father. Had I my life a second time, I would do everything that I have done again. Your arm, Captain. My ankles seem to be suffering from a difference of opinion.

(*Slowly they begin to walk around the misty perimeter of the stage.*

As the mist clears, an ornate golden throne is revealed, surrounded by the golden Puppet Court.

The MOB appears, holding a roll of black silk that sways like a death wind. As RICHELIEU and the CAPTAIN pass the MOB, the silk almost muffles them. The CAPTAIN draws his sword and holds the MOB at bay.)

CAPTAIN: Forgive me, Eminence, but you have always been most generous to me and my musketeers.

RICHELIEU: (*Wryly.*) And you, Captain, must forgive me for not trying to escape. Sadly my running days are over.

(*RICHELIEU and the CAPTAIN reach the empty throne. RICHELIEU kneels before it. Silence.*

The MOB chants the single word 'Death' over and over. At first in a whisper, then, accompanied by stamping feet, building to a terrifying crescendo.

Trumpets blare out, silencing the MOB.

LOUIS appears, resplendent in his crown and golden robes, surrounded by his Puppet Court. LOUIS is holding the QUEEN MOTHER's hand. She is also wearing a crown.)

THE MOB: (*In unison.*) Louis the Thirteenth is a truly great and just king!

(*QUEEN ANNE follows in a river-green dress. She is on the arm of the decadent GASTON, who is in a glittering white costume. They are giggling together.*
LOUIS raises his hand. Everyone freezes. For the first time, the Court and the Mob are aware that the KING is indeed the KING. LOUIS' slightest gesture at this point is more effective than any of his previous tantrums.)

LOUIS: (*After ascending his throne.*) Cardinal Richelieu, I now pronounce...
(*The MOB cheer extravagantly. The Puppet Court applauds. LOUIS silences the Court with a look.*)

RICHELIEU: Before you pronounce my fate, sire, I wish to ask for your forgiveness for failing. No, truly. Had I succeeded, I would not be here now awaiting your judgement. And failure merits death.

QUEEN MOTHER: Indeed it does, priest.

MOB: Death! Death! Death!

GASTON: Yes, give him his heart's desire, my liege.

QUEEN MOTHER: And now, Louis, now! Free us forever from this nefarious beast!

ANNE: Why do you pause, my lord?

RICHELIEU: Yes, it is beneath Your Majesty, to toy with me thus.

LOUIS: I am not toying with you. (*Smiling.*) You may rise.

RICHELIEU: Sire?

LOUIS: (*Descending from his throne and helping the bewildered RICHELIEU to his feet.*) Here. Allow me to assist you – my friend.

QUEEN MOTHER: Louis, in the name of all that's Unholy, what are you doing?

LOUIS: What I should have done from the beginning. I am turning away from my family, mother. Clamping love in irons, mother. Yes, I am becoming – for the first time – the undisputed King of France.

QUEEN MOTHER: Then stop this absurd posturing and chop this traitor's head off!

LOUIS: Armand Jean du Plessis de Richelieu, Cardinal of France, in regal solitude we have considered your many services to our kingdom and to our crown, and we have found your statecraft and your homage to us, to be exemplary. You are our greatest servant, and you will remain so while we live. Herewith, I embrace you as my foremost subject and most profound counsellor.

(*The KING embraces the CARDINAL.*)

QUEEN MOTHER: God's blood! I will not breathe the same air as this instrument of Satan!

LOUIS: Indeed you will not, mother. Henceforward you are exiled.

QUEEN MOTHER: Exiled?

LOUIS: As your *erstwhile* son, I still bear a certain love for you, my mother, but in my divine role as Louis the Thirteenth, King of all the French, I know you now for what you are – and I turn my back on you.

(*LOUIS reascends the throne.*)

QUEEN MOTHER: (*Grovelling at his feet.*) Oh my dearest, sweetest son, how can you possibly renounce me? I am your mother! You issued from my womb. And I love you. Yes, sometimes I have been deceitful, vicious, hurtful – and knowingly; but only to ensure your continual greatness as Absolute Monarch of our beloved France. So, for pity's sake, my liege lord, now I am on my knees, I beg you – in the blessed name of the wondrous Mother of our Lord – show compassion to your *own* mother. Can't you at least look at me, Louis? I'm an old woman. I know less and less why I am here, why I breathe, why I... And now you reject me! And for what? For the Cardinal who is just a tortured clump of rock, streaked with all our country's tears. My pretty son, please don't send me away. I promise that I will live as you want, and do as you want. I will keep silent, be a shadow, embroider my own shroud...anything. If only you will...

LOUIS: (*Fighting his tears.*) Mother, oh mother. Everything you say is too facile, and too late. You protest you love me, but all I see before me is an old woman, grovelling in a welter of self-pity. But I will not join you in the pit. Captain! Escort the Queen Mother from our presence into perpetual exile.

(*The CAPTAIN moves to the QUEEN MOTHER.*)

QUEEN MOTHER: I'm quite able to walk without assistance, thank you, Captain. (*Pausing before RICHELIEU.*) Why are you so unnaturally silent, Your Eminence? I made you, and now you have unmade me. As for you, Louis – my sometime son – I wish you the best of that THING!

(*The QUEEN MOTHER leaves with the CAPTAIN.*)

LOUIS: Good bye, mother. Try to die well.

GASTON: Sire, I beg you to call our mother back!

LOUIS: Not in this life.

(*The MOB murmur dangerously.*)

France, do not provoke me, or I will prove a Hydra to you, too – because to rule is my Divine Right. (*Indicating RICHELIEU.*) And whomsoever I choose as my friend and adviser, my subjects will honour and obey. Even if my friend drives the chariot of France into the inferno of the sun, I want – I demand – smiling hearts! (*In anguish.*) And J-Jubilation! See, I l-laugh even as I suffer. Whatever the cost to my soul, Justice shall be seen to p-prevail.

GASTON: That was our mother you treated thus, Louis. *My* mother!

LOUIS: Silence, you malapert. Your life is no longer sacrosanct. Anne will give me an heir. (*To ANNE.*) Won't you, beloved? Do not fail me, wife. There will be no second chance.

RICHELIEU: (*Kneeling before his king.*) May I kiss the hand of the wisest of kings?

(*LOUIS extends his hand to RICHELIEU who kisses it fervently. LOUIS snatches his hand away as if he has been stung.*)

LOUIS: (*Under his breath.*) I wish you did not n-n-nauseate me, my f-friend.

(*LOUIS strides through the MOB who fall to their knees as he passes. LOUIS looks back at ANNE.*)

An Heir is imperative, wife. (*To GASTON.*) And, brother, remember – I have no brother.

(*LOUIS exits. GASTON and ANNE follow. They are visibly shaken. GASTON pauses before RICHELIEU.*)

GASTON: (*To ANNE.*) Go in, sister.
(*ANNE exits. Then the MOB murmurs as the Puppet Court exits. The MOB flaps off with its black drapery like a giant bat.*)
Your Eminence, let us have peace.
(*Father JOSEPH hovers.*)

RICHELIEU: With all my heart, Prince Gaston. (*Exiting with JOSEPH as he whispers in JOSEPH's ear.*) Have Gaston watched.

JOSEPH: Naturally.
(*Once alone, GASTON pads over to the throne like a predatory cat, and sits on it.*)

GASTON: Even if Louis does manage to make Anne pregnant, she's bound to have a girl. His blood's too thin to sire a boy. So the moment he casts his eyes on the child's smooth crotch, my elevation is sure. By Salec Law, no bitch can squat upon the throne of France. If a bitch tried to, there would be civil war before she could straighten her stockings. Then within the week, the diadem would be mine. But to ensure my success, there is a swifter way to possess the throne. (*Shouting.*) Cousin Montpensier!
(*MONTPENSIER, a handsome nobleman of the Blood Royal, armed for war, enters.*)

MONTPENSIER: (*Bowing.*) We are ready – Your Majesty.

GASTON: (*Rising from the throne.*) Good. (*He pats the throne.*)
Now you're all mine.
(*They move to go.*)

MONTPENSIER: But is your cause just, my lord?

GASTON: My mother exiled, Queen Anne threatened, my head in jeopardy, the Red Monster on the loose, and a tyrannical King in full sweep! By the Apocalypse, no cause has ever been more just. Now let me see your Army.
(*They exit. Drums begin to pound. The approach of marching feet is punctuated by GASTON's Troops singing.*)

SONG: We've come to gobble the King,
With a heigh-ho-ding-a-ding-ding.
We've come to right a wrong,
With a heigh-ho-ding-a-ding-dong!
The Cardinal's corrupted the King,
With a heigh-ho-ding-a-ding-ding.

So the throne belongs to Gaston,
With a heigh-ho-ding-a-ding-dong!
The Cardinal and the King will swing,
With a heigh-ho-ding-a-ding-ding,
On the end of a rope like a gong,
With a heigh-ho-ding-a-ding-dong!

(*Braying trumpets. LOUIS, with RICHELIEU beside him, enters at the head of his Troops who wear lion masks. The KING is in golden armour, with his sword at the ready, and his blue cloak swirling behind him. RICHELIEU's silver armour glitters beneath his red robe. Above their heads, numerous fleur-de-lys flap in the wind.*

The drumming intensifies like a quickened, amplified heartbeat. Trumpets and gongs clash. LOUIS is nervous, and excited while RICHELIEU remains emotionless.)

LOUIS: Your spies were right as always.

RICHELIEU: It's taken poor Gaston six months to assemble his insects. We'll crush them in as many minutes.

LOUIS: (*To his Troops.*) Prepare!

(*His Troops sink on one knee, their pikes pressed against their thighs. The drumming has reached its crescendo.*

Large overhead mirrors distort the battle's smoky images.

Lithely, MONTPENSIER and his Troops sweep onto the stage. They are dressed in yellow and green like grotesque praying mantis. Their charges are comprised of great leaps like Russian Cossacks.

As MONTPENSIER's Troops charge, the KING's Army extends their long pikes, and then the KING's Musketeers fire. MONTPENSIER's Troops are either impaled on the pikes or killed by musket fire.

The battle is highly stylised. The KING's Troops step on their enemies' bodies, squashing them like insects. The drums and timpani are deafening.

The light becomes murky and green, reflected by the giant mirrors. Mist drifts in. The squeals of dying insects increase as the drums fade into an ailing heartbeat that becomes slower and slower.

One by one, MONTPENSIER's banners flutter to the ground like severed wings while LOUIS' rampant fleur-de-lys flaps over)

*the dead. The KING's banners are phosphorescent and flecked
with blood in the fading light.*

*GASTON appears in dazzling white. Two of LOUIS' Soldiers
charge at him. Acrobatically GASTON kills them like flies.*

*In the middle of the battle, MONTPENSIER's face is a welter
of blood.)*

MONTPENSIER: Gaston, for Christ's sake, be a King and
bring your Army!

(Everything freezes for a moment. GASTON laughs.)

GASTON: I do not know you, sir.

*(The bodies writhe. Withered death-cries echo over the battlefield.
Delicately GASTON walks over the wounded and the dying.
When GASTON is half-way across, he calls out to RICHELIEU
who has just piked an Enemy Soldier.)*

I come in peace, Cardinal.

(In the gloom, GASTON waves a white phosphorescent kerchief.)

MONTPENSIER: *(In extreme pain, to GASTON.)* You are not
worthy to be a prince of the realm, monsieur!

LOUIS: *(Holding up his hand.)* Sufficient death for today.

*(Both Armies freeze. The drumming heartbeats stop. Only
MONTPENSIER continues flailing his sword – but he kills
no one.)*

MONTPENSIER: Kill me, Louis. I am dishonoured. Kill me!

*(A Musketeer charges at MONTPENSIER but RICHELIEU
halts the Musketeer.)*

LOUIS: *(To RICHELEIU.)* Why?

RICHELIEU: Montpensier is for the block, sire. As a final
warning to your brother.

LOUIS: But Montpensier is my cousin!

RICHELIEU: No, he is merely a traitor.

LOUIS: You would even try to dispose of *me*, if it served your
ends.

RICHELIEU: You wrong me, sire. I am not Oliver Cromwell.

LOUIS: No, you are more dangerous. Craftily you manoeuvre
within the confines of the Law – which *you* are always
changing.

MONTPENSIER: Kill me!

RICHELIEU: In our good time.

(GASTON kneels on the dead before LOUIS.)

GASTON: Have mercy, my lord King. Please have mercy!

LOUIS: (*To the CAPTAIN.*) Escort Montpensier to the Bastille.

> (*The CAPTAIN seizes MONTPENSIER.*
>
> *Out of the mist, a baby's cry resonates. Everyone turns. The baby cries again.*)

What...?

RICHELIEU: Death.

> (*ANNE appears out of the mist, carrying a baby.*)

ANNE: No, this is not one of *your* gifts, Eminence.

LOUIS: (*Indicating the baby.*) Is it mine?

ANNE: (*Shaking her head and smiling.*) Ours.

LOUIS: A son?

ANNE: The future Louis the Fourteenth. For my King.

> (*GASTON snatches the baby from ANNE.*)

GASTON: It's a girl!

ANNE: (*Trying to pull the baby away from GASTON.*) No, no!

LOUIS: Give me my son.

> (*GASTON presses a dagger against the baby's throat. Everyone freezes.*)

GASTON: It is a girl, I tell you! (*GASTON unwraps the Baby as LOUIS steps forward.*) Genitals!

> (*ANNE rushes forward and takes the baby from GASTON.*)

RICHELIEU: (*Smiling.*) What a fine slip of a girl, my prince. The first in creation, with a King's implements.

GASTON: God curse you, priest, with your poxy plots. You've filched my inheritance from me.

LOUIS: Silence, miscreant.

GASTON: I will not be silent whilst that sleek rodent jibes at me.

LOUIS: You will! Forever. Now join our mother in exile before I have your severed head spiked on the gates of the Bastille.

GASTON: I'll be back. And not alone.

> (*GASTON exits, followed by MONTPENSIER and the CAPTAIN.*)

LOUIS: And now perhaps, Your Eminence, you will oblige us with a prayer of gratitude, for the wonder of my son.

RICHELIEU: With all my heart, sire.

(*RICHELIEU kneels among the dead. The Court follows suit.*)

Almighty God, we give you soul-felt thanks for the birth of this timely Prince who is your greatest gift to France, without whom Death would be the only heir.

(*Taking the baby from ANNE and holding the baby aloft.*) And now, here, before Your Invisible Throne, I dedicate this child, to the establishing of Heaven upon Earth. France is saved! Open the bells! Let the churches rock their steeples. I want to hear the tintinnabulation of our triumph!

(*The Troops and Court cheer the KING. The haggard figure of Father JOSEPH appears.*)

JOSEPH: (*Breathless.*) Your Majesty, Your Eminence!

LOUIS: Welcome, Father Joseph. I have a son, a real son!

JOSEPH: Congratulations, sire. (*Whispering.*) It is imperative that I speak with you both in private.

(*LOUIS, JOSEPH and RICHELIEU are isolated in a pool of light while the Court, Troops and ANNE are swathed in shadows.*)

RICHELIEU: Let's have the bad news.

JOSEPH: Gustavus Adolphus has been killed.

RICHELIEU: In God's name, how?

JOSEPH: He was trampled to death by his own horse in a cavalry charge.

LOUIS: Well, I, for one, am glad. It ill becomes a Catholic king playing the go-between-Jew to a Lutheran hog.

RICHELIEU: Hang your religious scruples, sire. Had Adolphus lived for one year more, we would have possessed half of Europe. (*To JOSEPH.*) How have the Swedish army taken it? How is their morale?

JOSEPH: Disintegrating. Like the French, the Swedes only respond to draconian leadership. Spain is already wasping over their guts. And *we* will be Spain's next victim.

LOUIS: (*To RICHELIEU.*) What shall we do?

RICHELIEU: Declare war first.

LOUIS: On Spain?

JOSEPH: Foolhardy!

RICHELIEU: On the contrary. I have been preparing for this moment from the day that I swore an oath to redeem France. And at last we are ready.

LOUIS: We still have only half a Navy!

RICHELIEU: Our Army is all we need. We will provoke Spain into having a military erection. Then we will cut her balls off.

LOUIS: For a cleric, your imagery is too dependent on codpieces, Monseigneur.

RICHELIEU: True, but from today I am a soldier.

LOUIS: There can never be enough death, can there?

RICHELIEU: There is always too much. But, sadly, war is the *only* road to ultimate peace. Then when all the battles are over, the real fighting begins – to make the peace permanent. And that is unbearably difficult. Like love.

JOSEPH: So speaks the congenital Cupid.

RICHELIEU: Peace can only be created out of coherent harmony, Father, not misplaced wit. And I, for one, am unsure whether we are ready, or even fit, for peace.
(*The church bells ring out.*)

LOUIS: It seems there is no time to enjoy my son, or the bells. Spain bloats on our borders, so perforce we must bleed her. War *is* the only road to peace. (*To his Troops who are once again illuminated.*) Sound the trumpets and drums. Bring the dead. Thank God, more blood! Death to the enemies of France!
(*LOUIS marches off in triumph with his Troops. The Court drags the bodies off.*
The bells have changed from jubilance to martial tolling.
Trumpets screech. The harsh dissonance of timpani is heard above the beating drums.
RICHELIEU is alone and spotlit.)

SOLDIERS' SONG: War! War! War! Always war!
That's all there ever is.
War! War! And more and more war!
We always have to live like this.
That's why we want to run away
Day in, day out, and every bloody day.
But war's the only game we're trained to play,

So merely being wounded is our idea of bliss
'Cause Death's the bride that we're always forced to kiss.
(*RICHELIEU kneels as the singing dies away. Silence. Then the
withering howl of a wolf echoes through the seething mist.*)

RICHELIEU: The desolation of the human spirit.
(*The cowled Father JOSEPH emerges from the mist like the
Grim Reaper.*)

JOSEPH: We must do what we must.

RICHELIEU: But are we right? Is Death the only way to
achieve a final peace? I have put all my faith into the State.
I have established France for a hundred years. Once Spain
is broken, the rest of Europe is ours for the taking. But is
that all?

JOSEPH: No. The veils of all the temples must be torn. Then
God will show himself.

RICHELIEU: But all who see God...die.

JOSEPH: Don't you understand even now? That – is – it!

RICHELIEU: Death?

JOSEPH: Yes. That is our final goal.

RICHELIEU: Only death?

JOSEPH: Only the *way* to death. You are born to die. That's
all you're born for. This France, this World, this Universe,
is only an image of God's Goodness. Only an experiment
in kindness, in Creation.

RICHELIEU: But nothing is kind! Everything is war. In love,
in family, in State, there is only habitual pain and killing.
Even animals rend and gorge. There must be something
more!

JOSEPH: Why??

RICHELIEU: Because there must!

JOSEPH: For a practical man, you have been over-using your
imagination again. You can only act what you are. And
you are the Rock on which others will build the temple of
France. You have saved France from anarchy. And when
Revolution comes – as it will...

RICHELIEU: Never!

JOSEPH: Oh yes. By making the King all-powerful, you have
ensured that the Revolution must come. But it will not
last long. Because, thank Heavens, the majority have little

confidence in themselves. They will always clamour to be
ruled by an enlightened despot. (*Father JOSEPH staggers.
RICHELIEU moves to support him.*) Yes… sadly…until the
end of time, we will always be on the look out for someone
like *you*, Armand.

RICHELIEU: You're in pain.

JOSEPH: The usual. So you had better be quick.

RICHELIEU: I don't understand.

JOSEPH: The Children are coming. They want us to
complete the foundation – however shaky. Then they want
us to die.

RICHELIEU: No!

JOSEPH: Yes, my friend. All your questions of right and
wrong, heart and soul, are irrelevant to the Children.
They have their own questions. You have followed Man's
cunning and subtlety to its apex, and have found that
anything is better than Anarchy. But unfortunately all the
scheming of our lives, all the work, all the energy, has
established nothing more than a tenuous compromise. A
Machiavellian modus vivendi. We must just keep things
going, that's all. So I'm glad that the Children are coming.
(*JOSEPH stumbles again. RICHELIEU tries to assist him.*)
No, I'd prefer to walk on my own. Thank you.
(*Father JOSEPH exits.
Shadows of wolves have gathered. A large mirror is lowered.
RICHELIEU prays to the mirror.*)

RICHELIEU: I believe. I have to believe. And yet I *don't*
believe. O Christ Jesus, give me assurance that the banner
that I have unfurled is for the glory of France, and not
merely for my own self-engrandisement. My soul is
stretched so fine that I can scarcely suck the night into my
lungs. That is why I can only see crucifixion on crucifixion
to the end of thought. That's when I can see anything at
all! Do not mistake me, Lord: I want to believe in Your
Resurrection. But it is the agonised image of You, wind-
lashed, on the cross, like a claw on the brow of a hill
who I really believe in. And sometimes…like now…that
claw has a face – and a mouth – *her* mouth…wanting…
wanting. And behind her, is the Queen Mother, forever

demanding…and always trying to possess me! Oh for
mercy's sake, breathe a corona of fire on me, or chastise
me with ice – but come to me in my abyss, and grant
me absolution. Yet why should You? Where did I lose
You, Lord? Through my political deviousness and the
expediency of statecraft? There are times when I feel that
I have never found You at all; so I can never lose what
I have never found. I know I seem to be crucifying You
daily in the name of the King. But I will repent the instant
that You consume me with the savagery of Your Love.
(*Pause.*) Yes…I suppose that is what it is. What I need most.
Love. Something that I always pretend is an indulgence.
O Master, I am so helpless and bewildered that I do not
know *how* to give love. Even worse, I am too frightened to
receive it. But I swear when I stop, when it all stops inside
me, You can crucify *me* on the other side of the stars. Until
then – from Your Stentorian Silence – it seems I must
continue to do what I deem to be necessary, whatever the
consequences – or both Kingdoms will fail: Yours, and
mine. Amen.
(*During the prayer, the wolves' howling dies away. But at the
end of the prayer, the howling resumes, and it is more terrifying
than before. Above the howling, we hear the cries of wounded
and dying men: 'Retreat! Retreat!'*
*LOUIS lurches out of the crimson mist, in his tattered cloak, with
blood on his face. His Troops follow, trailing shredded banners.
The wounded are everywhere. The Soldiers chant their embittered
war-song. There are screams of 'The Spaniards are coming. The
whole bloody world is coming!'.*)

LOUIS: (*To RICHELIEU.*) Is this your road to Peace, sirrah?
My subjects are dying!
(*FANÇAN pushes his way through the Troops, dressed as a
soldier.*)

FANÇAN: Yes, it's all our precious Cardinal's fault. Why
doesn't he fight the sodding Spanish on his own?
(*RICHELIEU stands, stunned.*)

LOUIS: They're barely f-f-five leagues from Paris. Don't you
understand, priest? They've routed us, and now they're
going to destroy us!

FANÇAN: Well, don't stand there like a petrified turd. Lead us!

(*The Troops take up the cry above the wolves and the drums.*)

TROOPS: Yes, lead us, Eminence, lead us!

RICHELIEU: (*Holding up his hands for silence.*) For the first time in my political life – I am at a loss as to what to say – or do.

LOUIS: Advice, Monseigneur! I demand your considered advice!

RICHELIEU: I know! But I am outside my body, and my mind has JAMMED!

LOUIS: I've no time for your clerical masturbation. All I want is advice.

RICHELIEU: Well then, sire, you had best retire to Fontainbleu, and leave the Army and I to remain here in Paris, to do what we can.

LOUIS: Wrong, Cardinal. You're so very wrong.

RICHELIEU: What other choice is there?

LOUIS: A monarch's choice, sir! You made me into the King, and now I will *be* the King. Your politics have betrayed you. Your God has forsaken you. Your deviousness and spies have failed you. As a consequence, most of my infantry are now hanging in gobbets of flesh on the hedgerows from here to Corbie. But *I* do not rely on serpentine scheming for my inspiration. Because France is mine! And now my subjects need *me* to imbue them with courage and fortitude, and give them the ultimate will to triumph over their enemies. Retreat? Never! No French King has turned tail since Jeanne d'Arc pulled Charles out of Chinon. We must go on fighting until the Hapsburg Dynasty is utterly vanquished. You see, all that matters is to believe that we will win, and we *will* win. But *you* don't believe. However, I forgive you for your military impotence this once, because there will not be another. I intend to create a New France in my image. And Joy, Cardinal, Joy will be its plumage. France, *my* France, tonight you will see Spanish blood stream across the sky. We will change the world because that is what the world is for.

(*The Troops cheer. Trumpets and drums sound.*)

Goodnight, Eminence. Sleep well.

RICHELIEU: Sire...

LOUIS: Try not to dream of what you *should* have said when I asked you for advice. (*To the Troops.*) Kill every enemy you see.

(*LOUIS marches off with his Troops. RICHELIEU is alone, menaced by the shadows of the converging MOB, materialising against the cyclorama.*

RICHELIEU is in obvious pain. The MOB creeps closer. Their faces are leper-white.)

MOB: We want war, yes, we want war

Never, never, never more.

But with you in charge, that's what's in store.

War and yet more war is your only law.

It was you who opened Purgatory's Door.

It was from your sanctimonious lips

That the order came for the demonic Four

Horsemen of the Apocalypse,

To ride forth and devastate the poor.

You've turned France into your personal whore.

You lied and lied and lied and lied,

And, as a result, our children died

To assuage your satanic Cardinal pride.

And now there's nowhere left for you to hide.

(*Father JOSEPH materialises from the shadows. Frightened, RICHELIEU turns to him.*)

RICHELIEU: They want me.

JOSEPH: They want your help, your encouragement.

RICHELIEU: I despise them.

JOSEPH: Walk among them. Talk to them!

RICHELIEU: Never.

JOSEPH: Tell them that the King will thrust the invaders back into the sea, and that there will be peace. My son, you must show them that you are not afraid of them! Or are you?

RICHELIEU: I think I've always been afraid of them. I will not go among them.

JOSEPH: You must!

(During this exchange, the MOB hiss like snakes.)

RICHELIEU: Louis may well be proved to be right for the first time in his skittish life. If so, he will not have the humility to admit that he is wrong ever again.

(Hissing, the MOB edges nearer. Their arms are outstretched like beseeching lepers.)

JOSEPH: Armand, you imposed your will on your country because you had to prove to yourself that you merited the prime place in the scheme of things. Out of self-doubt and fear, you did this. Now the time has come to exorcise your demons, and meet the people.

(Tentatively RICHELIEU approaches the MOB. The hissing stops. They wait, ready to pounce.

RICHELIEU extends his hand beneath a palsied BEGGAR's nose. The BEGGAR kneels and is about to kiss RICHELIEU's hand. FANÇAN appears out of the shadows and prevents the BEGGAR.)

FANÇAN: *(To RICHELIEU.)* Take your glove off first, priest.

RICHELIEU: And have his leprous muzzle slavering over my knuckles?

FANÇAN: Humble yourself, priest.

(RICHELIEU rises his hand to strike FANÇAN but Father JOSEPH catches his eye. RICHELIEU removes his glove, and extends his hand but he averts his eyes. Again FANÇAN prevents the BEGGAR from kissing it.)

How can you be so proud when your hand is stained with all that blood and shit?

BEGGAR: *(To RICHELIEU.)* Monseigneur, I would be most honoured if you would bless me.

(RICHELIEU looks at the BEGGAR, and for the first time RICHELIEU sees him as a human being.)

RICHELIEU: My friend, I did not realise…

BEGGAR: What, Monseigneur?

RICHELIEU: That you were…what you are. Forgive me.

FANÇAN: Humility hurts, doesn't it, Cardinal?

RICHELIEU: *(Still appraising the BEGGAR.)* Less than anticipated.

(RICHELIEU helps the BEGGAR to stand.)

BEGGAR: But I'm unclean, Monseigneur.

RICHELIEU: So am I. Your hand.

FANÇAN: Well, go on – say the magic word.

RICHELIEU: Please!

FANÇAN: Say it again. Well, you came here to get round us, didn't you?

RICHELIEU: No. I came to tell you that even now the King is destroying the Spaniards *and* the Austrians.

FANÇAN: Liar! (*Turning to the MOB.*) Tear this lying, bastard priest to pieces, and feed his entrails to your curs!

RICHELIEU: (*As the MOB murmurs dangerously.*) France! *You* are France, my friends. Without you, there is no France. I did not realise that until now. I thought you were just mindless animals.

FANÇAN: *You* are the excremental beast.

RICHELIEU: (*To the MOB.*) But you are human. And it's hard being that. I know – because *I* am not privileged to be one of you. I realise that I often appear to be callous and cruel but there is no other way to steer the ship of state. I have to ensure that we are not enslaved, by every means at my disposal. I believe the State is always in the right, even when it *seems* wrong. So I am merely the cypress tree whose only function is to catch the royal lightning from the sky, and then to fork it in each rebellious subject's heart.

FANÇAN: (*Pointing to the MOB.*) He means you! And you! And you! Everyone of you!

RICHELIEU: I plead for France. I demand for France. France is Louis. Louis is France. So Justice must kneel to the Law, and, in turn, the Law must grovel to Necessity!

FANÇAN: What about us? Our starvation? Our children?

BEGGAR: No, the Cardinal is right. We have to suffer! That's what we're here for. 'Til *our* time comes.

RICHELIEU: Then once we have established stability and order, change will come – for all of you. This I promise. So may the blessings of God the Father, God the Son, and God the Holy Ghost, be with you now and forever more. Amen.

MOB: (*As they shuffle off crossing themselves.*) God save you, Cardinal. You're a good man. An honest man. God save the King. God save the Queen. God save the Prince. God save...everybody.

(*FANÇAN remains. RICHELIEU crosses to Father JOSEPH.*)

RICHELIEU: Well?

JOSEPH: Brilliant. The only difference between you and me, Armand, is that *I* would have meant it.

FANÇAN: (*Calling after the retreating MOB.*) He's betrayed you again!

RICHELIEU: They are almost human. And this time I've betrayed them into believing what I *wish* could happen for them. Even though I know that the only change any of us are ever likely to feel – is the continuous acceleration of pain.

(*Two Musketeers enter. RICHELIEU signals them to arrest FANÇAN.*)

RICHELIEU: Close his mouth.

FANÇAN: You can't do that. You need me. I've got my rights.

RICHELIEU: You have no rights other than those designated by the State. You're far too greedy, my little man. (*To the Musketeers.*) Find him a dungeon where the rotting's slow. Good night, Propaganda.

(*FANÇAN is dragged off. Triumphant drums and trumpets resound, followed by loud cheering.*

LOUIS is carried in, on the shoulders of his Troops. RICHELIEU goes to LOUIS. JOSEPH watches.)

Sire, may I be the first to congratulate you...

LOUIS: You may – because *I* won, Cardinal. I defeated them.

RICHELIEU: Indeed, sire. Now we must work together. War is easy compared to the travails of Peace.

LOUIS: Too late.

RICHELIEU: But, my liege...

LOUIS: Your caution comes too late. I intend to found a new order of ecstatic Conquest and the rebirth of regal pride. Tomorrow I will lead my triumphant army on a Crusade. We will liberate Europe from the Satanic House of Hapsburg; bring unity to our beleaguered neighbours, and even greater glory to France. Don't you understand, Cardinal? Joy is not a mathematical equation. Joy is like

God. It dazzles the eyes and sears the soul. Joy is truly
terrible because it transforms us into angels.

RICHELIEU: Forgive me for stifling your vision, Majesty, but
once we've taken the fortress at Breisach, our borders will
be protected for the first time this century. So we cannot
indulge in further arbitrary conquest until we have first
consolidated the rebuilding of France from within.

LOUIS: National pride has to be rebuilt first, and war is the
only way to ensure that.

JOSEPH: (*Stepping forward.*) I agree. We must rout Spain while
she is retreating.

RICHELIEU: No. We must conserve. Learn to grow.
Constrain the blood.

LOUIS: You may conserve your piles, sir, while I do the
fighting. You see, every time I hear my heart jump, I realise
how transitory we are. Only through sublime fervour can
we transfigure ourselves, and escape from our...
(*LOUIS trails off, fighting for breath.*)

RICHELIEU: From our what, Highness?

LOUIS: From our d-d-dreams. And I would to God that I
could es-escape from my dreams.

RICHELIEU: Is it your mother who haunts you, my King?

LOUIS: I will never forgive you for always being right, even
when you seem to be palpably wrong.

RICHELIEU: Of course! It is Luyens who dominates your
nights, isn't it?

LOUIS: Yes. Even now. Although he is long gone. Luyens was
the only man who genuinely loved me. Cardinal, I promise
you that I will play the tyrant with my blood, if only to
keep my senses awake. Even my beautiful son can never
take the place of Luyens. I have so much life in me, and
yet I have no one to share it with. (*To the Troops.*) Home to
your wives! I'll see you are all well paid.

RICHELIEU: (*Under his breath as he blesses the Troops.*) Yes – in
Heaven.
(*The Troops salute as they pass.*)

LOUIS: (*To RICHELIEU.*) For France's good and yours,
sir, I recommend that you swiftly find me a captivating
distraction to occupy my mind.

RICHELIEU: If I do, you will not attack Spain, sire.

LOUIS: We will see. Well, now I suppose I must visit my wife.
(*LOUIS exits.*)

RICHELIEU: If only he'd take a mistress like a respectable
King.

JOSEPH: Armand!

RICHELIEU: (*Amused.*) Fortunately an acquaintance of mine
has the most lovely son. They call him appropriately Cinq
Mars. He's just what Louis needs. And if God is on my side
– which is highly unlikely – I can also use Cinq Mars to
spy upon the King. That way we will always be one jump
ahead of Louis' tantrums. What have we come to, Joseph?
We're nothing but royal pimps.

JOSEPH: Things could be worse.

RICHELIEU: How?

JOSEPH: You could be impeached and on trial for High
Treason.

RICHELIEU: (*Laughing.*) Yes, I suppose I could.

JOSEPH: Seriously. Even as we speak, the English Parliament
is trying King Charles' First Minister, Sir Thomas
Wentworth, for treason, and only because Wentworth tried
to make Charles into a god – as *you* have made Louis.

RICHELIEU: Yes, and my spies tell me that England is
girding up her greasy loins for an all-out Civil War.

JOSEPH: So the parallel has not escaped you?

RICHELIEU: There is no parallel, Joseph. Our countrymen
are too drunk, too cavalier and far too casual to ever desire
the democratic rigours of a real Parliament. We have no
tradition of freedom, thank Heavens.

JOSEPH: (*Laughing and coughing.*) Yes, there are times when
one is relieved to be French.
(*As his coughing fit convulses him, JOSEPH slumps to his knees.
RICHELIEU supports him.*)

RICHELIEU: Father, I'll call a physician.

JOSEPH: Too late. My heart's…erupting. Stay by me.

RICHELIEU: You're dying.

JOSEPH: Yes. God be praised, I'm about to find out
whether…I can fly.

(*JOSEPH passes out. The lights dim, then come up, then dim, then come up – like a wavering pulse. JOSEPH is in a fever.*) Has Breisach…fallen? Heaven on earth, the sky is filled with wolves… Has Breisach fallen?

(*Slowly MONKS enter, led by an elderly, patriarchal ABBOT. The MONKS are swinging censers and chanting in Latin. Black cowls shroud their faces. Their long shadows slide over the kneeling RICHELIEU and the dying JOSEPH.*)

RICHELIEU: Yes, my friend, Breisach *has* fallen.

JOSEPH: Blessed are the Saints of France. The Lord of Hosts is with us. France is saved!

(*JOSEPH dies. RICHELIEU is frozen in grief. The ABBOT steps forward, clutching a black cross.*)

ABBOT: France has *not* fallen, Cardinal!

RICHELIEU: I know. But it is only a matter of time.

ABBOT: You have just perjured yourself before God.

RICHELIEU: A trivial lie has given Father Joseph some much-deserved peace.

ABBOT: He was a priest, and in his dying there should only have been prayer. But like you, Father Joseph always clung to the temporal.

RICHELIEU: He made France!

ABBOT: Do not hide behind his sins, Your Eminence. Death gapes for you, too. Then you will also see the Face of God, when your soul is blasted to Hell!

RICHELIEU: (*Stripping his sleeve to show his withered skin.*) You don't frighten me, Abbot. I've been dying ever since I squirmed out of my mother's womb. I've lived my entire life in a freezing charnel house.

ABBOT: Pride! You are consumed by pride.

RICHELIEU: Yes. But although I'm rotting as I speak, I still have sufficient fire to set the grave alight, and conflagrate corruption where I find it. And I find it everywhere.

(*The MONKS, with the ABBOT at their head, form a semi-circle around RICHELIEU, as RICHELIEU takes JOSEPH in his arms and kisses him on the mouth.*)

In the cold pit – where I used to keep my mind – I had a love for you, my only friend. Indeed on one occasion, I almost hugged you in my arms, but then aversion forbade

me because I cannot bear to be touched. Yet now I taste
your death on my mouth. And the irony is, Christ has
never kissed me – even with disgust. For I am the Living
Dead. I know that now. I am a crimson vampire thrown
up amongst the wolves. But am I even that? (*Amazed.*) I
feel…GOD…heavy…in my blood.
(*The MONKS lift Father JOSEPH's body. Then they begin to
chant as slowly they carry his corpse into the shadows.*)
MONKS: Beware of Cardinal Pride. Beware Ambition.
Beware of Self Belief; the pathway to Perdition.
Beware of Power. Beware of Time.
Death is always unkind
To the jewelled mind.
Death is the Ringer, and Death is the Bell,
And all there is left before you ascend the stair
That winds down to the bowels of Hell
Is guilt, contrition, and unanswered prayer.
(*RICHELIEU walks behind the funeral cortège locked in
prayer.*
*LOUIS enters with CINQ MARS, his new favourite. The KING
makes no effort to speak to the grief-stricken RICHELIEU.
CINQ MARS, who bears a distinct resemblance to LUYENS, is
obviously bored with LOUIS. He is an extraordinarily handsome
youth in his early twenties. Bright curls frame his girlish face.*)
CINQ MARS: (*Yawning.*) Priests are dropping like flies these
days, thank Christ.
LOUIS: Cinq Mars, where have you been since yesterday?
CINQ MARS: Whoring. You should've come along. It was
highly stimulating. Mademoiselle de Treville knows more
libidinous tricks than Jezebel.
LOUIS: Why must you offend me so?
CINQ MARS: (*Yawning and playing with his curls.*) Can't you
do something about your complexion, Louis? It's like a
dried-up squash.
LOUIS: Don't mock me, my dear. I'm so obsessed by you that
whenever you desert me, I am always ill.

CINQ MARS: Hm! You're just like the Cardinal. He's habitually twittering on about the size of his piles. Still, he's not long for this life.

LOUIS: Why do you say that?

CINQ MARS: Richelieu is a traitor to you, Louis.

LOUIS: His Eminence? Nonsense.

CINQ MARS: (*Touching LOUIS' face.*) I'll do anything you wish.

LOUIS: Anything?

CINQ MARS: Yes, anything. If you will just present me with a platter – that has that traitor's head on it.

LOUIS: What new prank is this, 'Salome'?

CINQ MARS: If Richelieu is not a traitor, why did he force me to spy on you?

LOUIS: Oh come now, Luyens, he gave no... (*Realising what he has said.*) I meant, of course, Cinq Mars!

CINQ MARS: No, Louis, you meant 'Luyens'. But I don't care what you meant, on condition that you have that seditious priest beheaded.

LOUIS: On what charge? Where is the proof of his supposed treachery?

CINQ MARS: Who persuaded you to banish your mother and your brother? Who all but lost you the war against Spain?

LOUIS: Enough, boy!

CINQ MARS: Also there are growing rumours that your fungoid Cardinal has made a secret treaty with Spain, in order to usurp your throne.

LOUIS: I'll not believe it!

CINQ MARS: Do you wish to share the same fate as your sister's husband, Charles of England, who is now up to his perfumed ruffs in a bloody civil war? What's worse, Charlie is losing, Louis! The Puritan Anti-Christ, Cromwell, is marching his Ironsides through the King's tarnished crown. As Cardinal Richelieu will march his musketeers through *yours,* if you don't...
(*RICHELIEU is carried into view by Musketeers on an ornate scarlet bed. The Cardinal is very ill, clutching a document.*)

RICHELIEU: If he doesn't 'do' what, monsieur?

LOUIS: How dare you come into my presence without my permission?

RICHELIEU: Sire…

LOUIS: I hear you're dying.

RICHELIEU: That's not why I came.

LOUIS: Oh.

(*RICHELIEU bows his head in deference – as the QUEEN MOTHER enters. She is shrivelled in appearance but still possesses the remnants of regality, despite the blank look in her eyes.*)

Mother…what brings you to Paris?

QUEEN MOTHER: (*To RICHELIEU.*) I understand that you are the Cardinal, who was kind enough to…

LOUIS: Mother, I am the King now, and I…

(*LOUIS trails off as the QUEEN MOTHER looks at him blankly.*)

QUEEN MOTHER: I am most truly sorry, sir, but I did not see you. (*Indicating RICHELIEU.*) This…gentleman kindly allowed his musketeers to escort me to Paris, but I couldn't…find the grave…

LOUIS: (*Bewildered, to RICHELIEU.*) Whose grave?

RICHELIEU: I don't know, sire.

QUEEN MOTHER: (*To LOUIS.*) Do you mind, sir, if I…? (*She sits.*) Thank you. Mm… (*Indicating the surroundings.*) It's very grey. Even the brocade. When I ruled here, we had such…voluptuous tapestries…crystalline chandeliers. (*Laughing.*) I even had silver eyebrows.

LOUIS: Mother, for pity's sake…

QUEEN MOTHER: (*Overriding him, to RICHELIEU.*) I had Condé shot, you know. The clowns tore his face off. His blood was somehow different to what I had imagined… (*Turning to LOUIS.*) I do know you, sir.

LOUIS: Of course you do. I am your son, m-m-mother. (*Hugging his mother who remains motionless.*) Forgive me, please, for-forgive me. (*Stuttering badly.*) When I ba-banished you, I was de-deceiving my-myself.

QUEEN MOTHER: You *were* my son. In that other age. I'm glad they starch your ruffs properly now. They used to be yellow and frayed.

LOUIS: Are you ill, Mother? Your heart…

QUEEN MOTHER: No. I am dead, sir. Hadn't you noticed?

LOUIS: Oh God, don't pretend. I haven't the strength for your games.

QUEEN MOTHER: Do *you* know where his grave is, sir?

LOUIS: Father's?

QUEEN MOTHER: (*Shaking her head.*) My friend's.

LOUIS: Listen, Mother, there is something for years I've tried to tell you…

QUEEN MOTHER: Condé was a good man. And his charm…

LOUIS: For Christ's sake, can't you see that we've run out of time? Mother, I lo-lo-love…

QUEEN MOTHER: (*Overriding him.*) No, love is a gift, sir. And as a family, it has totally eluded us…so perhaps there is no grave.
(*The QUEEN MOTHER exits.*)

LOUIS: Mother, you can return to Court if only…

RICHELIEU: (*Interrupting.*) Let her go, Majesty.

CINQ MARS: No one asked you to wag your impertinent tongue, priest!

RICHELIEU: (*To LOUIS.*) I know what is twisting you. When my mother died, I…

LOUIS: (*Overriding him.*) Can you never progress beyond y-y-your mother, *your* l-life, *your* Fr-France? (*To CINQ MARS and RICHELIEU.*) I love her more than b-both of you combined are ca-capable of love! Yes, my mother is more to me than you, Cinq Mars, or Luyens, or my wife. And now she is beyond understanding, so she will never know what I… (*To RICHELIEU.*) And I banished her for you! God damn your soul, Cardinal.

RICHELIEU: (*Fighting for breath.*) Majesty, your love is… and must…continue to be solely for *France.* It is all we have left.

LOUIS: Too late. You taught me the other way, remember.
(*RICHELIEU hands LOUIS the document that he is holding.*)

RICHELIEU: Read.

LOUIS: How can you ask me to read at such a time?

RICHELIEU: Now! (*Coughing.*) I command you.

LOUIS: (*Perusing the contents rapidly.*) Were you not in your
death throes, Monseigneur, I'd… (*Breaking off as he continues
to read.*) A forgery. This is a forgery!

RICHELIEU: It is the truth.

LOUIS: I beg you, Eminence, to say this is not so.

RICHELIEU: You know it is.

LOUIS: You have shattered what is left of my world.

RICHELIEU: Be merciless, Louis. And now.

CINQ MARS: (*Yawning.*) What's all this nonsense about?

LOUIS: Y-you!

CINQ MARS: I don't understand.

LOUIS: It is *you*, not the Cardinal, who has made a treasonous
pact with Spain, to usurp the Cardinal! You, my dearest
friend. Oh sweet Jesus!

CINQ MARS: (*Laughing.*) What if I have, sire? The Cardinal
is not the King, so there is no treason involved.

LOUIS: (*To the CAPTAIN of the Musketeers.*) Captain, arrest this
traitor. Have him tried. Find him guilty. Then axe him, and
bring me his head on a platter!
(*CINQ MARS squirms out of the CAPTAIN's grip, and grovels
at LOUIS' feet.*)

CINQ MARS: My King, believe me! On my mother's bones,
I swear that I only plotted against His Eminence, never
against you! How could I? I loved you more than my own
life. You know this!

LOUIS: Don't you understand yet, boy? I *am* the Cardinal
– as the Cardinal is me!

CINQ MARS: Anything, sire, I will do anything if you will
only forgive me.

LOUIS: As a man, Cinq Mars, I am helpless before your
youth and your beauty.

CINQ MARS: Then free me, Louis, and as God's my witness,
I will do anything…

LOUIS: (*Cutting him.*) But as the King of France who – in
your own words – has callously banished his own mother
and his own brother, and who has learnt his implacable
wisdom from the man who makes his skin crawl; I do not
know you, Cinq Mars, I cannot hear you, and I will not see

you. Except as a degenerate traitor to me and mine, who must be executed now. Remove him, Captain.

(*CINQ MARS is dragged off whimpering.*
The Puppet Court enters like stilted shadows. Then the MOB,
dressed like statues, surround the Cardinal's bed. Picture frames
are lowered in front of some of the MOB, transforming them
into portraits. They become part of RICHELIEU's legendary
art collection. Both COURT and MOB freeze but there are
subliminal sniggers.
A MESSENGER enters.)

My mother…?

(*The MESSENGER inclines his head. LOUIS dismisses the*
MESSENGER who exits.)

(*To RICHELIEU.*) Are you satisfied at last – now that we are equal; mother for mother? Now that you have finally reduced my life to your own desolation. All I ever wanted was a mother to love me, and a faithful friend. If I had any gift at all, it was for friendship. But now – like you – I am totally alone. (*Watching RICHELIEU as the CARDINAL fights for breath.*) Are you frightened of going into the dark?

RICHELIEU: That, if I may say so, sire, is a matter between me and my Maker. Anyway, it's a personal question, and therefore unimportant.

LOUIS: Shall I redress your pillows?

RICHELIEU: No, listen, sire! We have made an uneasy peace with Spain, but it is relatively permanent. And we have planted the Royal Tree in good soil. The roots are webbed in blood, I know, and there is too much incense in the leaves. But the Tree is budding now. I feel the feathered green, swelling against my cheek. The buds are like…moist crystals. They hurt. Birth is coming. Rebirth! And your son will be the Sun King who will bring the blossoms into full fragrance. And soon. Very soon!

LOUIS: Saviour of F-France – my friend.

(*He extends his hand to RICHELIEU who kisses it.*)

RICHELIEU: If only you could mean that – my King.

(*There is the sound of the executioner's drum.*

CINQ MARS is brought in, blindfolded. The EXECUTIONER follows. The Puppet Court and the Statues giggle in anticipation. LOUIS moves to the Statues.
CINQ MARS is led directly behind the head of RICHELIEU's bed. CINQ MARS kneels. We can no longer see him.
The afternoon bleeds into a viridian twilight. The EXECUTIONER is silhouetted against the setting sun. He seems to be looking down on RICHELIEU. The sniggering of the Statues and the Court increases. The drumming stops.
QUEEN ANNE appears. She takes LOUIS' arm. They also snigger together as they wander between the Statues.)

ANNE: (*Pointing to an obscene Statue.*) I think I'll have that erected in my boudoir. It might give you some inspiration, dear.

LOUIS: (*Laughing.*) Yes, the Cardinal certainly had – has such exquisite taste. (*Kissing her hand.*) Your fingers are still as cold as on our wedding night.

RICHELIEU: (*Suddenly shouting.*) Why are they sniggering? (*The sniggering has now become full-blown laughter. RICHELIEU tries to block his ears.*) Captain! (*As ANNE and LOUIS continue to giggle their way around RICHELIEU's gallery, the CAPTAIN crosses to RICHELIEU.*) Captain, stop their infernal laughter!

CAPTAIN: No one's laughing, Monseigneur.

RICHELIEU: You dare to laugh in my face. (*The CAPTAIN bows and retires. RICHELIEU clasps his hands in prayer.*) Unmerciful Christ, here I am – waiting…content to subject myself to what is coming. I have sculpted France out of the veined marble, and given it the piercing features of *my* death mask for the next hundred years. But what is that in the sweep of Eternity? Especially when I wanted to *love* more than anything in the world, more than life itself. But the Law came before everything. Even before the promptings of my heart. Yes…and now I taste death in my mouth. There was my mother's milk, and then there was this taste. Always this taste. I was a little child. At least I think I was. And now I am an old, dying man. There has been little in between. Yet although I'm rotting as I pray to You, Lord, my mind is still the sharpest blade in France

– but now it has outworn its sheath, my curdled body. Father Joseph…Father…were you afraid when the coffin full of sand opened and…? Oh Lord, please take into Your Kingdom. Enough is enough.

(*The ABBOT enters and kneels beside RICHELIEU's bed.*)

ABBOT: (*Whispering.*) My son, do you wish to make a confession of your innumerable sins?

RICHELIEU: (*Laughing painfully.*) I've already confessed them, Father.

ABBOT: Do you forgive your enemies?

RICHELIEU: How can I? When I have none. None but the enemies of the State.

ABBOT: Beware of the illusion of pride, my son.

RICHELIEU: God will forgive me. Without me…Revolution and Chaos… And with me… Well, I tried…I tried.

(*Suddenly the laughter which had stopped, erupts again into a braying crescendo.*

The CAPTAIN gives the EXECUTIONER the signal. The axe scythes down.

RICHELIEU slumps back on his pillow, as if he has been beheaded. The moment the axe disappears below the bed, the laughter ceases abruptly – as if it was all in RICHELIEU's head.

ANNE pauses before the body of RICHELIEU.)

ANNE: (*To LOUIS.*) Just look at his face, my dear.

LOUIS: So waxen. (*Touching RICHELIEU.*) And infinitely cold.

ANNE: I still can't believe that 'It' is dead. The disease in the red robe is no more. Now don't scowl, Louis, and admit that you are relieved.

LOUIS: No. Richelieu gave his soul for France.

ANNE: Well, now he has lost both!

LOUIS: Anne, I would like to be alone with my friend for a moment.

ANNE: What hypocrisy. You hated him.

LOUIS: In a way, and yet in a way I… Please!

ANNE: Still, he bequeathed you most of his treasures, and the Palais Cardinal. So I suppose it was almost worth it.

(*ANNE exits as the MONKS, the Puppet Court and the Mob converge on the kneeling ABBOT, who is still at the foot of RICHELIEU's bed. LOUIS points at the Cardinal's corpse.*)

LOUIS: I'm free! France is free! Freedom!

(*Everyone takes up the chant of 'Freedom'! The MONKS start to sing, drowning the chanting.*)

MONKS: The swamp in the air,
And the bat's despair.
Death is the Ringer, and Death is the Bell.
If there is God,
Then there is Hell.
If there is not,
Then the Cardinal's well.
But there *is* God,
And there *is* Hell,
And Richelieu, like Satan, was proud and he fell
Down into the bowels of Hell.
For Death is the Ringer, and Death is the Bell.
But now you are dead, we wish you well.
Fare...well... Fare...well...

(*The MOB, COURT and MONKS are now only wraiths in the darkness. Spotlit LOUIS kneels beside the Cardinal.*)

LOUIS: Oh my ravaged Cardinal, did we achieve anything together? Only God knows. Now I must rule alone. But I've so very little feeling left. And certainly no sense of what is coming. With you gone...Armand...all I have to hold on to...are the rag-ends of prayer. Christ forgive you Armand – because you *knew* what you did. Christ forgive me. Forgive us all our mediocrity. Good night...Your Eminence.

The End.

PRINCE OF TRAITORS

*'Talleyrand, that prince of traitors, is nothing
but shit in a silk stocking'*
Napoleon Bonaparte

'I never betray anyone until they betray themselves'
Talleyrand

'Treachery is noble when its target is tyranny'
Racine

Author's Note

Prince of Traitors is a theatrical epic for six actors. Only the actors portraying Talleyrand and Napoleon have no other roles.

The set consists mainly of coat stands and tailors' dummies, on which there are draped numerous articles of costuming: for example, Napoleon's greatcoat, King Louis' cloak etc. During the play's action, the actors take the appropriate hat/coat/cloak/ sword/parasol from the coat stands/tailors' dummies to 'become' the various characters they are portraying. Each character's 'transformation' is achieved by the actor using only the stylised minimum in the way of costumes or props. The actors will wear basic, black period costumes, to which they will add the appropriate sash, cloak etc.

Characters

1

TALLEYRAND

2

THE VALET / MAJOR DOMO / SURGEON

3

NAPOLEON

4

TALLEYRAND'S FATHER / ROBESPIERRE /
BISHOP OF BORDEAUX / OUVRARD / THE POPE /
MARQUIS CAULAINCOURT / TSAR ALEXANDER

5

LOUIS XVI / ARTOIS / COACHMAN / COUNT EDMOND /
BARRAS / MARAT / ABBÉ DUPANLOUP

6

TALLEYRAND'S MOTHER / GERMAINE / DORETHEA

Prince of Traitors was broadcast by the BBC under the title of *Talleyrand, Prince Of Traitors* on 16 October 1978, with the following cast:

TALLEYRAND, Jerome Willis

NAPOLEON, Ian Hogg

DORETHEA, Virginia Stride

GERMAINE DE STAEL, Elizabeth Spriggs

CATHERINE DE GRAND, Catherine Kessler

COUNT ARTOIS, Michael Deacon

BARRAS, Geoffrey Matthews

BISHOP OF BORDEAUX, Hugh Dickson

ABBÉ DUPANLOUP, Manning Wilson

COUNT EDMOND, Terry Molloy

Director, Michael Rolfe

PART ONE

A circle of light reveals OLD TALLEYRAND, in his night cap and shirt, lying on a chaise longue in his candlelit study. He is very weak and in pain. Sitting beside him, and holding his frail hand, is DORETHEA, Duchess de Dino, his beautiful young mistress. The cadaverous figure of Abbé DUPANLOUP hovers in the shadows.

DUPANLOUP: Do you understand the dire consequences if you do not sign, Monsieur Le Prince?

TALLEYRAND: I believe so, Abbé Dupanloup. (*Smiling.*) Considering, in all probability, I shall be dead in a very few hours.

DORETHEA: Then, in mercy's name, Charles Maurice, sign now, so you can once again be enfolded in the forgiving arms of Christ's Beloved Church.

TALLEYRAND: I will sign, dearest.

DUPANLOUP: The Lord be praised!

TALLEYRAND: Between five and six o'clock.

DUPANLOUP: Five and six o'clock tonight?

TALLEYRAND: (*Amused.*) No. Tomorrow morning.

DUPANLOUP: But by tomorrow morning, Monsieur Le Prince, as you have aptly observed, you may very well be dead.

TALLEYRAND: Nevertheless...
As dawn suffuses the roofs with its cold fire,
I will sign my way to Heaven, and then expire.

DORETHEA: How can you make up asinine rhymes, my dear, when you might expire long before then?

TALLEYRAND: (*Gently mocking.*) I thought you were the one with the gift of faith, dearest. Please give me a little water to moisten my lips.

DORETHEA: You are truly impossible, Charles Maurice.

TALLEYRAND: I sincerely hope so.

DUPANLOUP: You must sign now, Monsieur Le Prince, or you will be damned for all eternity.

TALLEYRAND: Between five and six tomorrow is early enough.

DORETHEA: The Abbé is right, my love. Just because you have kept Robespierre, Napoleon and all the Bourbon Kings waiting upon your whims, surely you do not believe you can keep God in suspense as well?

TALLEYRAND: One must never be in a hurry, beloved. Even for the Almighty.

DUPANLOUP: Monsieur Le Prince!

TALLEYRAND: It is hysterical precipitation that leads to unsound policy, Monsieur L'Abbé. That's why I have always admired the English genius for filibustering. If only we French could simply talk, instead of act. Every apparently-wasted word could save a thousand lives. Remember, it is the zealots of this world who are always in a frenzied hurry. First they tyrannise their own souls, then they tyrannise the earth.

DUPANLOUP: Spare us your philosophy, I beseech you, and sign for your soul's sake.

TALLEYRAND: I will sign. But not until tomorrow morning. Between six and seven. So we had best pray that the Almighty keeps time as well as my clock.

(*TALLEYRAND slumps back on the chaise longue. There is the amplified sound of the ticking of a clock as TALLEYRAND, DORETHEA and DUPANLOUP are enveloped in darkness. The ticking clock grows in volume.*

A circle of light illuminates TALLEYRAND who is still asleep – but he is now in his high-backed chair. He is wearing a voluminous dressing gown. He whimpers in his sleep.

The lights come up to reveal a small desk on which there are various items, including bottles of wine and brandy, glasses, ink – and a telephone, and an electric torch!

In the shadows, there are two hat stands, with various hats, including Napoleon's and Germaine de Stael's, plus several wigs.

Overlooking TALLEYRAND and his furniture are a dozen Tailors' Dummies; dressed respectively, as Napoleon, Germaine, Louis XVI, Marat, Robespierre etc.

TALLEYRAND is snoring raggedly.

*The clock's ticking fades as Talleyrand's VALET appears, carrying
– of all things – a tape recorder. The VALET places the tape
recorder on a side table, and switches it on.*

*A random selection of sounds emerge from the tape recorder: a
nightingale, followed by plaintive wind over water. This, in
turn, is drowned by the sounds of a raging blizzard. Then the
blizzard is submerged beneath the roar of a thousand cannons
and the full welter of war.*

*The cacophony of sounds is amplified over the speaker system
in the theatre.*

*Still asleep, TALLEYRAND covers his ears, trying to blot out
the din.*

*Then the sounds of war are drowned by Napoleon's Coronation
Anthem which is gloriously deafening. The Anthem thunders to
a climax.*)

NAPOLEON'S SUBJECTS: (*On tape.*) God save Napoleon
the First, Emperor of all the French!

TALLEYRAND: (*In his sleep.*) No, no, no!

VALET: (*Smiling maliciously as he switches the tape recorder off.*)
Yes, yes, yes.

TALLEYRAND: (*Fighting his way awake.*) Am I dead? Or
dying? Or what?

VALET: (*Under his breath.*) God knows.

TALLEYRAND: Yes, of course. I must be dreaming this.

VALET: (*Again under his breath.*) Wouldn't be surprised. (*To the
audience.*) Working for him's always been a nightmare.

TALLEYRAND: Oh it's you, Pierre. I thought…

VALET: …That you were dead, Monsieur Le Prince?

TALLEYRAND: Well, it is conceivable. When I fell asleep
I was sure I was dying. So it is more than likely that I am
still dying. This has to be a dream. Yet I cannot afford
to dream my last moments away, when there are still so
many aspects of my 'Defence To Posterity' that I have not
completed. In the few hours I have left, it is imperative
that I finish my Defence. (*Indicating the wine bottle.*) Pour me
some wine, Pierre, for mercy's sake. Then perhaps I will
wake up. My mouth is filled with the taste of dead frogs.
(*Gulping down the wine.*) Why are my thoughts so muddled?
But is it surprising? One moment I am falling asleep

because I am dying. The next moment I am dreaming that I'm in a different sleep. So I must be dreaming a dream *within* a dream, because I can't remember what my original dream in my original sleep was! And if you can understand that, then you can understand anything.

VALET: (*Trying to hide his boredom.*) Oh everyone knows what you were dreaming of when you woke up just now, Monseigneur.

TALLEYRAND: Really?

VALET: (*Smirking and stifling a yawn.*) Yes, you always dream of your Presidential Oration to the Nation, at the end of the Napoleonic Wars.

TALLEYRAND: What if I do? One can never dream too much of a good thing. Well, turn the tape recorder on. You know there is nothing I adore more than listening to myself in my prime.

(*The VALET switches on the tape recorder.*)

YOUNG TALLEYRAND: (*On tape.*) People of France, on this auspicious day, in the year of Our Lord Eighteen Hundred and Fourteen, I, Charles Maurice de Talleyrand-Perigord, do herewith proclaim the immediate Deposition of the tyrannical despot, Napoleon Bonaparte. And in Bonaparte's stead, I invite Louis XVIII of the House of Bourbon to ascend the throne of France, on condition that the said Louis is willing to rule as a Constitutional Monarch in the English tradition.

TALLEYRAND: (*To the VALET.*) Enough! (*The VALET switches the tape recorder off as TALLEYRAND addresses the audience.*) Yes, you Judges in the Future, you heard correctly. I did say that Louis 'must rule as a constitutional monarch in the English tradition'. But then I am the only Frenchman, other than Voltaire, who has ever been an avowed Anglophile. And I'm the only Frenchman who the Duke of Wellington has actually praised in the House of Commons. (*Smiling.*) No wonder my fellow countrymen call me 'The Prince of Traitors'. But then I have always prided myself in being somewhat perverse in my tastes. (*Picking up the telephone on his desk.*) Hence my anachronistic penchant for telephones in my dreams. (*Picking up a torch.*) And torches with Long Life batteries. Not to mention tape-recorders. Fortunately this gift of prescience happens only in my dream world. Because if such a dangerous tool as a tape recorder was available to me in my waking hours, undoubtedly I would have been indiscreet enough to confide to it all my inmost thoughts. Which could prove to be disastrous. (*With a mischievous smile.*) As it will prove to be catastrophic for a certain American president in the future, when he has an horrendous problem with…Water and a Gate. Oh don't worry about Pierre smugly observing me from the shadows. When I go into my futuristic mode, he thinks I am rambling in my sleep. And he may very well be right.

(*TALLEYRAND shivers and slumps back in his chair.*)

But all I know is that a moment ago – in my dream within a dream – I was triumphantly telling the nation of my crucial role in the deposition of that despot, Napoleon. And the next moment – instead of being surrounded by my friends and the cheering crowd, I was being howled at by the mindless mob. Worse, I was kneeling on a blood-stained scaffold, staring up at the smiling lips of Madame Guillotine, and I was encircled by my numerous enemies. They were all there: King Louis and Queen Marie Antoinette, Robespierre, Marat, and His Holiness the Pope.

VALET: They're always there, Monseigneur. There or thereabouts.

TALLEYRAND: Even my numerous cast-off mistresses were jeering me.

VALET: Yes, even I've found that cast-off mistresses can become a bit of a problem.

TALLEYRAND: With your duties here, I wouldn't have thought that you had time for mistresses.

VALET: I haven't. That's why most of 'em have cast 'emselves off.

TALLEYRAND: (*To the audience.*) Only the Emperor was absent from my dream. But all the other revenants unsheathed their claws at me.

(*Two FIGURES in black materialise from the shadows and point accusing fingers at TALLEYRAND. Their voices are amplified and the effect is nighmarish.*)

FIGURES: (*In chorus.*) Talleyrand, the Great Betrayer, has finally betrayed himself!

(*TALLEYRAND covers his ears as the FIGURES raise their right arms above their heads.*)

TALLEYRAND: Then before I could defend myself, the guillotine's hissing blade above me swooped down like the Grim Reaper's scythe!

(*The FIGURES' arms slice down like guillotine blades.*)

And I cringed awake…back into this nether world. Wine, Pierre, more wine!

(*The VALET pours TALLEYRAND more wine as the FIGURES retreat into the darkness.*)

Why should I take such dreams to heart? But then again, why not? Every weed that burgeons in our sleep is a fungoid reflection of the sleeper. But why do most of my fellow countrymen call me the Great Betrayer, when I have done so much for the betterment of humanity? (*To the audience.*) That is why You – who are my Jury in the Future – are my only hope of gaining political redemption. So judge me now – but judge me fairly because I only have a very little time in which to convince you of my innocence. You must decide whether to acquit me because of my considerable humanitarian achievements, or whether to condemn me, as all my enemies do, because of what they call my innumerable 'betrayals'? The reason my enemies hate me is because I succeeded, while they all failed. There is no greater crime under the sun than being successful. And, equally, there is no greater tyranny under the sun than that exerted by the Critically Mediocre over the Creatively Strong. But then, had I not had the good fortune to fall off a clothes' chest when I was four years old, perhaps history would have also passed *me* by. You see, when I fell, I wrenched my foot irrevocably thus… (*Indicating his club foot.*) …and so I acquired this excellent horse's hoof. But my parents were not amused to discover that they now had a lame colt as their heir, so they promptly disinherited me in favour of my younger brother. Then they cantered me off to the country to be brought up by a gaggle of washerwomen. What a loveless, desolate childhood I had, hobbling through the snow, with the freezing sky above me, dead trees all around me – and nowhere to warm my mind. (*Indicating his empty wine glass.*) Refill, refill.

(*Stifling a yawn, the VALET obeys.*)

When I was ten, my parents, who had never visited me in the interim, suddenly remembered that they had a two-legged colt with a twisted hoof.

(*TALLEYRAND'S MOTHER and FATHER materialise out of the darkness.*)

FATHER: (*To the MOTHER, in gruff military tones.*) Nuthin' for it, wife. Since his lame foot makes Charles Maurice incapable of servin' in the Army, he must enter Holy Orders.

MOTHER: Oh, husband, surely there is some other…?

FATHER: (*Overriding her.*) Pointless carpin', m'dear. No other career is open to a youth of Charles Maurice's rank.

MOTHER: But, husband…

FATHER: 'But' me no 'buts', wife. He's to be a carrion-crow priest.

TALLEYRAND: Thenceforward every dawn this little cripple grazed his knees on the icy flagstones of the Chapel at Saint Suplice in the city of Rheims. Every dawn he stared into the sightless eyes of the crucified King of the World. But as my youth dissolved in incense and prayers, I made an important discovery that irrevocably changed my attitude to the Church. Like the great Cardinal Richelieu before me, I realised I could ride bare-back on the Church's shoulders. Then, when the time was propitious – like Richelieu – I was determined to vault into the saddle of real power. Thus I embraced my sacred profession in public, so that I could follow my profane ambition in private. Although being a crippled cleric did have its disadvantages in the beginning. (*Chuckling.*) Soon after I was made Bishop of Autun, I distinctly remember catching my cloven hoof in my cassock during Mass. No wonder the congregation took me for the Devil himself. And, of course, later, so did Louis the Sixteenth. Indeed I well remember His Majesty summoning me into his august presence one autumnal morning.

(*The VALET picks up the torch from the table and illuminates the face of LOUIS XVI who emerges out of the darkness.*)

LOUIS: You are the Devil himself, are you not, Bishop? So cease this pontificating, and face your accusers. Queen Marie Antoinette and I are tired of your prevarications.

TALLEYRAND: (*To the audience.*) Not as tired as I was of his peevish accusations. Mind, my mistress at the time, the seductive Germaine de Stael, was equally probing with her tongue. (*Suggestively.*) And I mean everywhere.

(*The VALET flickers the torch beam from LOUIS' face onto GERMAINE's face who materialises from behind the appropriate Tailors' Dummy.*)

GERMAINE: Yes, we're all here, you serpentine seducer. All your mistresses have come to charge you with the Betrayal of Love.

TALLEYRAND: (*Kissing her hand.*) Ah Germaine, Germaine, how enchanting of you to remember me from beyond the grave. I trust you are finding Hell to your liking.

(*The torch goes out on GERMAINE.*)

Periodically the ghosts of Robespierre and Marat also come and torment me.

(*The VALET, now with two torches, illuminates the head of ROBESPIERRE who is like a malevolent Tweedle Dum. Simultaneously the VALET illuminates his own face with the other torch; as the VALET becomes a Tweedle Dee-type MARAT.*)

ROBESPIERRE: Talleyrand!

TALLEYRAND: Yes, 'Citizen' Robespierre?

ROBESPIERRE: You are a traitor to the Revolution. So defend yourself against our charges.

TALLEYRAND: I am just about to, Citizen Robespierre.

MARAT: We should have chopped your head into the basket while we had a chance!

TALLEYRAND: It would have taken a better 'citizen' than you, Citizen Marat.

(*The lights go out on ROBESPIERRE and MARAT.*)

(*To the VALET.*) Congratulations, Pierre. No, no, truly. I would like to pay you the dubious compliment of being the spitting image of that leprous toad, Marat.

VALET: In dreams, Monseigneur, even the impossible is possible.

TALLEYRAND: (*In his own world.*) And, of course, I am forever stalked by the Emperor of Spectres, who is never far away.

(*NAPOLEON, torchlit, emerges from behind the appropriate dummy.*)

NAPOLEON: You betrayed my Empire, Talleyrand. You destroyed my glory. In God's name, why?

TALLEYRAND: Your Imperial Majesty, will you never cease haunting me? Every night of my life you besiege my dreams, accusing me of... (*Screaming out.*) '...HIGH TREASON!' But you can accuse me to kingdom come, and I will always outface you. For, in truth, it is not *I* who is guilty – but *you*. *All* of you! (*Pointing at his accusers who are torchlit by turn.*) Yes, it is you, King Louis, and you, Germaine, and you, Citizens Robespierre and Marat, and, above all, you, Napoleon Bonaparte, who should be on trial for High Treason tonight. I will prove – now and for all time – that I never betrayed anyone. Including you, my Emperor. Or any regime, including your monarchy, Louis. Or your Revolution, Robespierre. I never betrayed you – until *you* betrayed *yourselves!* From the outset, I made it clear – (*To NAPOLEON.*) – to anyone who would listen – that Liberty, Order and Peace were the prime goals of all true statesmen. Then you all, in turn, betrayed the implicit trust the French people had bestowed upon you. Instead of becoming Liberators, you became Tyrants. So I had no choice but to embody Racine's famous dictum: 'Treachery is noble when its target is Tyranny.'

(*The VALET switches on the tape recorder, and the night is filled with amplified voices screaming; 'Traitor! Traitor!'.*)

You may well scream 'Traitor' at me – because it is true;
I did use every means at my disposal to pull you tyrants
from your tarnished thrones. Then I cast you all into the
sea of ignominy. And you sank, and I survived.
(*The shouting subsides. Simultaneously, TALLEYRAND slumps
into a chair, exhausted.*)
For eighty-three years I have survived.

NAPOLEON: Indeed you have, but at what cost to others,
you charlatan?

TALLEYRAND: (*Blowing his nose.*) I may be many things,
Your Majesty, but I am no charlatan.

NAPOLEON: And I suppose those are not crocodile tears,
either.

TALLEYRAND: (*Blowing his nose even more vigorously.*)
Certainly not. I'm far too old for such a damp activity.

NAPOLEON: (*Laughing as he disappears into the shadows.*) Are
you indeed? But your time is shorter than you think. And
all that is waiting for you is endless perdition, you club-
footed traitor.
(*TALLEYRAND pushes himself to his feet.*)

TALLEYRAND: (*To the VALET.*) Pierre, assist me. I must
complete my Defence to Posterity with the little time and
strength that I have left.
(*The VALET removes TALLEYRAND's dressing gown, to reveal
that TALLEYRAND is wearing the elegant black costume of the
pre-Revolutionary period. TALLEYRAND assumes the physical
and vocal vigour of the YOUNG TALLEYRAND.*)
(*To the audience.*) I can still remember, with a dull sadness,
the very first time that I was accused of treason. I was
a mere thirty-five years old, and already the Bishop of
Autun. In which capacity I savoured more mistresses
than there are king-cups on the lake at Versailles. But I
digress. Or do I? In that shimmering summer of 1789,
the French nobility was equally rapacious. Decades of
royal tyranny and fiscal insanity had driven France to the
brink of starvation and bankruptcy. The Parisian mob,
incited by Revolutionaries like Marat and Robespierre,
went on the rampage. So I, being by nature a moderate

constitutionalist, decided to go to the King with a stratagem
that would save both the Monarchy and the French people
from the unspeakable terrors of an imminent Revolution.
(*The VALET hands TALLEYRAND his hat and cane.*)
After much petitioning, I was granted an audience at the
Royal residence at Marry with the King's younger brother,
the Count Artois – who was, as always, unbecomingly
swathed in peacock-blue.
(*Count ARTOIS, with a blue velvet cloak and a matching blue-
feathered hat, saunters into view. ARTOIS, who speaks with an
affected drawl, sits in the high-backed chair.*)

ARTOIS: You may approach the throne, sir.
(*TALLEYRAND limps forward, leaning on his cane. He removes
his hat with a flourish and bows.*)
Mm… Monsieur de Talleyrand, I see that my friend was
right about you.

TALLEYRAND: That a member of the Royal Household
is right about anything in these feverish times, Count, is
miraculous.

ARTOIS: However my friend was less struck by your
good features than by your habitual posture of serene
malevolence. Indeed he said it was as if he was looking
at the head of an angel, animated by the spirit of Satan
himself.

TALLEYRAND: (*Smiling and bowing again.*) Your Highness is
too kind.
(*The VALET switches on the tape recorder that emits the noise
of a howling mob.*)

ARTOIS: Indeed I am, because my friend also informed
me that you have a novel suggestion that will placate…
(*Indicating the shouting.*) …the rabid mob out there.
Apparently you believe that my royal brother, the King,
should instantly divest himself of his Divine Right to rule.
(*With petulant fury.*) And instead he should dwindle into a
constitutional monarch after the accursed English model!
You also advocate that we should create a two-tiered
Parliament, which, again, would be a French version of the
English Parliament.

TALLEYRAND: Yes, Highness, but…

ARTOIS: (*Cutting him.*) Do not presume to defend yourself, priest. There is no danger great enough to make any Frenchman want to espouse anything that is English. Indeed you should count yourself fortunate that you are able to leave my presence with your prating tongue intact, you seditious traitor!

TALLEYRAND: It is better, Your Highness, that I should be unfairly accounted an 'English' traitor than that our King should share the same gory fate as the English King, Charles the First. With Citizens Robespierre and Marat acting as our French Oliver Cromwells.

ARTOIS: Monsieur, how dare you mention such…?

TALLEYRAND: (*Overriding him.*) I only invoke the name of Cromwell to warn you of your imminent danger. So it were best you forget your regal dignity for once, and stare into the blood-shot eyes of reality.

ARTOIS: (*Indicating the howling mob.*) Reality's for peasants, not for kings.

TALLEYRAND: (*Pointing with his cane.*) Yes, and because you despise the peasants, the people of France are starving.

ARTOIS: Enough, Talleyrand…

TALLEYRAND: No, Highness, you will listen. If the coming harvest is as calamitous as the last, Robespierre, Marat, Saint Just and the other revolutionaries will incite that mob into roaring violence. Then they'll tear down these palace walls, and use their scythes to hack off your heads.

ARTOIS: (*Laughing.*) Madness, you spout nothing but madness.

TALLEYRAND: And once the torrent of ignorance and hatred is in full flood, it will be impossible for His Majesty to stem or reverse it. (*Kneeling.*) So I beg you, Highness, to persuade the King to immediately become a constitutional monarch, and to set up a Parliamentary system before the deluge engulfs us all.

ARTOIS: Not only do you presume upon my patience, Talleyrand, but with this treasonous talk of English Parliaments, you…

TALLEYRAND: (*Overriding him.*) I know you believe that I am betraying my class by saying this. But better that, than I betray my country – as *you* are doing, Highness.

ARTOIS: Leave my presence this instant, you nefarious snake.

TALLEYRAND: (*Rising hastily.*) Yes, well, I see that you are unconvinced, Highness. But *despite* yourselves, I will still try to save you *from* yourselves.

ARTOIS: Stay, priest!

TALLEYRAND: (*Returning.*) Highness?

ARTOIS: (*Laughing.*) How can a limping prelate possibly 'save us from ourselves'?

TALLEYRAND: Simple. I will be the first Cleric to do what no cleric has ever done before.

ARTOIS: With the Church's dubious record that will take some doing.

TALLEYRAND: Indeed, but even the most perverse of clerics has never agreed to work alongside the Tradesmen in the People's Assembly – as *I* intend to.

ARTOIS: The Devil in Hell!

TALLEYRAND: Hell is where the Devil is to be found, certainly. And if I do not succeed in winning over the Tradesmen to my cause, you may find yourself joining him there prematurely.

ARTOIS: You dare to…

TALLEYRAND: Yes! For the sake of France, I will also 'dare' to dirty my hands further – by pretending to join with the Revolutionaries in the People's Assembly.

ARTOIS: Horror upon horror.

TALLEYRAND: It will be, if I fail, Highness. So you had best pray that the Tradesmen and the Revolutionaries like the smell of incense. Because only from *within* the People's Assembly, can I hope to subvert the subversives, and thus hold back the mounting terror. At least for a week or so.
(*As TALLEYRAND bows his way out of ARTOIS' presence. ARTOIS rises and strides into the shadows.*)

ARTOIS: You are nothing but an arrant traitor, Talleyrand. And once my brother, the King, hears of your perfidy, you are a doomed man.

TALLEYRAND: (*To the audience.*) But as the King was already in political retreat, Count Artois thought it unwise to raise his royal hand against me. So I joined the Tradesmen and Revolutionaries in the People's Assembly. Of course instantly I was set upon by my fellow clerics. (*Amused.*) Particularly by the apoplectic, elephantine Bishop of Bordeaux.

(*TALLEYRAND places his hands on the back of a chair, using the chair as a speaker's podium. Simultaneously the portly, wheezing figure of the Bishop of BORDEAUX assumes a similar stance, with a similar chair, on the opposite side of the stage. They are both spotlit.*)

BORDEAUX: (*Addressing the Tailors' Dummies.*) I tell you, fellow clerics, Talleyrand has committed an act of sacrilege against the Son of God Himself! (*Gesturing at the audience.*) Therefore I demand that this Assembly hand this traitor over to the Holy Inquisition, so that he can be tried for his impious crimes!

TALLEYRAND: (*Mock innocence.*) My Lord Bishop, surely you are not condemning me to eternal perdition simply because I have nationalised all the Church's property?

BORDEAUX: You deserve more than eternal perdition, you scabrous, pox-infested rodent!

TALLEYRAND: How can you object, my lord, to the Church's property being given to the Nation? As Bishop of Bordeaux, I know you will be the first to acknowledge that your beloved flock, the French People, have already been taxed into penury. Whereas we, in the warm bosom of Mother Church, have grown nearly as obese as *you* are – at the People's expense. That is why I have proposed that we tax the Church, and nationalise its considerable property. Which, sadly, also includes your exquisite estate in Bordeaux.

BORDEAUX: Exactly, you mutineering mountebank!

TALLEYRAND: I fail to see what objection you can have to such an action, my lord; when you know full well that a man of the cloth, like your pious self, has no right to own property in the first place. At least not according to the beneficent dictums of… (*Crossing himself.*) …Our Lord Jesus Christ.

(*The VALET switches on the tape recorder. Strident echoing voices yell: 'We should nationalise everything, Citizen Talleyrand! Not just the Church, but also all the Land, the Banks, the Palaces, everything!'.*)

(*Holding up his arms to silence the clamour, and addressing the audience.*) In the name of Liberty, Citizens, I ask you to avoid too much feverish activity. Is it not enough that we now hold the King and Queen as virtual prisoners of the People, and that we are already drawing up together a Declaration of the Rights of Men? Surely to God we are moving much too swiftly as it is. Wild and impulsive reforms may lead us into new tyrannies that may yet prove to be more despotic than those we have banished. So, in Christ's Merciful Name, let us shun further violence. Nothing is more fatal to the cause of Freedom and Happiness than Violent Disorder. The problem with Revolutions is not to get them under way; but to *stop* them when they have gone far enough. And our Revolution has already gone further than far enough.

BORDEAUX: Talleyrand, you malefic blasphemer. If I had my way, I would encompass you in a circle of violence such as you have never known!

TALLEYRAND: (*Smiling beatifically at BORDEAUX.*) Oh, am I to understand that the good Bishop proposes to *embrace* me?'

(*The spotlight goes out on the apoplectic Bishop.*)

(*To the audience.*) Then, nonchalantly, I turned on my heel and left the Assembly. But despite my warnings, within the month, the Revolution was upon us, and I began to despair of the future. So I made my way to the salon of my latest mistress, the exquisite Madame Germaine de Stael, to seek solace in her alabaster arms. Once ensconced in her darkened bedchamber, like a true cleric, I set about tickling my lady's fancy – with my wit. And – other weaponry.

(*The VALET clicks his fingers and the theatre is plunged in darkness. GERMAINE giggles huskily in the darkness.*)

GERMAINE: Oh Monsieur de Talleyrand, if I could purchase your wit, I'd gladly go into bankruptcy.

TALLEYRAND: Hardly worthwhile, my sweet Germaine, when your lustrous beauty makes wit seem torpid.

GERMAINE: Oooh you silver-tongued seducer.

TALLEYRAND: (*Ardently.*) Germaine, Germaine…

GERMAINE: No, Charles Maurice, please. I need a moment's respite before we return to the amorous fray. Where ever did I put that candle?

TALLEYRAND: Well…

GERMAINE: Oh you naughty bishop! Ah. Here we are. Now where's the tinder box.

TALLEYRAND: I do believe I have my hand on it.

GERMAINE: Over the years, young gallants have called my Mons Veneris numerous things but never a tinderbox.

TALLEYRAND: I meant – in my other hand, dearest. Now let there be light!

(*Sound of a tinderbox being struck. The candle is lit and we see that TALLEYRAND is lying on the chaise longue, embracing the beautiful GERMAINE. The VALET is no longer present.*)

There's nothing quite like an ardent bishop to bring a service to a successful climax.

GERMAINE: Indeed there isn't. By the by, is it true that three days ago you were appointed as the official 'Chaplain' of the Revolution?

TALLEYRAND: Yes. God help me. Which I'm sure He won't.

GERMAINE: (*Laughing.*) I'll pray for you, my love, then He's bound to forgive you.

TALLEYRAND: It will take more than prayers, my sweet. This morning I compounded my sin, by consecrating three bishops in the name of the Revolution.

GERMAINE: You didn't!

TALLEYRAND: I did. What's more, in that torrential rain. But then God is occasionally precipitate. (*Fondling GERMAINE.*) If somewhat unsubtle.

GERMAINE: Whatever will the Pope say?

TALLEYRAND: The news will probably give His Holiness instant dyspepsia. Then, with luck, he may well defrock me.

GERMAINE: That would only be just. Well, *you* are always trying to defrock *me*.

TALLEYRAND: And I always succeed. Mind, the sooner the Pope defrocks me, the better. I have always wanted to be plain 'monsieur'. As long as I am an inordinately *wealthy* 'monsieur', of course. That's why, when I had completed the 'rain' ceremony with the three bishops today, being a devoted man of the cloth, I immediately retired to my favourite gaming house on the Rue Saint Germaine, and still in my vestments, I promptly broke the bank.

GERMAINE: (*Laughing.*) Enough, my love, enough. Come we had best return to love's joust before profane laughter overwhelms sacred desire.

TALLEYRAND: (*Nuzzling GERMAINE's neck.*) Sylvan poet as well as mistress; what more could a poor chaplain ask for?

GERMAINE: His mistress' personal fortune?

TALLEYRAND: Money definitely has its virtues. One does not think one's best when poor. Mmm…my little 'Saint' Germaine, your perfume enflames the senses. So much so, I feel I'm about to rise to the occasion. Yet again.
(*He kisses her passionately. There is a knock on the door.*)

GERMAINE: (*Breaking free from his embrace.*) For pity's sake, Charles Maurice, that could be my husband!
(*GERMAINE moves away from TALLEYRAND. There is another tentative knock on the door.*)
Come.
(*The VALET enters, with a letter.*)

VALET: This has just arrived for the Monseigneur, madame.

GERMAINE: Then give it to him, Claude.

TALLEYRAND: (*Taking the letter.*) Thank you.

GERMAINE: You may go, Claude. (*As the VALET is leaving.*) Oh, and, Claude – if the Master should return suddenly, you know the signal.

VALET: How could I forget it, madame?

TALLEYRAND: (*Reading the letter.*) Hm!

GERMAINE: What is it, my sweet?

TALLEYRAND: Another sulphurous belch from the Archbishop of Paris.

GERMAINE: (*Amused.*) It sounds even windier than his sermons.

TALLEYRAND: It's certainly more to the point. It seems he has already advised His Holiness to excommunicate me.

GERMAINE: Better and better.

TALLEYRAND: Indeed. So, my dearest tinderbox, we may as well get down to business in earnest and really strike a light, to celebrate my secularisation in style.

(*He snuffs out the candle, plunging the stage into darkness – and we hear the lovers 'getting down to it'.*

The sounds of their vociferous love-making are soon drowned by a rattling coach, bumping over a cobbled street.

The lights come up to suggest a moonlit street in Paris.

In the centre of the stage, four chairs are positioned to create the effect of being inside a coach. There is a chair at the front on which the coachman is sitting with his whip. 'Inside' the coach, TALLEYRAND is sitting opposite ROBESPIERRE and MARAT. They are swaying from side to side, simulating the coach lurching over the cobble stones.)

ROBESPIERRE: (*The hissing viper.*) It is very good of you to invite us into your opulent carriage, Citizen Talleyrand. Is it not, Citizen Marat?

MARAT: (*The belching frog.*) Indeed it is, Citizen Robespierre. Especially as we Jacobins dismantled your precious Assembly yesterday evening in your absence; thus throwing you out of political employment.

ROBESPIERRE: So what we want to know, is why you haven't fled to your beloved England, with the rest of the aristocratic filth who have escaped our clutches?

MARAT: Especially as you're a filthy aristocrat yourself!

ROBESPIERRE: And why did you beseech the People's Assembly last Friday *not* to execute the leprous King and his whorish Queen?

MARAT: Why did you also object to Madame Guillotine chopping up all the crapulous Clergy?

ROBESPIERRE: Why are you against our demand for a Military Dictatorship?!

MARAT: Because he's an English spy, Citizen Robespierre!

ROBESPIERRE: Yes, only an English spy would want a constitutional monarchy, Citizen Marat!

TALLEYRAND: False, Citizens, false! It is *you* who are betraying the Revolution, not me. It is you who are offering the People the hissing blade, instead of Liberty. And rotting entrails instead of Justice. And instead of Happiness…

MARAT: …We will offer them *you*, Monsieur de Talleyrand!

ROBESPIERRE: Yes, and, what's more, we promise you a personal 'Good Friday'.

MARAT: And with your blasphemous record, there will be no Easter Day!

(The stage is suddenly bathed in nightmarish crimson light. Simultaneously ROBESPIERRE and MARAT whoop with Satanic glee as their stranglers' hands leap for TALLEYRAND's throat.

They force TALLEYRAND to his knees, and then onto his back, making him fight for his life. He screams as the stage goes black.

In the darkness, via the tape recorder, there is an amplified, frenetic heartbeat. This slows down to a regular heartbeat. Then the heartbeat fades to silence.

A snowfall effect stipples the stage. The figure of TALLEYRAND is discovered, hunched over his desk, asleep.

The VALET watches his master from a discreet distance.

TALLEYRAND cries out in his sleep, then wakes abruptly. He sees the VALET.)

TALLEYRAND: Ah Pierre, for a moment I thought…

VALET: Is there something amiss, Monseigneur?

TALLEYRAND: No. Though I wish my dreams were not always filled with nightmare fangs tearing at my throat. *(Painfully he pulls himself to his feet.)* But then it is only three months since Danton generously saved my life, by sending me here to London as the Revolution's Ambassador. I find it hard to believe that my head is still upon my shoulders. *(Touching his neck.)* But I suppose it is. Just. And it's snowing – again – on Kensington Gardens. *(Pointing.)* Look, Pierre.

VALET: At what, Monseigneur?

TALLEYRAND: The robin on the window sill. Would you believe it? It's pecking at an icicle. Mind, here in England worms come in very strange forms.

(*There is a knock on the door. The VALET exits and returns with GERMAINE. TALLEYRAND embraces her.*)

Germaine my love, however did you manage to escape?

GERMAINE: France is so brimful of horror that when Danton gave me leave to visit you, I came post-haste.

(*TALLEYRAND pours GERMAINE and himself some cognac.*)

My dear, I have never seen you look so doleful. Aren't you enjoying being Ambassador in London?

TALLEYRAND: I like this house well enough. And I admire and respect the English. But sadly they do not reciprocate my feelings.

GERMAINE: Then it is true that the British Government has refused to listen to your defence of the Revolution.

TALLEYRAND: Can you blame them? The reign of illusion has ended in France.

GERMAINE: You're shivering, my dear.

TALLEYRAND: Since being here, I've done little else. But it's hardly surprising. For two whole years, my fellow countrymen have been trapped between terror and defiance. Little wonder they have degenerated into mute slaves! The people have become so accustomed to waterfalls of blood, it seems that they're only happy when they are exchanging one cannibalistic tyrant for another. Well, everyone, from Danton down to the ordinary citizen, all quake before the head-cutters. Oh Germaine, Germaine, wherever one turns in France today, one sees an endless chain of evil, caked with human entrails and filth.

GERMAINE: (*Embracing him to try to comfort him.*) Oh my poor darling, I did not realise you were in such distress.

TALLEYRAND: That is exactly what I told Lord Landsdowne and Lord Grenville about the present state of France. Not that their lordships listened. Sadly they regard me as a seducing schemer.

GERMAINE: (*Laughing and kissing him.*) The adjective is apposite, if not the noun.

TALLEYRAND: Unfortunately it is no laughing matter, my
dear. Not only did their snuff-taking lordships initially
condemn me for siding with the Revolution, but now they
equally criticise me for having betrayed it. But then how
can English roast beef savour French irony? (*Pouring himself
more brandy.*) It's pointless me explaining to them that I
have only betrayed the Revolution because the Revolution
has betrayed its original principles.

GERMAINE: So I was right in assuming that news of the
Revolutionary Tribunal's latest edict has already reached
these shores?

TALLEYRAND: What edict?

GERMAINE: You mean you have not heard?

TALLEYRAND: Heard what?

GERMAINE: The Tribunal has signed the order to have
Their Majesties executed on January the twenty-first!

TALLEYRAND: God in Heaven. When did those monsters
initiate this woeful barbarism?

GERMAINE: Two weeks ago.

TALLEYRAND: If only the royal simpletons had heeded
my prophecy, now they would not be tottering towards
oblivion. But more than their deaths, I mourn the final
demise of Constitutional Law in France.
(*He empties his glass and moves to go.*)

GERMAINE: Where are you going, my love?

TALLEYRAND: I don't know, Germaine, but for the first
time in my life I long to fight. Yes, I want to physically fight
these monsters! (*Pacing in agitation.*) I can't tell you what
pleasure it would give me to bestow a beating on those vile
wretches, Marat and Robespierre. Oh Germaine, I am in a
frightful state of mind that I scarcely know who I am.

GERMAINE: Calmly, my love, calmly.

TALLEYRAND: How can I be calm?

GERMAINE: Has something else happened which you have
not yet told me of?

TALLEYRAND: (*Nodding.*) To add insult to injury, the English
Government insist that I leave England, and never return
here.

GERMAINE: In God's name, why?

TALLEYRAND: It seems they regard me as a deep and dangerous man.

GERMAINE: (*Biting his ear provocatively.*) Well, sometimes you can go very deep, my love.

TALLEYRAND: (*Laughing.*) Yes, I suppose in contorted times like these, a man who believes in Freedom and Constitutionalism is indeed a dangerous subversive. Yet it pains me profoundly that the English, whom I have long admired and wished to emulate, should pack me hence as a seditious renegade. Somehow I must prove to the world that I love Liberty. That I always have, and always will.

GERMAINE: How do you propose to do that?

TALLEYRAND: If there is a counter-revolution in France, I must be there to lead it.

GERMAINE: And if there is not?

TALLEYRAND: I shall go to America.

GERMAINE: Nothing is ever that bad, Charles Maurice!

TALLEYRAND: Where I shall acquire a vast personal fortune.

GERMAINE: Then you shall go alone, my love.

TALLEYRAND: Why so?

GERMAINE: There are many things I would gladly endure to have the privilege of listening to your mind evaluating time and the wickedness of the world, but I draw the line at consorting with rapacious Redskins and prurient Puritans. (*GERMAINE retreats into the darkness while TALLEYRAND addresses the audience.*)

TALLEYRAND: So I went, alone, to Philadelphia where I accumulated a considerable amount of fiscal assets by playing the stock market. Oh, yes, and I also acquired an inordinately-luscious black mistress. While I was in America, I heard some wonderful news. The members of the Revolutionary Convention in Paris became so frightened that sooner or later they, too, would appear on one of Robespierre's death-lists that they banded together, and they arrested the Sea-Green Incorruptible. Then they bundled Robespierre off to the guillotine, and simultaneously they abolished the infamous Revolutionary Council. In its place, a certain Monsieur Barras set up – what he called – a 'moderate Directory'. On learning this, I sailed for France, because even though Barras was both a moral and venial pervert, at least he had no stomach for butchery. So I decided to insinuate my way into Barras' new Directory, in the hope that I could prevent him from betraying himself and the Nation into political perdition. (*The VALET re-enters, wearing the sash of a Court flunkey. Then, to the sound of the Waltz from Berlioz's 'Symphonie Fantastique', the VALET lowers a crystal chandelier that shimmers over the centre of the stage.*)

Three months after I had re-established myself in Paris, I went to the Luxembourg Palace to attend the last ball of the season.

(*GERMAINE waltzes into view with Count EDMOND – but the moment she sees TALLEYRAND, she finishes dancing with the Count.*)

GERMAINE: Oh Charles Maurice, everyone's dancing but you. Will I never persuade you to dance with me?
(*On the tape recorder, controlled by the VALET, the Berlioz Waltz changes abruptly to Strauss' 'Blue Danube'.*)

TALLEYRAND: My heart has been dancing with you, Germaine, from the moment I entered Paris. But as always my hoof refuses to keep time.

GERMAINE: And as always, despite your cloven hoof, you have contrived to attain one of the pinnacles of power in less time than the Devil could gallop a league.

TALLEYRAND: (*Now dancing with her.*) And as always, Germaine, it is you who has helped me to that pinnacle. For your own amorous ends, of course. Mmm…you have changed your perfume. (*Stepping on the hem of GERMAINE's dress with his club foot.*) My sincere apologies, my dear.

GERMAINE: I see your dancing hasn't improved in the interim years.

TALLEYRAND: That is what comes with having to practise the waltz to the thud of Mohawk tom-toms.

GERMAINE: Ouch! If anything, your dancing is even worse.

TALLEYRAND: Is it surprising? I loathe my present political role with such a passion that the little dancing rhythm that I once possessed, has now utterly forsaken me.

GERMAINE: (*Petulant.*) Surely you are grateful that I helped you to become Foreign Minister in Barras' Directory?

TALLEYRAND: On the contrary, Germaine.

GERMAINE: Charles Maurice!

TALLEYRAND: The Directory is the scandal of Europe. Barras is not only viciously dishonest, but also he's a pederastic voluptuary. He has merely replaced the bloody excesses of the Revolution with his own rapacious appetite for fiscal corruption and bum-boys.

GERMAINE: Then why ever did you persuade me to persuade him to persuade the other Directors, to appoint *you* as Foreign Minister in the first place?

TALLEYRAND: Because the Directory is a rotting corpse, pleading to be buried.

GERMAINE: (*Amused.*) And you intend to be its grave digger?

TALLEYRAND: Yes, and, what's more, we are now digging a very large grave indeed.

GERMAINE: 'We'?

TALLEYRAND: (*Winking.*) I am, of course, referring to my good self. And a certain iron general I know.

GERMAINE: (*Stopping dancing.*) What general?

TALLEYRAND: Oh, did I forget to mention that I've been in conference with General Bonaparte for the last three months?

GERMAINE: (*Appalled.*) No!

TALLEYRAND: How absent minded of me.

GERMAINE: You've been hobnobbing with that Corsican upstart! So that is the unsavoury reason you've avoided my salon during the whole of this season.

TALLEYRAND: Oh for beauty's sake, my sweet, don't encourage your azured orbs to bulge like that. It makes you appear unbecomingly pop-eyed.

GERMAINE: Is it surprising that I'm 'pop-eyed' when I learn that you have been clandestinely cavorting with that… minuscule military manikin?

TALLEYRAND: I had no alternative but to confer with
Bonaparte. If drastic action is not taken to bring down the
Directory, the Jacobins will regroup, and then they will
unleash a new Red Terror. Or, God save us, the Royalists
will unleash a White one. Either way, we'll be mangled in
a Civil War.
(*TALLEYRAND leads GERMAINE to the chaise longue. The
VALET brings them champagne.*)
(*Kissing her neck.*) But by allying myself with General
Bonaparte, together we can sweep away the factional dross
once and forever.

GERMAINE: A man of your considerable refinement, my
love, will not be able to control a fire-belching Gorgon like
Bonaparte. Remember, it was only yesterday your 'iron'
general threatened to march his army of eighty thousand
on Paris.

TALLEYRAND: (*Continuing with the seduction of GERMAINE
as a counterpoint to his political analysis.*) Yes…the precipitate
rise of one so audacious to such powerful pre-eminence, is
indeed wonderful to behold.

GERMAINE: It is rather a matter of the rise of an
uncontrollable juggernaut, Charles Maurice. Your iron
general has not only rebuilt the French Army into the most
formidable war-machine in Europe, but he has also chased
the terror-stricken Austrians from one side of Italy to the
other in less than six months.

TALLEYRAND: (*Amused.*) As I said: Bonaparte is the
Directory's perfect grave-digger.

GERMAINE: Yes, but the moment you try to transform him
into a peace-loving constitutionalist – and knowing you
as I do, you *will* try – it will be *your* grave that he will be
digging.

TALLEYRAND: I am prepared to take that risk, my sweet.
You see, History is not born. Like love, one has to make it.
(*GERMAINE breaks away from TALLEYRAND's amorous
embrace.*)

GERMAINE: You have betrayed my trust, Charles Maurice.

TALLEYRAND: To save France from Civil War, I had no
alternative.

GERMAINE: Don't touch me!

TALLEYRAND: As you will.

GERMAINE: You must choose between that peasant upstart and me.

TALLEYRAND: Then this must be our long au revoir, Germaine, because I know of no other way to save France. To quote the Great Corsican himself – (*Imitating NAPOLEON's gruff tones.*) – 'We must organise a coup against the Directory in such a way as that bum-bruiser Barras won't suspect a thing. In fact it might not be a bad idea if we convince Barras to personally *lead* the coup against his fellow Directors.' Then Bonaparte added, with his customary finesse: 'Barras and the Directory have but one use. It gives one profound pleasure to piss on 'em!'

GERMAINE: You think such crudity is amusing?

TALLEYRAND: It has its place, like everything else. So you will have to pray that I can control Bonaparte. For all our sakes.

GERMAINE: I will never forgive you if you do this, Charles Maurice.

TALLEYRAND: And I will never forgive myself if I do not make the attempt. (*Kissing her hand.*) So –
'Farewell, my lovely; farewell, my sweeting,
Because there will not be another such meeting.'
(*GERMAINE moves off into the darkness.*)

GERMAINE: (*Turning back.*) It is you, Charles Maurice, who will live to regret flirting with the peasantry, because I prophesy that the time will come when the Corsican will demand your blood, to spice his bestial appetite.
(*TALLEYRAND laughs and blows GERMAINE a kiss as she disappears. Then he crosses to his desk and rests his hand on the telephone.*)

TALLEYRAND: (*To the audience.*) And so – Ladies and Gentlemen – we come to the Coup. Monsieur Barras is in the Luxembourg Palace, with his Finance Minister Ouvrard – and I am awaiting their call in the Louvre. (*Indicating the telephone.*) As I observed earlier, I've always had a penchant for futuristic gadgets.

(*Simultaneously, BARRAS minces into view, flapping a lace handkerchief and dabbing himself with scent. He is followed by OUVRARD, the Financier.*

The VALET, using a pulley-system, lowers the cut-out of a latticed window. BARRAS peers through the window.)

BARRAS: Oooh Ouvrard, me dear, do join me here by the window. What's going on in the courtyard is highly droll. Well, it is such a turn-on to see all our fellow Directors being arrested at one fell swoop, isn't it?

(*OUVRARD doesn't move. He is more interested in the large brandy that the VALET is pouring for him.*)

You can savour yer brandy later, ducky. Now come and take a teensy-weensy peek at history being made.

(*The VALET, via the tape recorder, provides the sounds of the MOB cheering in the courtyard.*)

Oh you must troll over here and have a quick butcher's at what's happening. The mob's actually cheering the soldiers on. But then Parisians are always so deliciously fickle, don't you find? Although seriously, sweetness, I can't thank you enough for financing this bijoux little coup of mine.

OUVRARD: Think nothing of it, sugar-puff.

BARRAS: Oh, but I do, I do. Bumholes! I nearly forgot.

OUVRARD: What?

BARRAS: I promised I'd give old Hobbley-Horse, Talleyrand, a call. Well, if I don't call her up, she's such a venomous old tart – before I can say 'knife' – she'll start sharpening her talons to claw *me* into the Bastille, too. (*To the VALET.*) So fetch me the telephone, hunbunch, and quickish.

(*The VALET produces a telephone on the silver salver. BARRAS dials.*

TALLEYRAND's phone on his desk rings. TALLEYRAND picks it up.)

TALLEYRAND: The Louvre 1812, yes?

BARRAS: That you, m'dear Talleyrand?

TALLEYRAND: It certainly isn't Marie Antoinette.

BARRAS: Ooh, you are a wag. Just thought I'd give you a little tinkle to tell you that me coup's going a real treat.

TALLEYRAND: *Your* coup, Monsieur Barras?

BARRAS: (*Petulant.*) Alright, if you prefer it, Queenie, *your* coup!

TALLEYRAND: I don't. Because it isn't.

BARRAS: Well, if it isn't your coup and it isn't my coup, *who's* frigging coup is it?!

TALLEYRAND: It's General Napoleon 'Frigging' Bonaparte's coup.

BARRAS: (*Apoplectic.*) General…?! All the Saints defend me!

TALLEYRAND: They are the only ones who will.

BARRAS: What d'you mean?

TALLEYRAND: The General's coup also embraces *you*, Monsieur Barras.

BARRAS: Me?!

TALLEYRAND: Yes, and one word from Bonaparte, and the mob will tear down the Luxembourg Palace, with you still inside it.

BARRAS: Oooh Talleyrand, you've set me up, you big butch, silken serpent you! Wherever did I put me smelling salts? (*Shrieking into the phone.*) You've betrayed me, you old queen!

(*The VALET produces the smelling salts on the silver salver.*)

TALLEYRAND: (*As BARRAS takes a huge sniff of the salts.*) On the contrary, monsieur, it is your cupidity and your love of vice that have betrayed you.

BARRAS: How dare you accuse me of corruption, you Infant Jesus of Hell?

TALLEYRAND: Fear not, Monsieur Barras, in order to sweeten your imminent self-sacrifice, and thus encourage you to become the First Patriot of France, the New Republic is prepared to offer you the modest sum of THREE MILLION FRANCS, the moment you step into your coach and are driven into perpetual retirement.

BARRAS: (*Unable to believe his luck but trying to disguise the fact.*) THREE MILLION FRANCS??

TALLEYRAND: Exactly.

BARRAS: Oh that puts matters in quite a different light, ducky.

TALLEYRAND: We thought it might.

BARRAS: Yes well...if I've got to be the First Patriot of France...I suppose I've got to be.

TALLEYRAND: We knew France could count on your unswerving, patriotic self-sacrifice.

BARRAS: However, when I write me memoirs, which rest assured I will, I will inform the whole world who is the real traitor!

TALLEYRAND: Then your memoirs will read like everyone else's.

BARRAS: I don't follow you.

TALLEYRAND: (*Smiling.*) On the contrary: you have never done anything else, monsieur.

BARRAS: Well, I don't give a fig for what you think, you old trout. On the backs of me three million francs, I will retire to Italy. Always fancied those divine Sistine Chapel choir boys. So now I suppose it's nighty-night, sweetie-pie.
(*BARRAS hangs up and hooks his arm in OUVRARD's. They saunter off together.*)
(*As they disappear, to OUVRARD.*) Well, it's a good thing that we're both of a religious bent, isn't it, baby doll?
(*The VALET flies the window out.*)

TALLEYRAND: (*To the audience.*) Which brings me to the Great Man himself; General Napoleon 'Frigging' Bonaparte.

VALET: (*Approaching TALLEYRAND with a bottle of white wine and re-filling his glass.*) Yes...what was the Emperor really like, Monseigneur?

TALLEYRAND: Well, to be honest – (*Smiling.*) – and I am occasionally – I was never quite certain. (*Savouring the wine.*) Mmm...chilled to perfection. You see, Pierre, for most of my life I have always managed successfully to manipulate my fellow creatures. Indeed sometimes I feel that the Count Artois of this world, and the Robespierres, Marats and Barras, were only born so that I could bend them to my will.
(*While TALLEYRAND is talking, the VALET sets the table for two.*)
But not so with Napoleon. He was a true genius. I never succeeded in manipulating him. And, believe me, I tried.

(*The VALET adjusts TALLEYRAND's chair as TALLEYRAND takes his place at the table.*
Simultaneously NAPOLEON enters and is, in turn, seated by the VALET. The VALET serves the fish course.)
(*To the audience.*) So, here we are, having our celebratory-post-Coup-dinner. At this moment everything about General Bonaparte is demanding to go forward into the future. Only his hair-line is in retreat. His tragic folly in Russia is still years away. See how voraciously he eats. And he drinks even faster. Yet he seems totally unaware that he is doing either.

NAPOLEON: (*With his mouth full, to the VALET.*) Bread, sirrah, more bread.

TALLEYRAND: (*Eating delicately.*) No doubt about it, General, the petit pois are slightly overdone.

NAPOLEON: (*Gruffly, as he shovels down the food.*) Yes, you're right, the peas are disgusting. (*Grinning.*) Not unlike that shirt-lifter Barras and his crapulous Directory. Mind, I still can't believe that he accepted our bribe with such alacrity.

TALLEYRAND: He's not a self-confessed gentleman for nothing, General.

NAPOLEON: (*Picking his teeth as he talks.*) Why do fish always have to have bones?

TALLEYRAND: (*Watching NAPOLEON's piggery with growing distaste.*) Perhaps the bones are intended to prolong one's savouring of the turbot, which, in turn, then gives one a remote chance of digesting one's dinner.

NAPOLEON: Haven't the time to digest. Save all that for when I'm dead, and the worms are at me.

TALLEYRAND: Quite. (*Eating fastidiously.*) General, I understand, in my absence, that you had a little skirmish with the Council at Saint Cloud.

NAPOLEON: (*Talking with his mouth full.*) It was nothing to speak of. When my brother Lucien arrived with my troops, some of the voluble members of the Council began to shout out seditious slogans like: 'No tyrants, no dictatorship!'

TALLEYRAND: Such ejaculations were certainly somewhat premature.

NAPOLEON: Damn right they were. Especially as the
Council then threatened to outlaw *me*! Still, it all ended
democratically enough.

TALLEYRAND: Really?

NAPOLEON: 'Course. I just sent in my troops, and dissolved
the Council.

TALLEYRAND: (*Laying his cutlery down.*) Superb.

NAPOLEON: Glad you approve.

TALLEYRAND: I was referring to the turbot, General. But in
regard to the vegetables, I can only assume that your chef
has fennel on the brain.

NAPOLEON: A pox on the fennel! You still haven't said
whether you accept my offer to become my Foreign
Minister? (*Shovelling in more food.*) Well, do you accept,
Monseigneur, or don't you?

TALLEYRAND: Possibly.

NAPOLEON: You're a very cautious man, Monsieur de
Talleyrand.

TALLEYRAND: I intend to survive, General. Despite my
'friends'. Purely for France's sake, of course.

NAPOLEON: Of course. (*Helping himself to more food and eating
with gusto.*) Now the first thing we must do is draw up a
New Constitution, which needs to be short. (*Grinning.*) And
very confusing.

TALLEYRAND: (*Toying with his wine.*) I approve of the former
but distrust the latter.

NAPOLEON: Oh come now, man, France is crying out for
a little civilised confusion after a decade of barbarous
simplicity.

TALLEYRAND: What France needs is leadership that is *seen*
to be leadership.

NAPOLEON: Couldn't agree with you more.

TALLEYRAND: So, in my opinion, General, *you* should be
made First Consul of the New Republic.

NAPOLEON: (*Disappointed.*) First Consul...? Well, I suppose
it's a start.

TALLEYRAND: And once you've been elected as our
temporary 'sovereign', General, *together* we will begin the
reconstruction of our beloved country.

(*NAPOLEON noisily attacks a stick of celery.*)

NAPOLEON: (*Doubtful.*) Mm…I may still need to make
further conquests.

TALLEYRAND: (*Spluttering on his wine.*) Surely to God there's
no necessity to conquer any more…?!

NAPOLEON: (*Overriding him.*) Stop frothing at the gills,
my friend, and face facts. (*Belching.*) England and Austria
will never allow France to grow strong again if they can
prevent it.

TALLEYRAND: We should only go to war if the peace of
France is threatened.

NAPOLOEN: Hm!

TALLEYRAND: Under no circumstances must we become
traffickers in nations.

NAPOLEON: (*Shaking his head.*) War is indispensable if we're
to bring all our enemies to their knees.

TALLEYRAND: That is where you are wrong, General. The
only true superiority that an enlightened man, like your
good self, should wish for – is to be the master of his *own*
nation. One should never make the ridiculous claim that
one has the right or the ability to be the master of *other*
nations.

NAPOLEON: (*Amused.*) So you *can* be passionate when you
want, Monsieur de Talleyrand. I've long wondered at what
point your silk glove seizes the bayonet.

TALLEYRAND: You agree with me, then?

(*Noisily NAPOLEON assaults another stick of celery.*)

NAPOLEON: No question about it: celery definitely tastes
better after the first frost.

TALLEYRAND: General, do you agree with me or…?

NAPOLEON: (*Interrupting with a grin.*) Don't look so worried,
my friend. I feel we can work together, yes.

TALLEYRAND: As long as our interests follow the same
river, General, I will continue to sail alongside your
military genius.

NAPOLEON: Good. (*Pouring more wine.*) So why don't we
drink to our new partnership, then?

TALLEYRAND: With pleasure. (*Clinking glasses.*) To the First
Consul of the New Republic.

NAPOLEON: (*Clinking glasses.*) And to his illustrious Foreign
Minister.

TALLEYRAND: (*Raising his glass.*) Now let us toast our
beloved France.

NAPOLEON: (*Putting his glass down.*) No need, my friend.
(*Grinning.*) We've already done so. (*Rising.*) Now the
eating's done, time to get on with life. Can you lend me
some money?

TALLEYRAND: Yes…of course.

NAPOLEON: A hundred thousand francs should just about
see me through the month.

TALLEYRAND: A hundred thousand…? (*Recovering.*) I
suppose that seems reasonable, General.

NAPOLEON: (*Patting TALLEYRAND's shoulder as he passes.*)
Good man.
(*NAPOLEON exits. The VALET tops up TALLEYRAND's
glass.*)

TALLEYRAND: What's more, in the beginning, Pierre,
everything seemed reasonable. The five years of our
Consulate, from 1799 to 1804, were amongst the happiest
of my life. Together Napoleon and I created genuine
prosperity throughout France. The bloodthirsty Jacobins
were temporarily tongue-tied. Even the Royalists were less
inane than was their wont. And France was stronger than
it had been since the glorious days of the Sun King. Then
one blustery afternoon, things changed. Though, in truth,
they had been changing all the time. It was only *I* who had
stood still. I remember clearly how it all began. Bonaparte
summoned me to the Luxembourg Palace where he had
taken up residence.
(*NAPOLEON storms into view.*)

NAPOLEON: (*Shouting.*) It is my avowed intention to scrub
Paris free of vice! D'you hear me, Minister?

TALLEYRAND: Who could fail to hear you, General?

NAPOLEON: And you can keep your high-born sneers
to yourself, sir. I won't tolerate 'em. Anymore than I'll
tolerate so-called ladies, waddling round my palace,
displaying their tuberous tits in transparent gowns!

TALLEYRAND: I cannot be held responsible for the latest fashion in haute couture, General.

NAPOLEON: Well, someone has to be held responsible! Only last night, I was at the Opera, with the Lady Josephine – when who should burst into my box but that bucket of jiggling junket, Madame Talien, clad in nothing but a moth-eaten tiger skin!? So I told her straight to her striped pudenda that mythological fancy dress was no longer fashionable in my Court.

TALLEYRAND: I can only reiterate, General: I am not responsible for Madame Talien's striped pudenda.

NAPOLOEN: Nor, may I add, will I tolerate, sir, a Foreign Minister who is fornicating a lady who, by all accounts, is no fornicating lady!

TALLEYRAND: I trust you are not referring to my present mistress, Madame Catherine Grand.

NAPOLEON: I'm certainly not referring to her poxy grandmother! So you'd best abandon your Grand 'Madame' forthwith, and once more don your Episcopal robes.

TALLEYRAND: Never!

NAPOLEON: You have no alternative, monsieur.

TALLEYRAND: On the contrary. The happiest day in my life was the day that the Pope divested me of that accursed bishopric. So I have no intention of taking up a profession which I not only dislike, but also for which I am supremely unsuited.

NAPOLEON: All right. You don't have to be a bishop.

TALLEYRAND: Thank you.

NAPOLEON: You can be a cardinal instead.

TALLEYRAND: A cardinal?

NAPOLEON: Yes, like your patron saint, Cardinal Richelieu. Besides, a scarlet robe would suit you admirably.

TALLEYRAND: I'm sorry, General, but I prefer the world to see my cloven hoof.

NAPOLEON: You refuse?

TALLEYRAND: Absolutely.

NAPOLOEN: I thought one of your principles was never to do anything in haste?

TALLEYRAND: Yes, but there are limits, General. Especially to principles.

NAPOLEON: True. So if you refuse to be a cardinal, you must agree to marry that whore, Catherine Grand instead.

TALLEYRAND: (*Now flustered, mopping himself with a handkerchief as he retreats.*) Oh come now, General, you know perfectly well that Catholic Bishops can't marry.

NAPOLEON: (*Whirling round, with his famous Napoleonic scowl.*) Secularised, excommunicated, lecherous Catholic Bishops can! So stop hobbling away from me like a dying daddy-longlegs and face your matrimonial destiny!

TALLEYRAND: (*Again on the limping move.*) I cannot possibly wed Catherine Grand. His Holiness the Pope will have an instant attack of St Vitus' Dance if he ever hears of my doing such a thing.

(*NAPOLEON clicks his fingers. The VALET appears with a huge Map of the World which he unrolls in the middle of the stage.*)

NAPOLEON: (*Striding across the map.*) You seem to have forgotten, 'Monseigneur', that I have already conquered Italy once. (*Putting his boot down heavily on Italy.*) So I feel certain that the Court of the Vatican will see everything my way. Including your forthcoming nuptials. Oh by the by, I have another surprise in store for you, my little ex-cleric. Well, sit down 'Mister' Passionate Anglophile because I'm sure your Kensington club foot needs a rest.

TALLEYRAND: Am I to gather, General, from my new scabrous title that you now intend to provoke England even further?

NAPOLEON: I'm going to more than provoke her, my little Londoner. Your beloved England has presumed too much upon my patience already.

TALLEYRAND: General, for pity's sake…

(*NAPOLEON strides across the map like a latter-day Tamberlaine.*)

NAPOLEON: Did Nelson show any 'pity' when he routed the Danish fleet to ensure that the English not only control the Channel, but now control the Baltic as well?

TALLEYRAND: Yes, General, but it is still unwise…

NAPOLEON: (*Relentless.*) And to add insult to injury, Tsar Alexander has had the Slavic temerity to side with

England, so now I have no choice but to conquer England and Russia simultaneously!

TALLEYRAND: General, in God's name!

NAPOLEON: No, Monseigneur, I will conquer them in MINE!

TALLEYRAND: You promised we would not become traffickers in nations.

NAPOLEON: Your memory deceives you, man. I promised nothing. What's more, I intend the most difficult undertaking ever conceived in Foreign Policy. (*Indicating the map with his boot.*) With the help of some foggy weather, and more or less favourable conditions, within the month I will land with my army in England.

TALLEYRAND: General, you cannot possibly…

NAPOLEON: (*Overriding him.*) And three days after landing I will be master of London, Parliament and the Bank.

TALLEYRAND: Jesus in Heaven!

NAPOLEON: Then when I have subdued all those spineless English shopkeepers, I will consume the rest of Europe. And once my Empire is established, I will impose a new Pax Napoleana.

TALLEYRAND: *Your* Empire? God's teeth, this is unadulterated madness!

(*Impatiently NAPOLEON clicks his fingers. The VALET hands him a scroll.*)

NAPOLEON: And because the latest assassination attempt on my life has necessitated the execution of the Duc d'Enghien, I have decided to put forward this Resolution to the Senate that will deter men from even thinking treasonous thoughts. And also it will stabilise France for all time. (*Handing the scroll to TALLEYRAND, with a smile.*) Why don't you glance through it and comment on the style? Well, style is your forte, is it not?

TALLEYRAND: With pleasure.

NAPOLEON: Perhaps if you read it aloud, it might assist your critical judgement.

TALLEYRAND: (*Appalled by what he is reading.*) In the name of all that's unholy!

NAPOLEON: Dear me, Minister, you've gone quite pale. Does our airless palace oppress you?

TALLEYRAND: You cannot be intending to propose this to the Senate!

NAPOLEON: I've already done so. What's more, as you can see by their signatures, it has already been ratified. So read it aloud. You'll find it has a pleasing ring.

TALLEYRAND: Must I?

NAPOLEON: It will prove treasonous to do otherwise.

TALLEYRAND: (*Reading.*) 'The Senate proposes the following resolution... that hence forward Napoleon Bonaparte be named...EMPEROR...'
(*TALLEYRAND breaks off.*)

NAPOLEON: Do stop gasping, my friend, like a hooked carp, and continue.

TALLEYRAND: '...And in that exalted capacity, Napoleon Bonaparte shall be solely responsible for the governance of the French Republic and all its tributaries.'

NAPOLEON: (*Reciting from memory.*) 'And, further, the title of Emperor shall be made hereditary in his family, from male to male by primogeniture, even to the ending of the world'! (*After a long pause.*) Minister, your silence does not become you in this instance.

TALLEYRAND: Is there anything that does – 'Your Majesty'?

NAPOLEON: (*Amused.*) There's no necessity to kneel. Yet.

TALLEYRAND: I was not proposing to kneel!

NAPOLEON: Come now, there's no need to scowl – Prince of Benevento and Grand Chamberlain of my Imperial Court.

TALLEYRAND: I do not follow your drift?

NAPOLEON: You will. When I make you the Prince of Benevento, and you kneel before me – as my Grand Chamberlain – in Notre-Dame Cathedral on my Coronation Day.
(*The VALET turns on the tape recorder and we hear Napoleon's Coronation Anthem. Simultaneously a lighting effect simulates the colours of the stained-glass windows of Notre-Dame.*

As the Anthem resonates through the cathedral, the VALET lights two tall candles on the dressing table that now is transformed into the High Altar. Simultaneously the POPE appears in his full regalia, carrying NAPOLEON's Coronation robes.)

Yes…and on that auspicious day, the whole world will tremble at my feet, when they behold me in my triumphant glory.

(The POPE swathes the Coronation robes around NAPOLEON's shoulders.)

For I live for posterity. Death is nothing. But to live, defeated – and without glory – is to die every day. So I can give you everything but time, Talleyrand. If I lose a minute, I will lose my destiny. See…even as I prophesied, we are in the echoing splendour of Notre-Dame. And His Holiness the Pope, with trembling fingers, offers me my shining birthright; the circle of golden laurel leaves.

(The POPE obeys NAPOLEON's command.)

And now…amidst the perfumed curls of incense and the haloed candles, with the dark glowing of Notre-Dame's stained glass above me, I hold Caesar's golden laurel crown above my imperial head. And now! NOW!!…*I* crown *myself*: Napoleon the First, Emperor of all the French, and Saviour of the World!

(As the Coronation Anthem reaches its thunderous climax, TALLEYRAND sinks to his knees. NAPOLEON crowns himself. On the tape recorder and amplified throughout the theatre, we hear Napoleon's SUBJECTS crying out in ringing unison.)

SUBJECTS / TALLEYRAND: God save Napoleon the First, Emperor of all the French! God save the Emperor!!

(Instant blackout.

A moment later, the VALET with his torch illuminates TALLEYRAND's face. But he is once again OLD TALLEYRAND, in his night-cap. This should remind us of the opening of the play. With his other torch, the VALET illuminates the face of the EMPEROR.)

TALLEYRAND: *(To NAPOLEON.)* That is why I betrayed you! If I had not, you would have destroyed the whole world!

SUBJECTS: (*On tape.*) MAY THE EMPEROR LIVE
    FOREVER – AS THE SAVIOUR OF THE WORLD!
    (*Blackout.*)

PART TWO

The same setting as Part One.

TALLEYRAND is spotlit, swathed in a heavy cloak and sitting on a bench. He is asleep in the grip of a nightmare. TALLEYRAND is now sixty years old but looks haggard and distraught. He is surrounded by the menacing shadows of the Tailors' Dummies that are dressed as dignitaries of the Emperor's Imperial Court.

The VALET is fiddling with the tape recorder – from which we hear the 'glorious' panoply of war, with the cries and moans of dying soldiers.

Flailing his arms to ward off the demons in his sleep, TALLEYRAND screams awake.

TALLEYRAND: Why do you terrorise me even in my sleep, Pierre?

VALET: (*Switching off the tape recorder.*) Your pardon, my Prince, but I am merely a minion in your dreams, conjuring up the Year of Our Lord 1811 – as part of your on-going Defence to Posterity, to the Jury of the Future.

TALLEYRAND: I know, I know! But my dreams of death, and death itself, have become so entangled in my mind that I am no longer certain which is which. Although to my eternal chagrin, I do remember that the Year of Our Lord 1811 was also the year that the Lord of this World, with his World Wars, traduced God's Earth to a mountain of reeking corpses. But, thank Heaven, during those blood-boltered times, I was too old to fight. Instead, in the twilight, I would sit impotently on my dew-strewn lawn... overlooking the Seine.
(*The VALET turns on the tape recorder that emits river noises at dusk. A lapping water-effect dapples TALLEYRAND's face. A twig cracks behind him. He rises uncertainly, then he opens his arms in relief.*)
Dorethea, my dearest. I was worried that you had decided to return to your husband. Not that I would blame you. I am twenty-five years your senior. And your husband is my nephew.

(*The beautiful DORETHEA, Duchess de Dino, materialises out of the shadows. She moves into TALLEYRAND's arms.*)

DORETHEA: Yes, but your nephew does not begin to emulate you as either a lover or a doyen of culture, dearest. Not forgetting your rapier wit, of course, and your consummate charm.

TALLEYRAND: My lovely beloved, you ravish my soul. If my nephew had not brought you to Paris as his unwilling bride, I swear my present life would be as sluggish as the river at our feet.

DORETHEA: Yes, but what would your lady wife make of such ardent protestations?

TALLEYRAND: You are right to rebuke me. A married man should not talk so. But you forget that I was forced into the adamantine bonds of matrimony by the Emperor. Besides, my wife is as stupid as a mushroom.

DORETHEA: (*Laughing.*) The things you say, Charles Maurice.

TALLEYRAND: Well, marriage is such a sublime institution that one should spend one's whole life contemplating it.

DORETHEA: Sometimes I wonder, when you play these games with words, whether you truly love me.

TALLEYRAND: Here, take my cloak, beloved. The night wind is chilly. (*Swathing her in his cloak.*) There.

DORETHEA: *Do* you love me, Charles Maurice, or am I merely the plaything of...

TALLEYRAND: ...An elderly statesman?

DORETHEA: I did not say that.

TALLEYRAND: But you thought it.

DORETHEA: No, my love. An evening with the wonders of your mind is worth a lifetime of banter with the most handsome hussar in France.

TALLEYRAND: Do you mean that?

DORETHEA: With all my heart. So do you truly love me?

TALLEYRAND: Yes, dearest. You are my Evening Star. Now I know that I need wander no further. You are my last mistress.

DORETHEA: (*Kissing him.*) My love.

TALLEYRAND: All I have ever dreamed of possessing, is swathed in the folds of my cloak.

DORETHEA: (*Touching his face.*) Sometimes you seem so distant.

TALLEYRAND: I only appear so because one must not love too much. Love confuses. It lessens the clarity of one's vision, and makes one vulnerable.

DORETHEA: Yet – without love...

TALLEYRAND: ...Life would be nothing but a decaying sepulchre in a woman-forsaken desert. (*Suddenly pointing.*) Oh, look.

DORETHEA: At what?

TALLEYRAND: No, no – over there. In the west.

DORETHEA: The swan?

TALLEYRAND: Yes...its white wings are so radiant in this half light. See there...where the mist has parted...the swan's sunset flight is mirrored in the Seine. Now the swan is no more than a glimmer of blood-stained snow in the advancing dark. It is like our beloved France now that she has lost her peace and liberty. And it would never have happened if our 'God' Emperor had taken my advice. But, no, as always, his blood-lust had to be assuaged. Christ damn his soul!

DORETHEA: Charles, please...!

TALLEYRAND: Oh don't frown, Dorethea. Being alone with you in our garden, with the water lapping the reeds, has done much to cheer my spirits.

DORETHEA: Then why are you still so melancholy?

TALLEYRAND: I should have harkened to Germaine's warning.

DORETHEA: I see you intend to make me jealous.

TALLEYRAND: (*Shaking his head.*) She prophesied that I would finally dissolve into Napoleon's shadow. But I refused to listen. So whenever I was in the Emperor's 'august' presence, I only heard what I wanted to hear. And when he pretended to be interested in the peaceful Pacification of Europe, I not only believed him, but as his Foreign Minister, I journeyed to every capital to promote peace and harmony in his name.

DORETHEA: You must not dwell on this, my love.

TALLEYRAND: How can I not? When all the time – while I was travelling from country to country – behind my back, the Saviour of the World was avidly sowing the seeds of his longed-for World War! Now his weeds of death are choking the life out of civilisation. So I can only pray that soon the nettles will turn against the Sower, and sting him to his doom.

DORETHEA: Charles Maurice, what are you saying? Such dangerous sentiments are…

TALLEYRAND: …High Treason, I know, child. But the question is: *who* is the traitor?

DORETHEA: For pity's sake, you could be overheard.

TALLEYRAND: What if I am? *I* did not wrench the title of Emperor from a cowed Senate, or rapaciously cut Peace and Liberty out of the nation's heart. But now Bonaparte's dragon pride has grown so rank that he no longer even pretends to listen to my advice. I might as well be invisible.

DORETHEA: Oh come now, Charles, it is only your unnatural brooding that makes you exaggerate.

TALLEYRAND: No, it is true, dearest. When he defeated the Austrians at Austerlitz, I begged him to restore to Austria her monarchy, so that she would then join with us in withstanding Russian barbarism. But oh no! Napoleon the First knew better. Instead of re-building Austria, and gaining an invaluable ally, the Emperor wilfully lacerated Austria's wounded limbs. And, worse, a month ago, he did the same to the defeated Prussians. It is not Tsar Alexander who is the barbarian, but 'Tsar' Napoleon.

DORETHEA: At least the Emperor has not invaded the country of your dreams, my Prince.

TALLEYRAND: Only because there has been a shortage of fog in the Channel.

DORETHEA: From your passion, am I to assume that you are about to commit some dangerous act against the Emperor?

TALLEYRAND: One thing is certain: I can no longer stomach the waste of human life, the stench of carnage, and the rape of Liberty!

(*An owl hoots close by.*)

DORETHEA: (*Clutching his arm.*) Hunting owls always make me shiver.

TALLEYRAND: I know the feeling, beloved. So there is only one thing I can do now.

DORETHEA: Which is?

TALLEYRAND: As France is being ruled by a treacherous Christ, I will have to play Judas – and betray the Betrayer.

DORETHEA: You cannot be foolish enough to betray him!

(*The owl hoots again.*)

TALLEYRAND: I must save France from being picked clean by the night owls. And I must save her now. You had best go in, and leave the conspirator to his seditious thoughts.

DORETHEA: Will you come to bed soon, my love?

TALLEYRAND: (*Smiling.*) As Napoleon once observed in his more reasonable days: 'Just try and stop me, Josephine.'

(*Laughing sadly, DORETHEA retreats into the darkness.*)

(*To the audience.*) And so, Ladies and Gentlemen of the Jury, that autumn, in my role as the Emperor's personal emissary to St Petersburg, I visited Tsar Alexander, Autocrat of all the Russias, in his frost-lit Winter Palace.

(*There is the stippling effect of snow falling. TALLEYRAND bows before the imposing figure of Tsar ALEXANDER, who surges forward out of the darkness, in a fur hat and a fur-collared greatcoat.*)

…So I can only reiterate, Your Majesty: the Emperor is proffering peace to you with one hand, but planning to douse Russia in its own blood with the other.

ALEXANDER: I am sorry, Monsieur Le Prince, but I find what you say hard to accept.

TALLEYRAND: It is still the unpalatable truth.

ALEXANDER: (*Shaking his head.*) The idea of the Emperor Napoleon planning to invade Russia is beyond credence.

(*The VALET appears with a bottle of champagne and glasses.*)

(*To the VALET.*) Pour to the brim, fellow, then leave us.

(*As the VALET obeys.*) Well, it seems only yesterday that Napoleon announced to his Court: 'I'm so fond of Tsar Alexander that if he were a woman, I'd make him my mistress.'

TALLEYRAND: (*Savouring his champagne.*) The Emperor is congenitally volatile with his affections.

ALEXANDER: Do not fret, Monsieur Le Prince. Despite my protestations, I know you speak the truth. Or why else did Bonaparte have the temerity to tell you that he intends to spend next Christmas here in my Winter Palace?

TALLEYRAND: What is more, uninvited, Your Majesty.

ALEXANDER: The satanic arrogance of the man. (*Downing his glass.*) You can rely on me to play my part, Monsieur Le Prince.

TALLEYRAND: Then you will sign this Treaty with Bonaparte, agreeing to come to his aid if Austria attacks France?

ALEXANDER: Absolutely. And when Austria *does* attack France – as she surely will – I will follow your advice and *join* the Austrians in their attack *against* Bonaparte. Then together we will wipe this Gallic Genghis Khan off the face of the earth, because you are right to quote your poet Racine: 'Treachery is noble, when its target is Tyranny.' (*ALEXANDER moves into the darkness as TALLEYRAND addresses the audience.*)

TALLEYRAND: So I returned to Paris where I was peremptorily summoned to the Imperial Court. It was a bleak December afternoon when I found myself standing beside the Imperial Fireplace, awaiting the Imperial Presence.
(*The Imperial Fireplace, complete with poker and tongs, is lowered into view.*)
I was surrounded by the other Imperial Dignitaries, including my friends, Count Edmond and the Marquis Caulaincourt.
(*Count EDMOND appears between the Tailors' Dummies, with the Marquis CAULAINCOURT. TALLEYRAND and Count EDMOND exchange bows.*)

EDMOND: Welcome back to Court, Monsieur Le Prince.

TALLEYRAND: Thank you, Count Edmond. It is pleasing to return from the icy wastes. (*Smiling and addressing CAULAINCOURT and the Tailors' Dummies.*) Well, we are all here, gentlemen, so where, in Hades, is the Emperor?

(The VALET appears, dressed as the MAJOR DOMO, carrying a staff which he beats on the ground three times.)

VALET: Pray silence for His August Majesty, the Emperor, Napoleon the First!

(From the tape recorder, a prolonged trumpet fanfare rings out, followed by a flurry of drums. NAPOLEON, in his full regalia, strides into view.)

NAPOLEON: *(Addressing the Tailors' Dummies and Courtiers.)* So all the Grand Dignitaries of my Empire have generously deigned to await my Imperial Coming. It is most kind of you, gentlemen. Although, on second viewing, perhaps not; considering most of you look more like tailors' dummies than faithful subjects!

CAULAINCOURT: How have we have offended Your Majesty?

NAPOLEON: You *think* too much, Monsieur Le Marquis! You all think too much. But I know what stratagems you're plotting behind your painted smiles. And I don't like plotting! *(Prodding Count EDMOND in the chest.)* What's more, I won't have it, Count Edmond. *(Prodding a Dummy.)* From this time forward all you wooden tops must cease to give rein to your private thoughts. They smell of arrant perfidy.

EDMOND: I beg you, sire, to give us leave to defend…

NAPOLEON: Silence, sirrah! You seem to forget that you 'Grand Dignitaries of the Empire' exist by *my* will alone. You are nothing more than the Emperor's opaque reflections, created by the Emperor's beneficence, for the maintenance of *his* Empire.

CAULAINCOURT: Naturally, Majesty, we appreciate…

NAPOLEON: *(Cutting him.)* And to doubt the Emperor is to betray the Emperor, and to differ with the Emperor, even in the smallest scruple, is unmitigated treason! Indeed I'm certain that Treason has already reared its Hydra head here in this very room.

EDMOND: Who would dare commit treason, sire?

(NAPOLEON whirls round and points at TALLEYRAND.)

NAPOLEON: The diffident Monsieur Le Prince there! – who even now leans so nonchalantly against my Imperial mantelpiece. Mind, he has to lean because his cloven hoof has unbalanced his judgement. Does he think that I don't know that he has been plotting with the Tsar behind my back? Does he believe that I am unaware that even now he's trying to convince Russia and Austria to attack me simultaneously? Does he really think I am so blind? (*Pause.*) But note, my lords, note how he refuses to acknowledge my presence, let alone refute my accusations. See how he continues to gaze absently into the flames, in the vain hope that his contrived disdain will divert my Imperial anger. But it will not! Nothing will stand between the Royal Lion and the Slavic Lamb. Do you hear me, you Ruskified, syphilitic traitor? You rapacious, hobbling atheist! (*Pause.*) Do not my words sear through your seditious skull, you jake-house Judas? (*After a pause.*) Well, look me in the face, villain! (*Roaring.*) What? Will you still pretend that I'm not here? (*Now out of control.*) I'll not endure it! Still he does not deign to move a single muscle. His lizard's visage is barren of expression. I might as well hurl curses at the furniture for all the…! (*Regaining control.*) You thing of filth, I will provoke you into fury yet. Surely even an impotent cripple like you, will publicly cringe when I announce to my Imperial Court that there is no one alive as pox-ridden as your whorish wife who – even as I speak – is being mounted by some hung-like-a-horse Spanish signor, to give you cuckold's horns as high as the Halls of Hell itself! (*Pause. NAPOLEON is now breathless with disbelief.*) Mary Mother of Christ, does nothing move you? Still the same sly smile, the snake-inverted eyes. (*Bellowing.*) I insist you defend yourself, Elephant Foot! (*Moving even closer to TALLEYRAND, then whispering.*) Why are you so silent, man? (*Pleading.*) What is it you want of me? Don't you understand I could have you exiled? Hanged! I could break you into a thousand pieces. I have the power. But I hold you in too much contempt to take the trouble. (*Sneering.*) Do you know what you are, Prince of Benevento, Vice Grand Elector of the Empire, Grand Chamberlain of the Imperial Court? D'you know what you *really* are? You are nothing but SHIT IN A SILK STOCKING! (*Pause.*)

Doesn't even the truth move you? Well, have it your own way, you trappist turd. With or without your approval, I will ransack Russia, and I will toss your louse-infested Tsar out of his Winter Palace into the freezing snow. Then the Imperial House of Bonaparte will rule those barbaric moujiks until the ending of the world. (*Moving away, then turning back.*) And remember this, Monsieur Le Horse's Hoof, if you foment a Revolution against me in my absence, I will ensure *you* will be the People's first offering to Madame Guillotine!

(*NAPOLEON storms out. TALLEYRAND continues to gaze absently into the fire. Count EDMOND and CAULAINCOURT stare at TALLEYRAND in disbelief.*)

TALLEYRAND: (*After a long pause and without looking in the direction of NAPOLEON's departure.*) Is the Emperor's 'Retreat' complete, Count Edmond?

EDMOND: Assuredly, Monsieur Le Prince.

CAULAINCOURT: We trust you will not take His Majesty's extraordinary tirade to heart?

TALLEYRAND: Yes, it is indeed a pity that so great a man should be so ill-bred because he is the final loser, my lords. Not I.

CAULAINCOURT: How so?

TALLEYRAND: When my friends of the Ançien Regime hear of his scatalogical abuse, their indignation will bury mine. But then the foremost in the land have been annihilated by the tongues of my friends, far more than have ever been destroyed by the cannons of the Emperor.

EDMOND: But how could you bear to stand there in silence, Monsieur Le Prince, and allow him to berate you so vilely?

CAULAINCOURT: Yes, why did you not snatch up a chair, the poker or…those fire-tongs, and smash them over his head?

TALLEYRAND: (*Amused.*) I confess the idea did occur to me, but frankly I was too indolent.

EDMOND: We are appalled that you should lose your esteemed position in so unseemly a manner.

TALLEYRAND: I have lost nothing, Count Edmond. Save a little time.

EDMOND: Surely…?

TALLEYRAND: (*Interrupting.*) The Emperor still needs me to give him the illusion of respectability. And also, occasionally, to tell him the truth about himself. By tomorrow, he will have regretted his vituperative spleen. But then, I have often told him that he would be wise to follow my example, and do nothing in haste. Including getting dressed of a morning.

CAULAINCOURT: How can you be so frivolous, Monsieur Le Prince?

TALLEYRAND: On the contrary, dressing is an intensely serious matter. Indeed, on occasions, my toilette has been known to take up the better part of a whole day. So do not fear for me, my lords. It is the Emperor who is hastening to invade Russia, which, in turn, will hasten the beginning of his end.

EDMOND: Surely not?

TALLEYRAND: Yes, and the season is not far hence when he will come to me for advice. And then…

CAULAINCOURT: And then?

TALLEYRAND: Ah, then…I pray that *God* will help him… because assuredly *I* will not.

(*TALLEYRAND moves down to address the audience as Count EDMOND and CAULAINCOURT are submerged in the darkness.*)

As I prophesied, Napoleon's Wolf Hour came the following year. This time it was the Emperor who deigned to visit me in my palatial Parisian house…in the forever-falling snow.

(*TALLEYRAND limps back to his chair by the fire and refills his glass with cognac.*

There is a knock on the door.)

Come.

(*The VALET appears.*)

VALET: His Majesty the Emperor is here and…

(*NAPOLEON, in his greatcoat, and looking haggard, barges past the VALET.*)

NAPOLEON: (*To the VALET.*) Out, you knave! Close the door behind you. And no eavesdropping, or I'll have you drawn and quartered!

(*The VALET bows and scurries out. TALLEYRAND, now on his feet, welcomes NAPOLEON.*)

TALLEYRAND: (*Ushering him to a seat.*) Come in and warm yourself by the fire, Your Majesty.

NAPOLEON: (*Warming his hands.*) Hm!

TALLEYRAND: It is truly a villainous night.

NAPOLOEN: It is bitter cold indeed.

(*A raking cough momentarily possesses NAPOLEON. TALLEYRAND hovers, unsure what to do.*)

Slap my back, man, for God's sake, slap it!

(*Tentatively TALLEYRAND obeys. NAPOLEON recovers.*)

Enough, sir, enough.

(*NAPOLEON subsides into a chair by the fire and pours himself a large cognac.*)

Don't mind if I help myself, d'you, old friend?

TALLEYRAND: It is your Empire, sire. So what is mine is yours.

NAPOLEON: If only I could believe that. (*Emptying the glass and refilling it.*) Of late I can't drink enough of this stuff. But not even cognac heats my blood these days. (*Coughing.*) Well, don't just stand there like a mocking shade. Say something.

TALLEYRAND: I thought I just had, sire.

NAPOLEON: All right, if that's the way you want it. Don't look at me like that.

TALLEYRAND: How would you prefer me to look at you, sire?

NAPOLEON: Hell knows. But differently. (*Coughing.*) Mind, since my return from Russia, everyone seems to give me the same look as they creep around me like wraiths. Even you, Monsieur Le Prince, seem almost invisible. Yes, I know what you're thinking.

TALLEYRAND: And what, pray, is that, Majesty?

NAPOLEON: You think it is I who have blurred at the edges, and become a haggard spectre of my erstwhile greatness. And it's true. Since Moscow, I have not been myself. (*Crying out.*) Moscow! Moscow!! (*Coughing and warming his hands against the fire.*) God rot that white Hell. Although when we reached the city, it was already a world of flames.

But the searing heat failed to warm us because the Siberian wind ate into our souls. And your precious Tsar, Monsieur Le Prince, was already two hundred miles away, having vacated Moscow to the furnace, but he still had the gall not to acknowledge his defeat. (*Coughing.*) So...with the Russian winter about to clamp us into ice, we had no choice but trudge for home. By the time my Grand Army had wearied its way to Smolensk, the snow was like iron filings, flailing into our blizzard-raw faces. It was so far below freezing, our guns and swords were welded to our hands.

TALLEYRAND: Sire, what is it you desire of me?

NAPOLEON: (*Oblivious.*) Still the snow howled round us day in, night out. Thousands died of exposure. Thousands more were butchered by marauding moujiks, or massacred by Cossacks. (*Coughing/anguished.*) And all that indiscriminate slaughter was *my* Imperial doing.

TALLEYRAND: Your Majesty, it is very late, so I would be obliged if...

NAPOLEON: (*Overriding him.*) I've never seen such carnage. Never. Bodies strewn over the endless white waste...like giant blood-stained icicles. My Grand Army of half a million of the bravest soldiers in Christendom were reduced to thirty thousand frost-bitten ghosts.

TALLEYRAND: Sire, please...

NAPOLEON: (*Desperate fury.*) What's to be done, man? In the Devil's name, what is to be done?

TALLEYRAND: Negotiate with the Tsar.

NAPOLEON: Negotiate with that posturing braggart?

TALLEYRAND: Yes, sire. And *tonight* – while you still have something to bargain with. Tomorrow you may have nothing. Then you will be able to offer nothing.

NAPOLEON: I asked for advice, not imbecility!

TALLEYRAND: Your only hope is to inform the Allies that you are willing to withdraw your Imperial forces to the boundaries established at the Treaty of Luneville.

NAPOLEON: (*Coughing and pouring more brandy.*) Alright, alright, say I do negotiate; in return, will *you* once again agree to take upon yourself responsibility for the Foreign Ministry?

TALLEYRAND: I cannot, sire.

NAPOLEON: Why not?

TALLEYRAND: I am no longer acquainted with the affairs of Your Majesty.

NAPOLEON: You know 'em well enough, Monsieur Le Prince. But you're planning to betray me, aren't you? (*Coughing.*) Aren't you?

TALLEYRAND: Think what you will, sire, but I cannot assume office in your government.

NAPOLEON: Why not?

TALLEYRAND: Your policies are contrary to my conception of the safety and happiness of my beloved country.

NAPOLEON: (*Swigging back his brandy and trying to appease.*) Oh come now, my dear Talleyrand, there's no need for us to fall out. I didn't really mean that about you being a traitor.

TALLEYRAND: Didn't you, sire?

NAPOLEON: (*Laughing.*) No. If I thought that you were a traitor, I'd never allow you to attack me as often as you do in print. Besides – were you a *real* traitor, you would have paid me lip-homage in public, then behind my back you'd be plotting my downfall with the Tsar of Russia and every other Mongol bumpkin that came your way.

TALLEYRAND: (*Hint of a smile.*) How do you know that I am not practising subterfuge *within* subterfuge?

NAPOLEON: (*Coughing.*) What?

TALLEYRAND: Perhaps I am abusing you in public, *and* betraying you in private.

NAPOLEON: Don't play the perverse double dealer with me, Monsieur Le Prince. I'm too cold in the marrow for such games. My nose tells me I can trust you. I want to trust you. (*Coughing.*) So much so, I insist you become my Foreign...

TALLEYRAND: (*Cutting him.*) I cannot, Majesty.

NAPOLEON: You must face reality, man, and accept my...

TALLEYRAND: (*Overriding him.*) I *have* faced reality. It is *you* who no longer have a tangible hold on the real world. Oh yes, until recently I was little more than an extension of your shadow: but now – before my very eyes – you are fast dwindling into *my* shadow.

NAPOLEON: Join me as my Foreign Minister, my friend. Then, together, we can once again…

TALLEYRAND: Too late, Majesty. It is impossible for me to be your Foreign Minister. My only concern is the salvation of France.

NAPOLEON: But *I am* France, man!

TALLEYRAND: You *were* France, sire.

NAPOLEON: Don't you fear my vengeance, Talleyrand?

TALLEYRAND: Yes, sire – I fear your vengeance on France. I am too much of a national cripple for you to waste your vengeance on me.

NAPOLEON: (*Lurching to his feet.*) You're right! You're nothing but a deformed incubus, a hobbling traitor and a Devil-hoofed thief. You don't even believe in God. You'd sell your own mother for a mess of pottage. I hope you rot in your own icy hell when your time comes! And come it assuredly will. And much, much sooner than you think. (*NAPOLEON lurches into the shadows.*)

TALLEYRAND: (*Calling after him.*) And equally, sire: now that your time is here, I pray that the Almighty will protect you – from yourself. (*TALLEYRAND clicks his fingers and the stage is plunged in darkness.*) (*In the dark.*) And this, Ladies and Gentlemen of the Jury, is the Darkness before the Dawn. (*In the darkness, we hear sounds of laughter and love-making.*)

DORETHEA: Oh my rampant Prince. How can you possibly make love at such a time?

TALLEYRAND: I can make love at all times, Dorethea. Given such an arousing mistress. What are you doing?

DORETHEA: With all this erogenous exertion, I have developed an exceeding thirst.

TALLEYRAND: Then allow me to quench it, beloved.

DORETHEA: (*Quickly.*) For wine, Charles Maurice.

TALLEYRAND: Oh that.

DORETHEA: Now light the candle, you naughty man, so I can see what I'm doing.

TALLEYRAND: Oh excellent, i'faith. We'll continue love's tilting by candle-light.

(*TALLEYRAND lights the candle. Then he tries to pull DORETHEA back into his arms but she eludes him and pours herself some wine.*)

DORETHEA: You are truly insatiable, Charles Maurice.

TALLEYRAND: At least I only hunger for *you*, my sweet. Unlike the Emperor, who has learnt nothing from history, and habitually hungers for interminable gore and glory.

DORETHEA: I still cannot believe that you are denouncing the Emperor so vociferously in public, and simultaneously betraying him in private.

TALLEYRAND: (*Pouring himself some wine.*) The Emperor doesn't believe it either. Thus, politically, he damns himself to perdition.

DORETHEA: Oh come now, Napoleon's recent defence against the Allies was breath-taking.

TALLEYRAND: Yes, and in the process he spilt even more French blood, so yet again his militaristic venture proved vaingloriously futile. And now the Allies have him completely encircled. But then what other man in history has had the mindless hubris to make implacable enemies of Austria, Prussia, England and Russia at one and the same time?

DORETHEA: Do you feel no pity for him?

TALLEYRAND: None.

DORETHEA: Charles!

TALLEYRAND: I warned him not to put his warrior's pride before the peace and the liberty of the Republic. But he, of course, knew better. Now he is being chastened by a cat-of-nine-tails of his own making, so he has no alternative but to crawl into his hole and die.

DORETHEA: You have destroyed him, dearest. History will never forgive you.

TALLEYRAND: I care not a pinch of snuff whether History sneezes at me or not. Napoleon is the tyrant who has destroyed himself. But not today. Not last year. It was almost a decade ago when he set out to prove to the world that he could rule nations, other than his own, better than the countrymen of those nations. Like Lucifer, Napoleon was once an incandescent angel. His dark radiance dazzled the universe. And like Lucifer, he was in love with falling… endlessly falling…through a weeping firmament. Until his spectral darkness clotted into a human meteor – which even as we sit here in this midnight stillness – plunges downwards…ever downwards…into the imperial wastes of desolation.

DORETHEA: You almost…love him, don't you?

TALLEYRAND: 'Almost' is a thousand leagues away from 'loving' anything, or anyone – save you.

DORETHEA: What will become of us, my Prince?

TALLEYRAND: We will survive. That is an art in itself.

DORETHEA: So when the Tsar marches triumphantly into Paris tomorrow, what will you do?

TALLEYRAND: Persuade the Tsar to help me re-establish the Bourbons on the throne of France.

DORETHEA: You cannot be serious!

TALLEYRAND: Never more so.

DORETHEA: Then you will be personally responsible for establishing a new 'Ançien Regime', with all its attendant vices!

TALLEYRAND: (*Smiling.*) Will I, my golden one?

DORETHEA: Yes.

TALLEYRAND: Enough of tomorrow, beloved. Now, in love's ardent name, let us do battle in honour of tonight. (*TALLEYRAND extinguishes the candle flame between his finger and thumb. The stage is plunged in darkness.*)

DORETHEA: (*In the darkness.*) Oh Charles Maurice, my diabolical Prince of Peace…
(*The sounds of their love-making are soon replaced by TALLEYRAND's voice ringing out in the darkness, from the tape recorder.*)

TALLEYRAND: People of France, on this auspicious day, in the year of Our Lord 1814, I come before this Assembly with the blessing of the Tsar of All the Russias and his beneficent Allies. In my new role as the President of the

Provisional Government, I Charles Maurice de Talleyrand-Perigord, do herewith proclaim the immediate and irrevocable Deposition of the Tyrant, Napoleon Bonaparte. (*The Assembly cheer.*) From this moment onwards, the People and the Army of France are freed from their oath of allegiance to the Corsican despot. To ensure that Bonaparte will never again abuse the destiny of our illustrious nation, forthwith we invite Louis XVIII of the House of Bourbon to return home from exile, and be our new King. But the said Louis must accept that henceforward he rules as a Constitutional Monarch after the English model. Furthermore, before Louis Bourbon ascends the throne, he must also swear to uphold the People's Constitution which this Assembly will prepare for his signature. Under no circumstances can there ever be a return to the Ançien Regime.

(*Applause and cheering in the darkness.*
The applause fades and is replaced by the ominous ticking of a clock.

A shaft of moonlight illuminates TALLEYRAND's sleeping face as he struggles in the throes of a nightmare. He is lying on his chaise longue, and wearing his night-shirt. He has dwindled into the OLD TALLEYRAND of the beginning of the play.)

No, my Emperor, you must believe me! I had no alternative! (*NAPOLEON steps into the moonlight, with a mocking smile.*)

NAPOLEON: Well, well, my dear Talleyrand, now we, who are with the Dead, are eager to see if *you* know how to die. Because die you will, and very soon.

(*NAPOLEON retreats into the darkness again.*)

TALLEYRAND: (*Still in his sleep.*) Once my Defence to Posterity is completed, I am not afraid to die.

(*DORETHEA enters, with a lighted taper that she applies to the candles beside the chaise longue.*)

DORETHEA: (*Trying to wake him.*) Charles Maurice, Charles Maurice.

TALLEYRAND: (*Still asleep.*) Death will come as a relief, believe me.

DORETHEA: Wake up, my dear. You are afflicted by a nightmare.

TALLEYRAND: (*Waking.*) Oh Dorethea, your pardon. I did not realise you were… I must have fallen asleep. Yet again. While I was writing my Defence to Posterity. I have even broken my quill. Which is a shame when I was just recording my glorious exploits at the Congress of Vienna.

DORETHEA: (*With a half smile.*) And one of your glorious exploits at the Congress, if memory serves, was your betrayal of the Allies.

TALLEYRAND: They invited betrayal! Well, how could I allow the Tsar to snaffle up Poland? And old Metternich was far too tricky for Austria's good.

DORETHEA: And Lord Castlereagh?

TALLEYRAND: Yes, even England occasionally elects an isolationist fool. Still, all in all, the Congress was the greatest triumph of my political career.

DORETHEA: Yes, who but the Prince of Benevento could have succeeded in subtly *dividing* the 'mighty' conquering Allies *against* themselves? Thus ensuring that France regained her rightful place in the forefront of world affairs. Not to mention preserving the independence of all the smaller nations in Europe. Indeed, it can be said that never before in human history have the Vanquished so completely dictated terms to the Victors.

TALLEYRAND: But my mental anguish remains, Dorethea. Will Posterity remember me for my libertarian achievements? Or will they call me 'the Prince of Traitors' because of what they ignorantly believe are my innumerable 'betrayals'? I only did what I did to save the world from a god who became a devil. The thought that my name will always be linked with the concept of treachery continually haunts me. (*Gasping in pain.*) The Virgin preserve me!

DORETHEA: My dear, what is it?

TALLEYRAND: Another pain spasm in my spine. But it's unimportant. The Napoleon of my nightmares is right: very soon we shall see if I know how to die.

DORETHEA: My Prince, do not entertain such morbid thoughts. They cut me to the heart.

TALLEYRAND: Come, come, my dear. There is nothing to weep about. After all, death is not a serious matter.

DORETHEA: You cannot die, you cannot!

TALLEYRAND: Why not? My wife has. Most of my friends have, so I might as well. Being eighty-three is inordinately wearisome. Unless you like playing patience – which I don't.

DORETHEA: Oh my dearest. What will I do without you?

TALLEYRAND: You will probably run off with that dashing Austrian Count again, so I can become the butt of all those malicious Parisian gossips.

DORETHEA: I wish you wouldn't remind me of my foolish assignation.

TALLEYRAND: I don't blame you. It was not until you ran off with the Count that I realised how intensely I needed and loved you. Indeed I was so tortured by jealousy that my friends believed I would die of a broken heart.

DORETHEA: Please, Charles Maurice…

TALLEYRAND: But you did come back to me, dearest. Although I have never been certain as to why. Was it because you could not resist governing 'a famous *old* man', who blindly doted on you?

DORETHEA: No!

TALLEYRAND: I'm no longer afraid of the truth. Did you sacrifice love for ambition, my golden one?

DORETHEA: As God is my witness, I came back because the glories of your mind were more seductive than all the Austrian Counts in Christendom. You must believe me when I say this.

TALLEYRAND: I do, my dear. (*Holding her hand.*) In this tormentful life, it is rare to find two minds that think alike. Where there are no mental reservations. No secrets. (*Suddenly unsure.*) Have you any secrets from me, Dorethea?

DORETHEA: No. You must stop torturing yourself with unfounded jealousy.

TALLEYRAND: I will, I will… (*Crying out as he clutches his spine.*) If only this damnable pain would leave me – or wrench me hence! You had best call the physician.

DORETHEA: Is the pain so great?

TALLEYRAND: Put it another way; if it were possible, I would ask you to fetch a priest.

DORETHEA: You know that is not possible, my dear. Not until His Holiness agrees to re-admit you into the bosom of the Church that you have consciously abandoned.

TALLEYRAND: I know, I know. I had intended to do something about Rome before now. I've been thinking about it for some considerable time.

DORETHEA: (*Pleased.*) You have?

TALLEYRAND: Yes, now, for pity's sake, give me some wine. My tongue seems to be on fire. I can never lose this taste of dead frogs in my mouth.

DORETHEA: (*Pouring him wine and helping him to drink.*) If you have been thinking about Rome, why have you taken no action to rectify matters with the Pope?

TALLEYRAND: I've never been over-fond of clerical effort.

DORETHEA: The Archbishop of Paris admires you greatly. He would be more than willing to take your written submission, enumerating all your sins, to His Holiness – who I am sure will then forgive you.

TALLEYRAND: How do you know all this?

DORETHEA: I…have been making enquiries.

TALLEYRAND: (*Laughing.*) You sly minx.

DORETHEA: Someone has to save you from yourself.

TALLEYRAND: (*Smiling.*) Now who is betraying who?

DORETHEA: Well, what is more important, Charles Maurice? That you die defending your political reputation to your imaginary judges in Posterity, who may or may not acquit you? Or that you expire without receiving absolution, and thus be found guilty by the Almighty Judge of committing a far greater treason? Or perhaps your soul has turned to dross, and you believe there is no Judgement to come?

TALLEYRAND: How could I believe such things, Dorethea? There is no sentiment less aristocratic than non-belief.

DORETHEA: Why are you always so flippant, my dear, when the salvation of your soul is at stake? Do you intend to betray that as well?

TALLEYRAND: (*Sadly.*) Then *you* also believe that I am the Prince of Traitors?

DORETHEA: No, Charles, I do not. But I fear for you. I fear for you greatly.
(*Feverishly TALLEYRAND rummages in the drawer of his desk.*)
Please listen to me. There is surely nothing in that drawer that cannot wait. What are you searching for?

TALLEYRAND: (*Handing her a letter.*) This.

DORETHEA: (*Examining it.*) It's addressed to His Holiness.

TALLEYRAND: Yes. Now fetch the physician and quickly.
(*DORETHEA runs out with the letter.*
The stage is bathed in a harsh surgical spotlight. The Dummies are like accusing shadowy sentinels – as the SURGEON (the VALET), in a white coat, appears, wielding his knife like the blade of the guillotine.)
Yes, I know, Doctor. If you do not remove the gangrenous carbuncle that is poisoning my lumbar region, I will surely die. (*Amused.*) But what matter if I do? Most men die many times before their hearts stop beating. Well, hack away, my friend, hack way!
(*The SURGEON moves behind TALLEYRAND. Without warning, he plunges the knife into TALLEYRAND's back. TALLEYRAND writhes with pain and screams.*)
AAAHHH! Good doctor, I doubt you realise the excruciating agony that you are causing me with your little knife!
(*Simultaneously a spotlight illuminates LOUIS XVI.*)
Your Majesty, you do not need to gloat over my pain.

LOUIS XVI: Now you know what it feels like to be under the blade of the guillotine, you revolutionary traitor.

TALLEYRAND: I did everything I could to save you and the Queen. I tried to prevent the Revolution but your brother would not listen.
(*Again the SURGEON applies the knife. TALLEYRAND stifles another cry of pain. The spotlight illuminates ROBESPIERRE.*)

TALLEYRAND: Ah… Citizen Robespierre, I knew you would not fail me.

ROBESPIERRE: Why should I? They sliced *my* head off, too, you Prince of Traitors! But unlike you, I was always the Sea-Green Incorruptible.

TALLEYRAND: No, Robespierre, you were the slaughterous Death's Head of the age. It was you that transformed the Revolution into an abattoir, not I.
(*Again the knife strikes home.*)
AAAAH! I never knew such pain was possible.
(*The spotlight illuminates GERMAINE de Stael.*)
Ah, Germaine, I wondered when you would come to torment me.

GERMAINE: You betrayed my trust for a Corsican butcher. I hope the good doctor cuts out your heart!

TALLEYRAND: I betrayed your trust to save France, Germaine.
(*The knife strikes home for the last time and TALLEYRAND slumps forward onto his face, howling in agony.*)
AAAAHHHHHHH! Even death would be preferable to this.
(*NAPOLEON is illuminated.*)

NAPOLEON: We have heard your Defence to Posterity, Talleyrand, and neither we – nor you – believe any of it to be true. Everyone knows that you betrayed the world to save your own neck, line your own pockets, and creep into other men's beds.

TALLEYRAND: No, sire. I did everything for France. Always and only for France.

NAPOLEON: No, you did it for Talleyrand! Always and only for Talleyrand!
(*All the ACCUSERS take up the cry but they are drowned by the final cry of desolation from TALLEYRAND himself.*)

TALLEYRAND: Doctor, you should have cut my brain out, to stop the endless ticking of my imagination!
(*Blackout. In the darkness the ominous clock starts ticking again.*
There is a knock on the door…as the moonlight illuminates TALLEYRAND's drawn, sleeping face. TALLEYRAND is now

lying on the chaise longue. DORETHEA moves towards him out of the darkness. She sits beside him. He awakens.)
(*Weakly.*) Oh…Dorethea? Is that you, dearest? I did not hear you enter. But then, since my operation, you seem to be in a different world. A world of shades and shadows.

DORETHEA: My dear, please…

TALLEYRAND: (*Interrupting.*) Yes, I know. You do not need to remind me. (*Picking up a document from the desk.*) If I fail to sign this recantation of my sins, His Holiness the Pope will not re-admit me into the bosom of Mother Church. Then I will die without the Last Rites, unshriven, and be forever consigned to Hell and damnation. With all my other ghosts.

DORETHEA: So why haven't you signed it?

TALLEYRAND: The time is not propitious.

DORETHEA: Do you then wish the Archbishop of Paris to visit you here at Valençay, and explain to you why he has amended certain portions of your recantation?

TALLEYRAND: Absolutely not.

DORETHEA: The Archbishop has said that he is only too willing to come and talk to you.

TALLEYRAND: Oh please, beloved, I can endure conversion but I cannot countenance boredom. (*Peering weakly into the shadows.*) Who else is there with you?
(*The cadaverous Abbé DUPANLOUP emerges from the shadows.*)

DUPANLOUP: Monsieur Le Prince, until you sign the recantation of your innumerable sins against the Church, I cannot possibly administer the Last Rites.

TALLEYRAND: Ah, so it is you again, Abbé Dupanloup. My sincere apologies. I was not aware that you were quivering there in the shadows, savouring the possibility of my damnation. But then, unlike my mind, my sight has a tendency to blur. Countess Dorethea and your good self are now little more than wraiths. I can peer…right through you both. Yes…and through the walls of my chateau…and the trees beyond…over the furthest hills…until I reach… the ocean. In my mind's eye, I can see over the booming

waves…to that final island of desolation…of which I made
Napoleon…the Emperor. Saint Helena.

DUPANLOUP: Forgive me for saying so, but you are…

TALLEYRAND: (*Irritably.*) …Wasting time, I know, Abbé.

DUPANLOUP: Do you understand the dire consequences if
you do not sign, Monsieur Le Prince?

TALLEYRAND: I believe so, Abbé Dupanloup. Considering,
in all probability, that I shall be dead in a very few hours.

DORETHEA: Then, in mercy's name, Charles Maurice, sign
now, so that you can be enfolded in the forgiving arms of
Christ's Beloved Church.

TALLEYRAND: I will sign, dearest.

DUPANLOUP: The Lord be praised.

TALLEYRAND: Between five and six o'clock.

DUPANLOUP: Five and six o'clock tonight?

TALLEYRAND: (*Amused.*) No. Tomorrow morning.

DUPANLOUP: But by tomorrow morning, Monsieur Le
Prince, as you have aptly observed, you may well be dead.

TALLEYRAND: Then we had best pray, Abbé, that the
Almighty keeps time as well as my clock.

(*TALLEYRAND slumps back on the chaise longue. There is the
amplified sound of the ticking of a clock as TALLEYRAND,
DORETHEA and DUPANLOUP are enveloped in darkness.
The ticking of the clock grows in volume. Over the ticking, we hear
TALLEYRAND's voice, and see his face, spotlit. He seems like a
spectre of himself. His eyes stare sightlessly into the audience.*)
So…at last, my Death Dream is coming to fruition. And
I will never know whether you, my Jury of the Future,
accept my Defence to Posterity, and acknowledge that
'Treachery *is* noble, when its target is tyranny'. Or will
you – like most of my peers – always judge me to be 'The
Prince of Traitors'? And, worse – it seems that I will not be
able to awaken from this deathly dreaming-sleep, to sign
my recantation. So it appears that Hell and Damnation are
to be my final destiny.

(*TALLEYRAND's eyes glaze over. He shudders, then falls back,
motionless.*

As the first rays of the rising sun touch TALLEYRAND's waxen features, DORETHEA enters, with DUPANLOUP. DORETHEA gazes at his sightless eyes, then she begins to sob uncontrollably.
A distant church clock strikes six. Then, to DORETHEA's amazement, TALLEYRAND moans and stirs.)

DORETHEA: Oh thank God. (*Clutching his hand.*) For a moment I thought you were…

TALLEYRAND: So did I.

DORETHEA: (*Laughing with relief.*) And it's six o'clock, and you're still…

TALLEYRAND: (*Amused.*) …Hanging on, beloved. So you see – it is not only *I* who have a sense of timing.

DORETHEA: Now will you sign?

DUPANLOUP: (*Handing TALLEYRAND the paper.*) Here is the recantation, Monsieur Le Prince.

TALLEYRAND: Thank you, Monsieur L'Abbé. So… (*Writing.*) …I sign. (*Handing the recantation back to DUPANLOUP.*) There you are, my friend.

DUPANLOUP: (*Puzzled, studying the paper.*) But today is May sixteenth, 1838, Monsieur Le Prince.

TALLEYRAND: Indeed it is.

DUPANLOUP: Then why have you dated your signature: March third, 1838?

TALLEYRAND: Because, on March third, I made a remarkably witty speech to the Academy, in which I expounded on the various qualities that are necessary in the perfect Foreign Minister.

DORETHEA: Which only *you* possess, my dear.

TALLEYRAND: Naturally. And after my oration, even my critics said: 'Behold, it is Voltaire, only better.'

DUPANLOUP: That still doesn't explain why you have erroneously dated your recantation March third, when it is now blatantly May sixteenth!

TALLEYRAND: I do not wish the world to think that I signed this in my dotage. Even if I have. They must believe I was at the height of my considerable powers.

DUPANLOUP: Then why did you not sign it on March third, when you *were* at the height of your powers?

TALLEYRAND: Because, on March third, I didn't know that I was going to die, you silly man. And I wanted to be certain that I would be gone from here moments after signing. And now, because of my immaculate sense of timing, I will. (*To DORETHEA.*) It is amusing, dearest. Well, what if I had signed, and then lived on for years? It doesn't bear thinking of, does it? Well, does it?

(*TALLEYRAND's laughter is cut short by a painful gasp. His head falls back. He is dead. Simultaneously the clock stops ticking. DORETHEA closes his eyes.*)

DORETHEA: (*Weeping.*) Oh my Prince…my diabolical Prince of Peace.

(*Slow fade.*)

The End.